LONDON

FODOR'S TRAVEL GUIDES

are compiled, researched, and edited by an international team of travel writers, field correspondents, and editors. The series, which now almost covers the globe, was founded by Eugene Fodor in 1936.

OFFICES
New York & London

Fodor's London:

Editorial Contributors: Patricia Harris, Frances Howell, Mark Lewes, John Mayor, David Tennant, Gillian Tindall

Editor: Richard Moore

Deputy Editor: Thomas Cussans

Maps and Plans: C.W. Bacon, Brian Stimson, Swanston Graphics

Drawings: Eric Fraser

FODOR'S

LONDON
1986

FODOR'S TRAVEL GUIDES
New York & London

The following Fodor's Guides are current; most are also available in a British
edition published by Hodder & Stoughton.

Country and Area Guides

Australia, New Zealand
  & The South Pacific
Austria
Bahamas
Belgium & Luxembourg
Bermuda
Brazil
Canada
Canada's Maritime
  Provinces
Caribbean
Central America
Eastern Europe
Egypt
Europe
France
Germany
Great Britain
Greece
Holland
India, Nepal &
  Sri Lanka
Ireland
Israel
Italy
Japan
Jordan & The Holy Land
Kenya
Korea
Mexico
North Africa
People's Republic of
  China
Portugal
Scandanavia
Scotland
South America
Southeast Asia

Soviet Union
Spain
Switzerland
Turkey
Yugoslavia

City Guides

Amsterdam
Beijing, Guangzhou,
  Shanghai
Boston
Chicago
Dallas–Fort Worth
Greater Miami & The
  Gold Coast
Hong Kong
Houston
Lisbon
London
Los Angeles
Madrid
Mexico City &
  Acapulco
Munich
New Orleans
New York City
Paris
Philadelphia
Rome
San Diego
San Francisco
Stockholm, Copenhagen,
  Oslo, Helsinki &
  Reykjavik
Sydney
Tokyo
Toronto
Vienna
Washington, D.C.

U.S.A. Guides

Alaska
Arizona
California
Cape Cod
Colorado
Far West
Florida
Hawaii
New England
New Mexico
Pacific North Coast
South
Texas
U.S.A.

Budget Travel

American Cities (30)
Britain
Canada
Caribbean
Europe
France
Germany
Hawaii
Italy
Japan
London
Mexico
Spain

Fun Guides

Acapulco
Bahamas
London
Montreal
Puerto Rico
San Francisco
St. Martin/Sint Maarten
Waikiki

CONTENTS

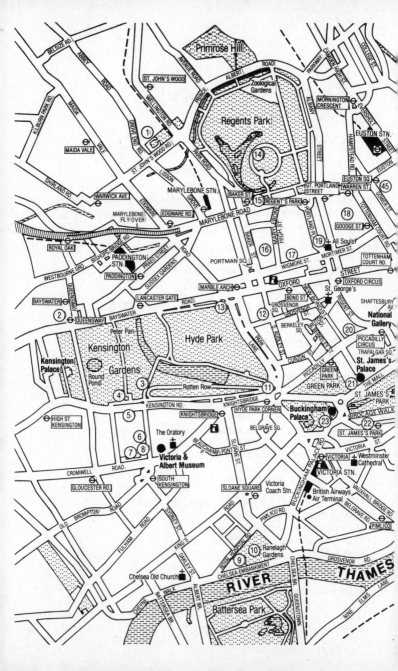

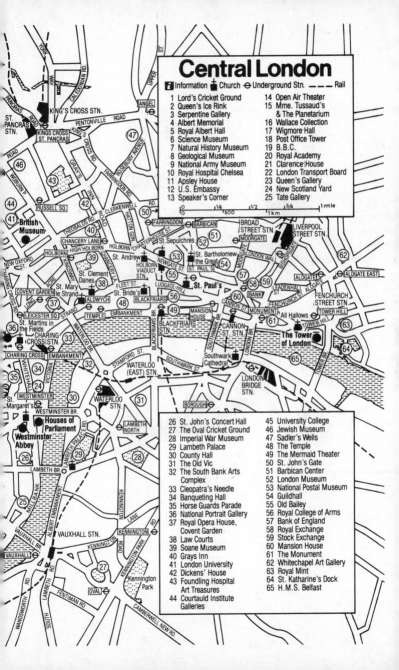

Central London

ℹ Information **✝** Church **⊖** Underground Stn. **— — —** Rail

1 Lord's Cricket Ground
2 Queen's Ice Rink
3 Serpentine Gallery
4 Albert Memorial
5 Royal Albert Hall
6 Science Museum
7 Natural History Museum
8 Geological Museum
9 National Army Museum
10 Royal Hospital Chelsea
11 Apsley House
12 U.S. Embassy
13 Speaker's Corner
14 Open Air Theater
15 Mme. Tussaud's & The Planetarium
16 Wallace Collection
17 Wigmore Hall
18 Post Office Tower
19 B.B.C.
20 Royal Academy
21 Clarence House
22 London Transport Board
23 Queen's Gallery
24 New Scotland Yard
25 Tate Gallery

26 St. John's Concert Hall
27 The Oval Cricket Ground
28 Imperial War Museum
29 Lambeth Palace
30 County Hall
31 The Old Vic
32 The South Bank Arts Complex
33 Cleopatra's Needle
34 Banqueting Hall
35 Horse Guards Parade
36 National Portrait Gallery
37 Royal Opera House, Covent Garden
38 Law Courts
39 Soane Museum
40 Grays Inn
41 London University
42 Dickens' House
43 Foundling Hospital Art Treasures
44 Courtauld Institute Galleries
45 University College
46 Jewish Museum
47 Sadler's Wells
48 The Temple
49 The Mermaid Theater
50 St. John's Gate
51 Barbican Center
52 London Museum
53 National Postal Museum
54 Guildhall
55 Old Bailey
56 Royal College of Arms
57 Bank of England
58 Royal Exchange
59 Stock Exchange
60 Mansion House
61 The Monument
62 Whitechapel Art Gallery
63 Royal Mint
64 St. Katharine's Dock
65 H.M.S. Belfast

TWA to Europe. (Why not get

the easy decisions out of the way first.)

Over the next several hundred pages, you're
going to be faced with any number of
tough decisions. Like what to see in
Europe. When to see it. Where to stay.
Where to eat. And so on.

Fortunately, deciding how to fly there
won't be one of them. Who else but TWA?

TWA has convenient nonstops to more
European countries than anyone else. With
our great TWA low fares.

At TWA's JFK Airport Flight Center, only
a short hallway stands between you and your
connecting TWA overseas flight.

Finally, there's TWA Getaway* Vacations –
by far the most popular vacation choice in
America. With over 100 value-packed tours.
And a vacation style to fit yours.

So call your travel agent or TWA.
Now that wasn't so hard, was it?

LEADING THE WAY. TWA.

INTRODUCING LONDON

A New Look at an Inner City

by
GILLIAN TINDALL

Gillian Tindall is a distinguished novelist and short-story writer with a highly successful parallel career as a "seasoned London-watcher." Her book, The Fields Beneath, *which traces the development of Kentish Town, the part of London in which she lives, is a new kind of local history that has completely changed the way in which many Londoners look at their own neighborhoods.*

For a Great City, London is very odd. It was once the largest in the world, and is still among the top half-dozen in both population and geographical extent, yet many parts of it do not feel or function like

1

a world city at all. Born Londoners, who know only London and not the other capitals of the world, do not usually realize how contrary its nature is: foreign visitors, especially New Yorkers or Europeans accustomed to their own capitals, often arrive in the place unprepared for its eccentricities and, in trying to find in it a city of a more classic kind, become frustrated. Those who take the trouble to understand how London works, and to appreciate what she does have to offer, frequently come to love it better than any other foreign place. Those who come expecting a version of a Continental city plus "quaint pubs" are doomed, if not exactly to disappointment—for pubs there are in plenty —but to confusion. Where is the "center" of London? She doesn't have one. Or rather she has half a dozen different centers, depending on your point of view, and they are not necessarily located where tradition officially places them. Which way is up-town and which down-town? But this transatlantic way of orientation does not work either, partly because no European city uses the logical American grid-pattern, but more particularly because London originally grew, centuries ago, from *two* ancient centers rather than one.

In addition, the life-style of London is eclectic, undramatic and, outside the main shopping streets, oddly private. Paris seems positively constructed for the visitor, so impressive is its street scenery and so easy is it to find a drink, a meal, a phone, at any hour. New York is almost as well-endowed, has its own brand of urban glamor, and possesses a street plan so simple that the outsider can feel knowledgeably at home there within a couple of days. Central Rome is a tightly packed open-air museum, Amsterdam has canals, Vienna—but I need not go on: all these different capitals are in their own ways, versions of a particular type of compressed, high-density, one-hundred percent urban environment.

London is not. To some extent she pretends to be—she is, after all, as well as many other things, the service city, shop-counter and showcase of a highly industrialized nation—and has in the last two decades acquired a sprinkling of international glass towers, housing multinational corporations. But in terms of London's true physical and social nature this is merely an imitative top-dressing, a prestige-gesture with no deep rationale behind it. For London doesn't really need high-rise blocks at all, it is not one of those places where people are crowded—out of doors and within—giving rise to earnest sociological comparisons with rats in confined spaces. In world terms, London is the archetypal spread-out city, with well over half its land-surface actually open to the air in the form of roads, gardens, back yards and parks. Its density of population, at just over 11,000 residents to the square mile, is only half that of Paris and well under half that of New York.

This is the most basic fact to grasp about the place and, in itself, goes a considerable way towards explaining the haphazard, uncity-like feel that London has as soon as you step outside your main business and shopping centers. Moreover, although her population density has declined to some extent in this century, like that of most other cities in the developed world, it was never that high even at its late-nineteenth-century peak. London was famous then, in its conceited Victorian heyday, as the "Mother Megalopolis . . . the greatest city the world has ever seen," but its greatness lay not in its architectural massiveness but in its sheer extent—street after street, square after square, mile after mile, not of tall, impressive piles of stone, but mainly of quite small houses of two, three or at the most four stories, each with its own narrow frontage, its own front-door, frequently with its own little plot of land. Nearly all of London, in fact, was not built to be part of a city at all, and even today, after the destructive efforts of German bombs in the Second World War and the equally destructive rebuilding boom that followed, this remains substantially true.

City Without Walls

But to understand the reasons behind this you have to go back earlier than the nineteenth century, for the prolific Victorian speculative builders, whose individual and piecemeal efforts created the townscape we still see, were simply working on a pattern that was already well-established. You have to go back to the Middle Ages to find London looking like other chief towns on the Continent of Europe—the days when it was a small, crowded, defensively walled settlement on the bank of the river. That originally walled square-mile is still there; today it is the business heart of London, home of the big banks, the insurance companies and the Stock Exchange. The spires of its elegant old churches still rise up, looking oddly tiny against their newer neighbors, but few parishoners are left to pray in them. Apart from the Lord Mayor, in his opulent house opposite the Bank of England, and a sprinkling of pub-keepers, office-caretakers and the like, The City, as this district is now confusingly called, has few residents. Today, this is quite normal for a business district—but the significant fact is that the exodus from The City began hundreds of years ago. At a time when walled Continental cities like Paris were only expanding slowly and concentrically, building new circlets of walls to contain the new districts, prepared right up to the late nineteenth century to regard themselves as potential fortresses that might have to withstand siege from an enemy, London, as the capital of Europe's main off-shore island, felt able to take a more relaxed view of town building.

Already, by the reign of the first Elizabeth in the mid-sixteenth century, England had suffered no invasion by an enemy for five hundred years. London's walls, parts of which dated from Roman times nearly fifteen hundred years earlier, were still in place but were decaying and full of gaps, being generally accepted as fulfilling no useful purpose. The town had jumped the walls, particularly on the west side, where it sprawled at ease along the line of present day Fleet Street and the Strand, heading for Westminster, that other city and seat of Royal government as opposed to the commercial rule of the City guilds. London and the smaller Westminster were, in fact, joining hands, and a belated proclamation in Queen Elizabeth's name that no more houses were to be built outside the City of London's walls had no appreciable effect, for towns have a tenacious life and nature of their own.

It has been estimated that the population of London more than quadrupled during Elizabeth's reign, but that by the end of it only one quarter lived actually within the City walls. Subsequent rulers tried to bring in further regulations, but these were persistently ignored or circumnavigated. Early in the seventeenth century we find Stowe, London's first historian and chronicler, complaining that a favorite lane running north from the City, which used to pass between hedges and elm trees and over stiles, was now lined with kitchen gardens, cottages, drying yards, bowling alleys and the like (the Shakespearian equivalent of gas-station-and-hamburger-joint townscape!) and that this was a wasteful and unnecessary use of the countryside.

His words went unheeded, as did the efforts of Cromwell, during the period when England had temporarily disposed of its Royal family; Cromwell even introduced retrospective fines for houses illegally built since 1620, but his laws against building proved about as effective as his laws against fornication.

With the Restoration of Charles II in 1660, a further building boom took place, and the disastrous Fire of London six years later, which destroyed a large part of the old City, simply gave further impetus to the move beyond the walls. Thus a trend was set in motion which continued unabated for the next two hundred and fifty years. There was no shortage of commentators to point out that if London's immediate countryside were cluttered with houses it would cease to *be* countryside —that such neighboring villages as Hackney, Islington and Bethnal Green were, because of all the building, rapidly losing the rustic appeal which drew new inhabitants to them in the first place.

But when has individual enterprise ever obeyed such warnings? Not till our own century, with the urgent planning restrictions of the mid-1930s, followed by the more imaginative post-War Green Belt legislation, was the growth of London effectively curbed by law, although, oddly enough, almost every generation throughout the eighteenth and nineteenth centuries seems to have imagined that London *had* reached by that moment her optimum size and that growth would shortly cease. And all the while London was spreading and spreading, lining the old routes away from the City and Westminster with houses, gradually in-filling the fields behind, burgeoning into elegant new districts of squares and crescents here, running up rows of workmen's cottages there.

Around the turn of our present century, a British writer (G. K. Chesterton) referred to London, which was by then enormous, as consisting of a series of "submerged villages." This remark has since become something of a cliché—it is very much part of the British character to enjoy thinking of oneself as living in a village, even a submerged one—but in fact it is only true for certain areas and not for the great mass of London's townscape. Certainly, by the time Chesterton was writing, at the beginning of this century, all the old villages that had once provided the hay, dairy cows, laundrymaids and country retreats for Londoners had been swallowed and had become the inner-London districts as we know them today: the "hamlets" of the East End, Islington, Kentish Town, Hampstead, Marylebone, Kensington, Chelsea, Battersea—all were once separate villages.

The Suburbs Arrive

But the greater part of the countryside over which London expanded in the eighteenth, nineteenth and early part of this century was just that—countryside which, till the houses came, had been open fields, market gardens or commons, with only the odd farmhouse or barn built upon it. What grew up on it, therefore, were not new villages in their own right, nor yet districts specifically designed as part of the town, but *suburbs,* spreading outwards one beyond another as the years passed, in ever-widening rings. The "garden suburb," now imitated all over the world, was a British invention, an archetypally British living place that is neither town nor country but which partakes (in theory) of the advantages of both, a toy countryside with town amenities.

"Commuter" is a word which originated in the United States and which has become part of the British language only in the last twenty-five years, yet the phenomenon of commuting was an English invention long before, and one which only in this century has been adopted as a way of life by other nations. Already, in the early 1800s, a French visitor to London (Louis Simond) was remarking on the odd way in which "London is stretching out her great arms on all sides, as if to embrace the whole countryside. Yet her population is not growing in proportion, it is simply displacing itself from the center to the outskirts. The center has become a trading counter, a place of business. Instead, the people live more spaciously in the suburbs, with better air, and more cheaply; the public coaches which pass by every half-hour make it easy to travel back and forth."

He also remarked that in traveling to Hertford, twenty miles north of London proper, "one travels half the distance between two rows of brick houses." Many of these small houses, or similar ones constructed in the same spirit a little later in the century, still stand today, though along the main roads they have usually been modified from their original appearance. The privet hedges or railings that once screened their neat front gardens from the road have gone and shops have been built out over these same front gardens concealing once-fine pedimented front doorways. Upper floors have become offices, workshops, store-rooms or just non-space, difficult of access, their twelve-paned windows veiled with dust, their bare wooden floors supporting little but card-board boxes and mouse-droppings. No specific census has ever been taken of the amount of under-used space existing today behind the facades of these once-genteel family homes, here in the capital city where space is supposed, in theory, to be some of the most expensive in the world, but there is no doubt that such a census would be highly instructive and would help revise a number of received notions about property values in London.

Off the main thoroughfares, however, the picture is different, and many of the houses are still—or rather, once again—lovingly tended family homes. For just as London's City and West End facade of a hustling modern world city disappears as soon as you look a little further afield, so, in individual districts, does the main road create a false impression which the side roads contradict. Blighted by noise, dust and traffic fumes, these ex-suburban High Streets often give the impression of being run-down and fit for little but urban renewal, yet less than fifty yards away in the side streets you may find quiet, careful-ly-painted houses that are clearly "valuable period properties" in Real Estate terms.

Up to the 1950s the situation was rather different, for the sooty dirt and consequent fogs of London had driven most middle-class occu-pants away from these one-time suburban streets to newer suburbs further out; but the gradual abolition of open fire-places and coal-fired railway locomotives during the 1950s and early '60s brought about a revolution in London's climate and appearance that has never been fully appreciated by foreigners. (I am sorry to disappoint all those arriving in the hope of genuine London fog—the traditional Dickensian "pea-souper"—but they have come thirty years too late!)

In the last generation moneyed middle-class residents have been returning steadily to inner London districts, wherever there are suffi-cient numbers of surviving Georgian or early-Victorian houses to be rehabilitated and cherished. Thus, imported transatlantic concepts of "decayed inner-city areas" do not really apply to London, any more than clichés about over-crowding or land-values do. Certainly there are some grimly derelict districts in London—notably the old East End and large tracts of land south of the river Thames—but these are, almost without exception, areas in which the town planners of the post-War era saw fit to demolish older houses and to destroy street patterns in favor of comprehensive redevelopments of State-owned dwellings. These are frequently tower-blocks set in desolate waste-lands of supposed "public open space," and are now generally admitted to have been one of the social failures of the century. Seek for the historic East End of the Siege of Sidney Street, of the Cable Street march in Blackshirt days and the Ripper murders of an even earlier date, and you will find only shreds and patches left. But move a couple of miles to the northwest, to Islington, which for a variety of reasons largely managed to escape the demolishers' ball and chain, and you will find the decor of nineteenth-century London still intact in street after street.

Backs to Nature

There is yet a further visual deception here, in these pretty stucco houses with their restored porticos and balconies. From the street they do indeed appear fairly urban, with their railed-in basements, not city-center houses but hardly country ones either. Yet the fact is that these cream-painted façades are indeed just that, façades. In most cases these frontages are stuck onto houses whose essential nature is much less classical, more utilitarian and domestic—what one distinguished for-eign commentator (Steen Rasmussen) has called "Queen Anne fronts and Mary Ann backs." For if you are invited into one of these houses on a summer evening, what do you find? The sense of being in a city abruptly disappears: the backs of the houses are revealed as the homely brick constructions they really are, sprouting chimneys and drainpipes and back-additions in odd places, the direct descendants of the country cottage. The basement has vanished, and typically the back room leads out into a flowery yard or even a garden with over-hanging hedgerow trees that may pre-date the house itself. On each side and ahead stretch other gardens; the back of adjoining terraces of houses form a green enclave, a world of washing lines and cats and roses and old deck chairs that seems separated by many miles or many decades from the traffic-choked High Road. It is in such private places, not in Piccadilly Circus or Westminster or Oxford Street that the true quality of London lies.

Of course a number of other capitals, including New York, once had such family houses near their center, but as pressures of space and preconceptions about the nature of cities led to urban growth upwards, such houses were for the most part torn down before the start of the present century, to be replaced by urban-style blocks. A hundred years ago New York's Fifth Avenue and London's Portland Place (a few minutes' walk from Oxford Circus) looked not unlike one another. Portland Place looks the same today as it did then—but where are the brownstones of Fifth Avenue? Equally, most Continental cities, when they finally got rid of their constricting walls in the latter part of the nineteenth century, indulged in a spate of rather grand and self-conscious town-planning, complete with boulevards and palatial vistas, which demanded a new kind of august, undomestic architecture to set them off. But London, though at that time the capital of the richest nation on earth, failed to construct herself a grandiose décor. Her one street designed for processions is the Mall, leading from Buckingham Palace to her only exhuberant, Continental-style piazza, Trafalgar Square; London has countless other squares (see them at their best in Bloomsbury and Belgravia) but these again are based on the essentially domestic concept of individual houses surrounding a garden. Nor, except in one or two instances, were broad streets driven through old, congested areas, and even where they have been (as with Kingsway, linking the Strand to Bloomsbury) the spacious concept soon peters out into a narrower, pre-existing street-pattern. A hundred years ago London was already too far committed—literally far, in terms of land-area —to the principle of development by spreading somewhere else, to be attracted to the idea of a homogeneously planned townscape.

It was also too late to persuade Londoners to abandon the free-range homes-in-the-ground, to which they had become accustomed over the past two or three centuries, and to attempt to cram them into the apartments that truly urban living inevitably requires. Of course blocks of purpose-built flats do exist in London, but they are mainly occupied by the rich and childless with country retreats elsewhere, by London's huge foreign community, or by the poorer sections of society who have been put into municipal blocks not of their own choosing. At no level of society is living in a flat regarded as the natural way of life in London, despite the persuasive arguments of several generations of town-planners.

In the same way, and in disregard of all the good intentions of those who drew up plans for her post-1945, London has remained peculiarly resistant to motorways (freeways). A ring, or rings, of such traffic arteries was confidently planned, and eventually in the late 1960s a few miles were built from Marylebone Road running westwards—but every yard of this runs, metaphorically, over the blood and bones of the protesters who, as it progressed, mounted a mass movement against the destruction of any further districts for the sake of the motor car. No more "improvements" of this type are therefore planned, and London's traffic problems seem no worse than those of any other major city.

Going West

I have already said that the old East End had been virtually extinguished, architecturally and socially, and that the City, the original heart, is now strictly a business district. This is very much in the tradition of great cities: all cities (at any rate in the northern hemisphere) tend to show a movement westwards that is both geographical and social, for reasons that have never been entirely explained—following the setting sun perhaps? In any case the tendency of London, over the centuries, to shift its center westwards, was naturally encouraged by the presence of the city of Westminster standing there waiting to be incorporated, with its Abbey, its palaces and Houses of Parliament. But what is not so well understood or recognised is the extent to which, in the last hundred years, London has continued its progression westwards, and has thereby left its old centers of commerce or fashion stranded, places with a famous name and past, but with a somewhat blurred rôle in the present.

What of the Strand itself, a one-time riverside path whose houseplots ran down to the unembanked Thames? Visitors reared on Dickens and on Music Hall songs ("Let's all—Go down the Strand" . . . "As I walk down the Strand with my hat in my hand . . . ") might be excused for expecting the Strand to be worth a visit, but in reality it is today a fringe street, on the edge of theaterland, just out of Fleet Street and Law Court country, not quite in the West End, a thoroughfare without much character. Those wanting fun and little restaurants would do far better to take the tube two or three miles westwards to Queensway in Bayswater, a once rather dull suburban street which now has all the amenities of late-night food and Sunday activity that visitors naturally seek. And yet the character of the Strand could be due to change again, for, by one of those counter-currents that complicate the pattern in big cities, Covent Garden, the erstwhile vegetable market lying directly to the north of it, has recently been revamped as a pedestrian area of boutiques and restaurants. The old market buildings have been sensitively re-used, and the place seems well on the way to becoming again what it has not been since the eighteenth century—a district of decorous and elegant pleasure.

Conversely Piccadilly Circus, half a mile away, which used to figure in old-fashioned Children's Encyclopaedias as The Heart of the Empire and once had its flower-sellers and expensive restaurants, is now a piece of "decayed inner city" with a vengeance—a lurid case of wet-rot, exemplified in sex-shops, "souvenir" stalls and the kind of public lavatory where it is as well not to linger. You won't get mugged there—or, for that matter, anywhere in central London—but you won't find anything there that is "typically London," or much in garish, declining Soho to the north of it.

Soho has a long history as a place of entertainment, and still has delicate, eighteenth-century house-fronts rising above the clamorous signs for All-Adult Video, but in recent years most of its real tradesmen and eating places have been driven northwards, across Oxford Street to Charlotte Street. Others have moved out of the West End entirely—miles farther west in fact, beyond Knightsbridge, to Kensington and Chelsea, where wholly separate worlds of shopping and entertainment have set themselves up, surrounded by some of the most attractive housing in the world. Many of the residents of these westward centers hardly move from them, finding everything they want close at hand. As a result there is a total lack of concensus among Londoners themselves as to where the "center" of London actually lies.

Trading in Futures

In recent decades there have been town-planning attempts to neaten the psychological map a little by dragging the South Bank into the picture as well, ignoring the historical fact that the South Bank has never been part of central London in the way that, say, the Left Bank has always been part of central Paris. The Festival of Britain was held on the South Bank in 1951, and since then its site has gradually been covered with an Arts Complex, including the National Theater. Inwardly effective and well-frequented, outwardly these lumpy buildings have not created an attractive habitat. Freelance roller-skaters and skate-boarders have taken to using the convenient under-belly of the Queen Elizabeth Hall, but otherwise street life there is non-existent. New plans have been afoot for some time to develop the remains of the area in such a way as to encourage Covent Garden style "fun" of an artistic kind, but seasoned London-watchers remain skeptical about the validity of such forced attempts to make London behave in a predictable manner.

More promising, but still vague, plans exist for revitalizing an area much farther to the east and much more of an unknown quantity—London's defunct docklands. (The trade, with the advent of container-shipping, has moved off to the mouth of the Thames at Gravesend.) So far, St. Katharine's Dock near the Tower of London—yet another very old center—has been attentively adapted as a tourist attraction, with shops and a museum; but a vast acreage lies farther east, sleeping land covered with ruined walls and rosebay willow-herb, waiting to be reawakened. What forces will re-awaken it, and in what form it will spring to life again, remains to be seen.

FACTS
AT YOUR
FINGERTIPS

FACTS AT YOUR FINGERTIPS

Planning Your Trip

All prices quoted in this Guide are based on those available to us at time of writing, mid-1985. Given the volatility of current costs, it is inevitable that changes will have taken place by the time this book becomes available. We trust, therefore, that you will take prices quoted as indicators only, and will double-check to be sure of the latest figures.

DEVALUATION—INFLATION. Current monetary problems make it impossible to budget accurately long in advance. All prices mentioned in this book are indicative of costs at the time of going to press (mid-1985), at which time the rate of exchange was about £1 = $1.15. We suggest that you keep a weather eye open for fluctuations in exchange rates, both while planning your trip—and while on it.

WHAT IT WILL COST. This is about the hardest travel problem to resolve in advance. A trip to Britain (or to Europe) can cost as little (above a basic minimum) or as much (with virtually no limit) as you choose. Budgeting is much simplified if you take a prepackaged trip. As an indication: a five-day stay in London, including hotel, meals except lunches, but with lunch included on two full-day sightseeing trips, visits in London and to Windsor and Hampton Court and theater, costs anything between £300 and £600 depending upon the hotel category required. A good-quality package 7-day mini coach tour, taking in the Welsh Borders, Lake District, Scottish Borders, Yorkshire and the Peak District, can be had for £280 (inc. half-board).

Sample Costs. Hotel and restaurant costs are discussed in the relevant chapters. A man's haircut will cost from about £3.50 (around £8.50 in a central London barbers); a woman's starts at around £6, a set is minimum £3.50. It costs about 50p to have a shirt laundered, from £1.25 to dry-clean a dress or £2.50 a man's suit. Newspapers will cost you around 23p, the Sunday ones a little more. A pint of beer is up to 90p and a small gin and tonic about the same. Your evening out means spending £4.50 to £12.50 for a theater seat (up to £16 for a top musical, to £34 for Covent Garden), £2.00 to £4.50 at the cinema, and about all you have at a nightclub—exact figures vary greatly, since you have to pay a membership fee to "join" a nightclub the first time you go, and the fee is highly elastic.

CREDIT CARDS are now an integral part of the Western Financial Way of Life, and, in theory at least, are accepted all over Europe. But, while the use of credit cards can smooth the traveler's path considerably, they should not be thought of as a universal answer to every problem.

Firstly, there has been a growing resistance in Europe to the use of credit cards. A great many restaurants, for example, object to paying the percentage which the parent organizations demand. If they are able to get American Express, etc. to lower their rates, then the situation may well change, but at the moment you would be well advised to find out if the restaurant of your choice does take credit cards. Otherwise you may find yourself in an embarrassing situation.

Another point that should be watched with those useful pieces of plastic is the problem of the rate at which your purchase may be converted into your home currency. We have ourselves had two purchases, made on the same day in the same place, charged ultimately at two totally different rates of exchange. If you want to be certain of the rate at which you will pay, insist on the establishment entering the current rate onto your credit card charge at the time you sign it—this will prevent the management from holding your charge until a more favorable rate (to them) comes along, something which could cost you more dollars than you counted on. (On the other hand, should the dollar or pound be revalued upward before your charge is entered, you could gain a little.)

We would advise you, also, to check your monthly statement very carefully indeed against the counterfoils you got at the time of your purchase. It has become increasingly common for shops, hotels or restaurants to change the amounts on the original you signed, if they find they have made an error in the original bill. Sometimes, also, unscrupulous employees make this kind of change to their own advantage. The onus is on you to report the change to the credit card firm and insist on sorting the problem out.

WHEN TO GO. The regular tourist season in Britain runs from mid-April to mid-October. The spring is the time to see the countryside at its fresh greenest, while in September and October the northern moorlands and Scottish highlands are at their most colorful. June is a good month to visit Wales, the Lake District and Ireland. July and August are the months when most of the British take their vacations and that is when accommodation in some popular resorts is at a premium. The winter can be rather dismal for wandering around the country at large, but in London it is a time full of interest with theaters, opera, concerts and art exhibitions going at full speed. In the main, the climate is mild, though the weather is changeable and unpredictable. London has summer temperatures in the 80s at times, and can be humid. You should remember that London buildings have very little in the way of aircondi-tioning, and dress accordingly.

Annual rainfall varies from about 23 inches in London and most of the southeast, to upwards of 60 inches in the Lake District and west Highlands.

Temperatures. Average max. daily temperatures in Fahrenheit and centigrade:

Jan.	Feb.	Mar.	Apr.	May	Jun.	Jul.	Aug.	Sep.	Oct.	Nov.	Dec.
45	45	50	55	63	68	70	70	66	61	50	45
7	7	10	13	17	20	21	21	19	16	10	7

ANNUAL EVENTS. These are some of the major happenings in London each year.

January. *International Boat Show* at Earls Court.
February. *Crufts Dog Show* at Earls Court.
March. *Camden Arts Festival.*
　　Oxford and Cambridge Boat Race, on the Thames from Putney to Mortlake.
March-April. *Daily Mail Ideal Homes Exhibition* at Earls Court.
　　London Marathon.
　　Chelsea Antiques Fair, Old Town Hall, Chelsea.
May. *Royal Windsor Horse Show,* now held at Ascot.
　　Chelsea Flower Show, in the Royal Hospital grounds.
　　Football Association Cup Final.
May to August. *Summer Exhibition,* at the Royal Academy.
June. *Royal Ascot.* Major race and a society event.
　　Derby, at Epsom. Similar society event.
　　Trooping the Color at Buckingham Palace/The Mall/Horse Guards Parade. *The Garter Ceremony* at Windsor.
June to July. *Lawn Tennis Championships* at Wimbledon.
July. *City of London Festival.* Numerous musical events.
　　Royal International Horse Show at Wembley. Showjumping.
July or August. *Royal Tournament* at Earls Court.
July to September. *Henry Wood Promenade Concerts* at the Royal Albert Hall—1986 being their 92nd year.
August. *Greater London Council Horse Show* at Clapham Common.
September. *Thames Day,* in Jubilee Garden.
　　Battle of Britain week. RAF aircraft fly over Westminster.
October. *Burlington House Antiques Fair,* at the Royal Academy, Piccadilly.
November. *State Opening of Parliament* by the Queen.
　　RAC Veteran Car Run from Hyde Park Corner to Brighton.
　　Remembrance Sunday. Moving ceremony in Whitehall.
December. *Royal Smithfield Show* at Earls Court.

OUT OF TOWN. The following is a list of annual events taking place within easy reach of London.
April. *Badminton Horse Trials* at Avon. Five-day equestrian event.
April to December. *Shakespeare season* at Stratford-upon-Avon.
May to June. *Bath Festival* of music.

May to August. *Glyndebourne Opera,* at Lewes, Sussex.
May to September. *Drama Festival* at Chichester, Sussex.
June. *Aldeburgh Festival.* Musical festival made famous by Benjamin Britten, its chief creator.
July. *Henley Regatta,* at Henley-on-Thames.
September. *Farnborough Air Show,* Kent.

 TRAVEL AGENTS. Once you decide where you want to go, your next step is to consult a good agent. If you haven't one, the American Society of Travel Agents, 4400 MacArthur Blvd., N.W. Washington, D.C. 20007, (202) 965–7520, or the Association of British Travel Agents, 55 Newman St, London WIP 4AH, can help. Whether you select *Maupintour, Diners Club-Fugazy, American Express, Cook's,* or a smaller firm is a matter of preference. They all have branch offices or correspondents in the larger European cities. The *American Automobile Association World-Wide Travel,* 8111 Gatehouse Rd, Falls Church, Va. 22047, (703) 222–6000, also runs escorted tours.

A good travel agent can help you avoid costly mistakes due to inexperience. He can help you take advantage of special reductions in rail fares and the like that you would not otherwise know about. Most important, he can save you *time* by making it unnecessary for you to waste precious days abroad trying to get tickets and reservation. Thanks to his work, you are able to see and do more.

NORTH AMERICAN AGENCIES SPECIALIZING IN BRITISH TOURS

American Express, Travel Division, 822 Lexington Ave., New York, N.Y. 10021, (212) 758–6510; and 12 Richmond St. East, Toronto, Ontario, Canada M5C 1M5, (416) 868–1044.

Barclay Travel Ltd., 261 Madison Ave., New York, N.Y. 10016, (212) 557–5600, specializes in individual, small-group, out-of-the-way and special-interest (e.g. mansions, gardens, antiques) tours of Britain. These are individually tailored, not for large groups, so contact Barclay directly.

Caravan, 401 North Michigan Ave., Chicago, Ill. 60611, (312) 321–9800.

Cartan, One Crossroads of Commerce, Rolling Meadows, Ill. 60008, (312) 870–2222.

C.I.E., 590 Fifth Ave., New York, N.Y. 10036, (212) 944–8828.

Cosmos of London, P.O. Box 862, 69–15 Austin Street, Forest Hills, N.Y. 11375, (212) 268–7000.

Fugazy International Travel, 600 Madison Ave., New York, N.Y. 10022, (212) 572–8480.

Esplanade Tours, 38 Newbury St., Boston, Mass. 02116, (617) 266–7465.

Fourways Travel, 878 Bridgeport Ave., Shelton, Conn. 06484.

Globus-Gateway, 69–15 Austin St., Forest Hills, N.Y. 11375, (212) 268–7000.

Kuoni Travel-Scottish Omnibuses Ltd, 11 East 44th St., New York, N.Y. 10017, (212) 687–7190.

Lynott Tours, 350 Fifth Ave., Suite 2619, New York, N.Y. 10118, (212) 760–0101.

Maupintour, 1515 St. Andrew's Dr., Lawrence, Kansas 66044, (913) 843–1211.

Trafalgar Tours, 21 East 26th St., New York, N.Y. 10010, (212) 689–8977.

SOURCES OF INFORMATION. A large selection of brochures, booklets, and general information may be had from *B.T.A. (British Tourist Authority),* the national tourist organization, which has over 20 overseas offices.

In the US

40 West 57th St., New York, N.Y. 10019, (212) 581-4700;
875 North Michigan Ave, Chicago, Ill. 60611, (312) 787–0490;
612 South Flower St, Los Angeles, Calif., 90017, (213) 623–8196;
Plaza of the Americas, North Tower Suite 750, Box 346, Dallas, Texas 75201, (214) 748–2279.

In Canada

94 Cumberland St., Suite 600, Toronto, Ontario M5R 3N3, (416) 925–6326;
409 Granville St., Suite 451, Vancouver, B.C. V6C 1T2.

HANDICAPPED TRAVEL. One of the newest, and largest, groups to enter the travel scene is the handicapped. There are millions of people who are physically able to travel and who do so enthusiastically when they know they will be able to move about with safety and comfort. A growing number of travel agencies specialize in this market. Generally their tours parallel those of the non-handicapped traveler, but at a more leisurely pace, with everything checked out in advance to eliminate all inconvenience, whether the traveler happens to be deaf, blind, or in a wheelchair. For a complete list of tour operators who arrange such travel, write to the *Society for the Advancement of Travel for the Handicapped,* 26 Court St, Brooklyn, New York, 11242 (tel. (718) 8585483). An excellent source of information in this field is the book *Access to the World: A Travel Guide for the Handicapped,* by Louise Weiss, available from Facts on File, 460 Park Ave. South, New York, N.Y. 10016.

Another major source of help is the *Travel Information Center,* Moss Rehabilitation Hospital, 12th St and Tabor Rd, Philadelphia, Penn. 19141, (215) 329-5715. *Access Travel: Airports* is a brochure for listing design features, facilities, and services at 220 airports in 27 countries. For a copy, write to: *Consumer Information Center,* Pueblo, Colorado 81009. It is published by the

US Dept of Transportation. For an international directory of access guides, write to *Rehabilitation International,* 1123 Broadway, New York, NY 10010.

The London Visitor and Convention Bureau publish *London—A Guide for Disabled Visitors,* in full color (80 pages). It is available from LVCB Tourist Information Centers or by post from LVCB's Sales Department, 26 Grosvenor Gardens, London SW1. However, it has not been revised for several years. More up-to-date is *London Made Easy* (40p, 60p by post), whose 55 pages include a useful section for the handicapped. There is also an *Access Guide to London,* published by *Access,* 39 Bradley Gdns., West Ealing W13, £3 in the UK, £5 for US residents (inc. postage).

The *Royal Association for Disability and Rehabilitation* (*RADAR* for short), 25 Mortimer St., London W1, publishes an excellent handbook, *Holidays for the Physically Handicapped,* and acts as an information service.

TRAVEL DOCUMENTS. Apply several months in advance of your expected departure date. **US residents** must apply in person to the US Passport Agency in Boston, Chicago, Detroit, Honolulu, Houston, Los Angeles, Miami, New Orleans, New York, Philadelphia, San Francisco, Seattle, Stamford (Conn.), or Washington DC, or to their local County Courthouse. In some areas selected post offices are equipped to handle passport applications. If you still have your latest passport issued within the past eight years you may use this to apply by mail. You will need 1) Proof of citizenship, such as a birth certificate, 2) two identical photographs, in either black and white or color, on non-glossy paper and taken within the past six months; 3) $35 for the passport itself plus a $7 processing fee if you are applying in person (no processing fee when applying by mail) for those 18 years and older, or if you are under 18, $20 for the passport plus a $7 processing fee if you are applying in person (again, no extra fee when applying by mail); 4) proof of identity such as a driver's license, previous passport, any governmental ID card, or a copy of an income tax return. Adult passports are valid for 10 years, others for five years. When you receive your passport, write down its number, date and place of issue separately; if it is later lost or stolen, notify either the nearest American Consul or the Passport Office, Department of State, Washington D.C. 20524, as well as the local police.

If you are a resident alien you must file a Treasury Sailing Permit, Form 1040C—if a non-resident alien file Form 1040NR—certifying that all Federal taxes have been paid; apply to your District Director of Internal Revenue for this. You will have to present various documents: (1) blue or green registration card; (2) passport; (3) travel tickets; (4) most recently filed Form 1040; (5) W-2 forms for the most recent full year; (6) most recent current payroll stubs or letter; (7) check to be sure this is all! To reenter the United States, resident aliens with green cards file Form I-131 45 days before departure, if remaining abroad for more than 364 days. If abroad less, your Alien Registration Card will get you in on return. Apply for the Re-entry Permit in person at the nearest office of the Immigration and Naturalization Service, or by mail to the Immigration and Naturalization Service, Washington D.C. (Naturalized American citizens may now stay abroad an unlimited time, even in the country of their origin.)

Canadian citizens entering the United Kingdom must have a valid passport. In Canada, apply in person to regional passport offices in: Edmonton, Halifax, Montreal, Toronto, Downsville (Ontario), Vancouver or Winnipeg. Or, write to: Canadian Passport Office, 200 DuPortage 6th Floor, Place du Center, Hull, Quebec K1A OG3. A $20 fee and two photos are required. Canadian citizens living in the US need special forms from their nearest Canadian Consulate.

VISAS Not required for entry into Britain by American citizens, nationals of the British Commonwealth and most European and South American countries. Citizens of EEC countries do not need passports but must be able to prove their nationality.

HEALTH CERTIFICATES are not required for entry to Britain, unless you arrive from Asia, Africa or South America.

WHAT TO TAKE. The first principle is to travel light. The restrictions, either by size or weight, that are imposed on air travelers, act as added incentives to keep baggage within bounds of commonsense. Don't forget, too, that you may have to carry your cases yourself. Porters are very scarce indeed these days.

Britain is sometimes cool even in midsummer. You will want sweaters and you will certainly need rainwear. The kind of raincoat which has a detachable warm lining might have been invented with the British weather in mind. In keeping with the climate, ordinary everyday dress, especially for traveling, runs very much to the casual and to sportswear; tweeds and non-matching jackets for men, mix-and-match separates for women. If you are going to be doing a lot of walking, even if it is the indoor variety in museums, then be sure that you are well equipped with comfortable, supportive shoes. Dressing in the evening during summer is not practiced widely in England these days.

If you wear glasses or contact lenses, take along the prescription or, even better since opticians charge the earth in Britain, take along a spare pair. There is no difficulty about getting medicines, but if you have to take some particular preparation, better bring a supply. Emergency hospital and emergency dental treatment is not free, contrary to popular belief. In most cases you will be required to pay on a private basis; however, this is usually considerably cheaper than in America.

Baggage. The transatlantic airline baggage allowance is based on size rather than weight. First-class passengers are allowed two pieces of baggage, the sum of the height, width and length of each piece not to exceed 62 inches. The two together must not exceed 124 inches. Economy-class passengers are allowed two pieces, neither piece to exceed 62 inches and the two together not to exceed 107 inches (somewhat illogically). Under-seat baggage allowance is the same for both classes, one piece which must not exceed 45 inches. The charges for excess are high; New York to western Europe $65 per piece. If, after breaking your journey, you are going on to the Continent or beyond you will not be able to take more than one piece, the total dimensions of which must not exceed 62 inches. This applies to both first class and economy. Moreover, there are some domestic flights in Europe that allow only 15 kg or pay extra. The only exception to the rule is passengers who are in transit after a transatlantic flight. Perhaps the day will come when all airlines on all routes adopt the same system for baggage!

Important Note: Be sure to put your address (both your home address and your vacation destination) inside your suitcase, and your identity tag on the outside of the case.

Getting to Britain

FROM NORTH AMERICA

BY AIR. London is the busiest international air center in the world, with its main airport Heathrow and Gatwick the number two, now much enlarged and a superb entry or leaving point. From the U.S.A. to either Heathrow or Gatwick (and in a number of cases to both) there are direct flights from the following cities—Boston, New York (JFK), Newark, Philadelphia, Baltimore, Washington (Dulles), Pittsburgh, Detroit, Chicago, St. Louis, Kansas City, Atlanta, Tampa, Miami, New Orleans, Denver, Dallas/Fort Worth, Houston, Minneapolis, Seattle, San Francisco, Oakland, Los Angeles, Anchorage and Honolulu. In addition there are through-plane flights from a number of other cities including Phoenix, Cincinnati and Portland (Ore). From Canada non-stop or through-plane flights go from Vancouver, Calgary, Edmonton, Winnipeg, Toronto, Montreal, Halifax and Gander.

Add to these the direct flights from New York, Toronto, Miami and Tampa to Manchester, and from Glasgow (Prestwick) to Boston, Montreal, Toronto, Halifax, Winnipeg, Vancouver, Edmonton, Calgary and Miami. These are all scheduled flights of one kind or another. In summer there are also limited charter flights from various U.S. and Canadian points to London (Gatwick), Birmingham, Manchester, Prestwick, Newcastle, Cardiff and Belfast. Check on all these trans-Atlantic routes as a number may change both before and during 1986.

The prime route, of course, is from New York (JFK) to London with Heathrow having the more flights, among which is Concorde operated by *British Airways* and taking under 3½ hours for the journey.

But whether you are in the 1st-class-deluxe travel league or in the cheapest-possible-fare sector, you have a very wide choice of flights between the two countries—and all subsonic flights are by wide-bodied jets.

Although there are some daytime flights, most services tend to depart from east coast cities during evening hours in order to arrive early the next morning (U.K. time, that is); flights from more westerly points are timed accordingly. The one major drawback to this arrangement is that some hotels may not allow you to check in before noon or even 1 p.m., and that can leave you feeling exhausted with no place to nap or unwind for several hours. In-flight travel time from the east coast is usually between five and six and a half hours.

Fares. Air fares from the U.S. to Britain are in a constant state of flux, and there are a bewildering array of special fares ranging in price from the relatively inexpensive to the astronomically costly. Our best advice is to consult a travel agent and let him or her make your reservations for you. Agents are familiar with the latest changes in fare structures, as well as with the rules governing various discount plans.

Generally, on regularly scheduled flights, the basic breakdown is as follows: Concorde and First Class fares run at the very top of the cost scale. The substantial extra money involved—often well over twice that of other fares (at presstime, a one-way ticket for the Concorde hovered just under $2,500!)—will buy all on-board amenities at no extra cost, a shortened flight time (about 3½ hours on Concorde flights), and a more comfortable seating arrangement. No restrictions are put on these tickets, i.e. you may book, travel, and change flight dates at any time, and have stopovers when required.

Economy fares are less pricey than the above, but can still be expensive. As with First Class tickets, there are no restrictions, though there may be an additional charge for stopovers.

APEX (Advance Booking Excursion) fares are just about the best bargains available. These fares offer enormous reductions on the price of a First Class or Economy ticket. But in exchange for the lower cost, a number of restrictions are imposed. The basic requirements are a 21-day advance booking and payment, plus a minimum stay of seven days. APEX tickets are only available on round-trips, and once booked, flight dates may not be changed.

Special Offers. The cut-price (around $190 one way) fares by People Express from Newark to Gatwick with daily flights each way, started in 1983, has proved a big success and the frequency may be increased for 1985. As we went to press, a similar cut-price offer was being promoted by Virgin Atlantic Airways, who were awaiting government approval. The main airlines were holding their fire about their response, but it is likely that they will counteract with a series of cut-price bargains. We advise you to keep in close touch with your travel agent about the latest developments which will change rapidly. You could save a lot of money.

Stand-by fares were abandoned by all airlines in 1983, but were then revived in the summer of '84. They are sometimes available, though they do not always represent a savings over APEX. Similarly, some airlines offer APEX-equivalent fares if passage is booked two days in advance of departure.

Although the number of charter flights across the North Atlantic is less than it was, say, in 1980, there are still quite a few available. Some of these are on a "seat only" basis, others as part of a package holiday with accommodation, some meals and excursions included. Details from travel agents.

BY SEA. The only regular transatlantic service by liner is that provided by the *Queen Elizabeth 2* (Cunard Line) which does a dozen round trips from April to October often interspersed by one or two short cruises from Southampton. The voyage from New York to Southampton, usually with a call at the French port of Cherbourg, takes five days. Operating officially as a two-class ship (but with substantial intermingling) the cost of a one-way fare is between $1,000 and $6,500 with many variations. There are also excursion returns and an air-sea return fare allowing you to sail one way and fly the other.

There are also a *very* limited number of berths available on passenger-freighter vessels which carry up to a maximum of 12 passengers on each voyage. Reservations for these are made many months in advance, up to two years in some cases. They operate from ports on both the Atlantic and Pacific coasts. We suggest that you consult a good travel agent, one that is involved in shipping activities, for the latest position on freighter travel.

Failing a handy, well-versed travel agent, the determined can consult *Air Marine Travel Service,* 501 Madison Ave., New York, N.Y. 10022, (212) 371–1300, publisher of the *Trip Log Quick Reference Freighter Guide;* or *Pearl's Freighter Tips,* 175 Great Neck Rd., Great Neck, N.Y. 11021, (516) 487–8351, for details on freighter passage.

FROM THE CONTINENT AND IRELAND

BY AIR. Between the services of the main U.K. airlines and those of Continental carriers, London and over a dozen provincial cities have links with some 65 European destinations, either by non-stop or through-plane flights. For example, every European capital—with the exception of Tirana (Albania)—has a direct flight to London; from France there are flights from no fewer than 14 cities plus Paris. With a very few exceptions, all of these operate throughout the year, mostly on a daily basis but on the busier routes anything from three to a dozen flights daily.

Besides London (Heathrow and Gatwick) the following U.K. cities have direct flights from Continental destinations—Birmingham, Manchester, Newcastle, Glasgow, Edinburgh, Cardiff, Bristol, Leeds, Norwich, Southampton, Aberdeen, Belfast, Exeter and Plymouth. From Ireland there are flights into London, Liverpool, Manchester, Glasgow and a number of other cities—mostly from Dublin and less so Cork and Shannon.

The variety of fares offered is very wide indeed. Consult your travel agent and airlines. Remember, too, that if you have a full-fare ticket from the U.S.A./Canada to a European destination it can often allow you a stopover in the U.K.

BY SEA. Although the talk of a Channel Tunnel linking England with France still goes on, the reality remains somewhere in the future. However, with over 70 drive-on, drive-off car ferries operating to no fewer than 13 ports in England it is a very easy matter to get there either by car or as a foot passenger using road or rail services.

Here are the main routes on the drive-on, drive-off services, all of which carry foot passengers. They are ordered from the northernmost one, round the coast of Europe to Spain—

Bergen (Norway) to Newcastle-upon-Tyne

Kristiansand (Norway) to Harwich

Gothenburg Sweden) to Newcastle-upon-Tyne, Harwich

Esbjerg (Denmark) to Newcastle-upon-Tyne, Harwich

Hamburg (West Germany) to Harwich

Rotterdam (Holland) to Hull

Hoek van Holland (Holland) to Harwich

Zeebrugge (Belgium) to Hull, Felixstowe, Dover

Vlissingen (Holland) to Sheerness

Oostende (Belgium) to Dover, Folkestone

Dunkerque (France) to Ramsgate, Dover

Calais (France) to Dover, Folkestone

Boulogne (France) to Dover, Folkestone

Dieppe (France) to Newhaven

Le Havre (France) to Portsmouth

Cherbourg (France) to Weymouth, Portsmouth

St. Malo (France) to Portsmouth

Roscoff (France) to Plymouth

Santander (Spain) to Plymouth

In addition to these there are Hovercraft services operated by *Hoverspeed* from Dover to both Calais and Boulogne. And the newest of the "surface skimmers"—the *Jetfoil*—operates from Ostend to Dover. The latter carries passengers only.

Between Ireland and the U.K. the following services operate—

Belfast to **Liverpool**

Larne to **Stranraer, Cairnryan** (both in southwest Scotland)

Dublin to **Liverpool**

Dun Laoghaire (near Dublin) to **Holyhead**

Rosslare to **Fishguard, Pembroke**

All are drive-on, drive-off ferry services.

Arriving in London

 CUSTOMS REGULATIONS. In general all articles you are carrying with you for your personal use may be brought in free of duty if you are visiting for less than 6 months, but the following restrictions apply. *If you live outside Europe:* you may import duty-free from any non-Common Market country, or from *within* the EEC provided goods are obtained duty and tax *free,* the following, 400 cigarettes or 200 cigarillos or 100 cigars or 500 grams of tobacco; 1 liter of alcoholic drinks over 38.8° proof or 2 liters of alcoholic drinks *not* over 38.8° proof (or fortified or sparkling wine), and 2 liters of still table wine. Also 50 grams of perfume (2 fl. oz), ¼ liter (9 fl. oz) of toilet water and £28 worth of other goods.

Entering Britain from any other *Common Market* (EEC) country, you may, *instead* of the above exemptions, bring in the following, *provided you live outside Europe,* or provided goods are obtained duty and tax *paid within* the EEC, and you can prove the goods were *not* bought in a duty-free shop: 300 cigarettes or 150 cigarillos or 75 cigars or 400 grams of tobacco; 1½ liters of alcoholic drinks over 38.8° proof or 3 liters of alcoholic drinks *not* over 38.8° proof (or fortified or sparkling wine), plus 4 liters of still table wine; 75 grams of perfume (3 fl. oz) and 0.375 liters (13 fl. oz) of toilet water and £163 worth of other normally dutiable goods.

Note that provided you are visiting Britain for less than six months, you are also entitled to bring in, free of duty and tax, all personal effects which you intend to take with you when you leave (except tobacco products, alcoholic drinks, perfume and toilet water).

 PETS. There are extremely rigid controls on the importation of animals into Britain, caused by the rapid spread of rabies on the Continent. If you are likely to be taking animals into Britain (from the Continent or elsewhere), make very sure you have checked on the quarantine (*always* 6 months) and other regulations. Infringement of these regulations can lead to a heavy fine or imprisonment.

 GETTING INTO TOWN FROM THE AIRPORTS. From Heathrow it is easy to reach London by taxi, Underground or airport bus. Taxis will cost in the region of £16, excluding tip, but you must beware of ripoffs— keep an eye on the meter. Underground (Heathrow Central and Terminal 4 on the Piccadilly Line) costs around £1.50 to the middle of London. But be warned —you have to tote your bags a long way. London Regional Transport's Airbus goes to a couple of stops near Victoria Station (also very handy for the Coach Station), and to Euston and Paddington stations. The A1 to Victoria runs around every 20 minutes, and the A2 to Paddington around every half-hour;

6.30 in the morning until 9.30 at night, 7 days a week. The A3 to Euston runs hourly from about 8 until 3 P.M. Fare £2.50.

From Gatwick, rail is the quickest method (to Victoria Station). There are trains every 15 minutes, the fare is around £3.70. Other British airports are well served with bus and local taxi services.

$P£ **MONEY.** You may take into the United Kingdom any amount of currency of any kind in the form of travelers' checks, letters of credit and so forth and any amount of notes in any currency. You may take out of the country foreign currencies in the amount you brought in, or any amount in sterling.

When you change dollars or travelers' checks, you will probably lose a few cents on the dollar, from 1c or 2c at banks, to 4c at hotels and shops, as the former convert at "bank rates" and the latter at any rate they feel like. The small *bureaux de change* that are springing up throughout central London usually have a minimum charge of about 50p.

British Currency. The decimal currency is based on the pound sterling, but is divided into 100 *pence*. Bank notes are in values of £50, £20, £10, £5 and £1 (the latter is supposed to be on the way out, though the coin replacing it has proved singularly unpopular). The decimal coins are: £1, 50p (seven sided), 20p, 10p (the old 2 shilling piece, still legal, has the same value), 5p (equivalent to the old 1 shilling piece, also still legal), all cupro-nickel (silver); 2p and 1p, bronze.

Exchange Rates. Rates of exchange are extremely volatile these days. We advise you to check carefully on the exchange while you are planning your trip and then, while traveling, keep an eagle eye on what is happening to the dollar or pound. It's a simple precaution, but it can pay handsome dividends, both in peace of mind and hard cash.

Traveling in Britain

 BY CAR. Any visitor who is a member of an automobile club in his own country can, when bringing a car to Britain, have the assistance of the two principal motoring clubs, the *Automobile Association,* Fanum House, Basingstoke, Hants., (tel. 954 7373), and the *Royal Automobile Club,* 49 Pall Mall, London SW1, (tel. 839 7050), for a small charge. Rescue services are operated for members of both these organizations, but they are conditional, unless you join their special recovery services (about £35 a year, including basic membership fee of £19.50).

Both the AA and the RAC have their highly organized touring departments represented at all the principal ports and in a number of provincial towns. It is, however, a good idea before leaving home to get advice from your own automobile club concerning procedure and documentation. Providing that you have with you your car registration papers, a nationality plaque and a current driving license, visitors are free to drive their own cars in Britain. If they have no registration papers or plaque, they will be issued with temporary papers and what are called "Q" plates, i.e. special registration plates for visitors. These cost £10.50. (*Note:* new legislation may change all this—check with auto club.)

Rules of the Road. In Britain one drives on the left-hand side of the road and tries to sort out the various speed limits. In the center of cities and most built-up areas, it is 30 mph; on some suburban roads it is sometimes 40; on dual carriageways and motorways 70; and on all other roads 60 mph. The beginning and end of all limited sections are marked with round warning signs, except the 60s. When a suburban road is limited to 40 mph, or is derestricted, it carries small applicable signs on the lamp posts. Hardly any foreigners can make head or tail of all this, and nor can many British drivers. The AA and RAC maintain highway services to help in emergencies such as a flat tyre or no-go engine, but they no longer patrol the roads. Instead they are equipped with walkie-talkie and can be summoned by telephone.

Maps. To get about Britain with any degree of success it is essential to have maps. Simple maps giving sightseeing information are available, mostly free, from the British Tourist Authority. Good overall planning maps come inexpensively from the AA, while the RAC covers the whole country in 11 excellent sectional maps at 3 miles to the inch (except the two Scotland maps, which are 4 miles to the inch). They also put out a good map of the whole of England, Scotland and Wales, which clearly shows motorways, primary and secondary routes. In fact, England now has motorways running almost the length of the country in both west and east, with three links connecting them in the south, midlands and north. The network is excellent for covering, toll free, long distances between one touring area and another, but they convey almost nothing of the countryside.

Alternatively, advantage can be taken of British Rail's car-passenger trains, known as *Motorail*. At press time, there were eight scheduled routes, all out of London, to destinations including Inverness, Aberdeen, Stirling and Edinburgh north of the border, Penzance in the West Country, and Newcastle in the North East. For an example of prices, Euston to Inverness starts at £90 single and £170 return; these rates are for car and driver—additional passengers from £35 (single), £64 (return). All above prices include sleeper accommodation on train. Check with BR for latest rates (tel. 387 8541, 837 4200).

When planning a motoring holiday in Britain it is necessary to realize that once you get off the motorways travel is slow. To keep up an overall average of 35 mph is not easy. In Wales it is more difficult than in England; in some parts of Scotland it is impossible. Similarly it should be noted that motor travel in Scotland and the North might be impossible from January to March because of sudden bad weather laid on top of difficult roads.

Gas. The price of gasoline (petrol in Britain, though everyone understands "gas") is approximately £2.05 a gallon as we go to press. Lubricating oils average around £1.20 a liter. Remember that the British imperial gallon is substantially larger than the American, four of the former equal five of the latter. But you may find, anyway, that metrication has changed all that.

Car Hire. Buying or renting a car is preferable to bringing your own, as American models are unwieldy on narrow English roads and consume more gas than do the small native models. There are many firms specializing in the hire of self-drive or chauffeur-driven cars, by the hour, day, week, or month. Prices vary according to the size of the car and length of hire. With unlimited mileage, you can hire a Ford Escort (automatic) for £224 per week (up to £428 for classier model). All firms require a deposit, plus the estimated cost of hire, unless you use a recognized credit card, with which all charges can be paid later. You must also pay a collision damage waver in most cases (£19.60 in case of Escort above). Winter rates can be lower. Rates for chauffeur-driven cars: expect to pay from £94 per day for up to about 40 miles/8 hours, inclusive (to around £230 for a Rolls Royce). *All plus VAT.* It is possible to arrange for a self-drive car to be waiting for you at your port of arrival, or any railway station.

Don't forget when planning your trip that there are great advantages in leaving your car at the end of your tour at a different city from that in which you picked it up.

Avis Rent-a-Car, International Reservations, Trident House, Station Rd., Hayes, Middlesex (848 8733).

N.C.P. Car Park, Orchard St, Swansea, Wales (0792 46 0939).

4 Saunders Rd, Piccadilly Station Approach, Cardiff, Wales (0222 42111).

100 Dalry Rd, Edinburgh, Scotland (031 337 6363).

Gateway Garage, Station Approach, Manchester (061 236 6716).

For chauffeur hire (01) 897 2621.

Godfrey Davis Europcar, Bushey House, High St, Bushey, Watford, Hertz (950 4080).

Monaco House, Bristol St, Birmingham (021 622 5311).

1/11 Byron St (off City Rd), Cardiff, Wales (0222 497110).

24 East London St, Edinburgh, Scotland (031 661 1252).

Hertz International Reservations Center, Radnor House, 1272 London Rd, Norbury, London SW16 (679 1799).

Terminal Building, Edinburgh Airport, Scotland (031 333 1019).

47 Corporation St, Manchester (061 834 4806/437 8321).

7 Suffolk St, Smallbrook, Queensway, Birmingham (021 643 5387).

Kenning Car Hire, Central Reservations, Manor Offices, Old Rd., Chesterfield, Derbs. (0246 7724).

London Airport, Skyline Hotel, Bath Rd, Harlington, Hayes, Middx (759 9701).

Circle Self-Serve, Crew Rd South, Crew Toll, Edinburgh, Scotland (031 343 3377).

210 Cheetham Hill Rd, Manchester (061 834 8151).

Swan National, 305 Chiswick High Rd, London W4 (995 4665).
2 City Rd, Cardiff, Wales (0222 496 256).
19–21 Glasgow Rd, Corstorphine, Edinburgh, Scotland (031 334 9245).
New Cross Service Station, Oldham Rd, Manchester (061 834 3020).
In the US, 1133 Broadway (corner of 26th St), New York, NY 10010, (212) 929–0920.

 BY TRAIN. In spite of the severe financial restrictions put on British Railways (a state-owned but independently operated organization) by various governments, the U.K. has one of the best railway networks in the world —though you will hear many criticisms from the British, especially the commuters. Today however for speed, safety, comfort and time keeping British Rail (or B.R. as it is usually known) is second to none.

Pride of place must go to the InterCity network which links London with every main city and many of these with each other. Fast diesel or electric trains provide a high-density service, all trains carrying both first and second class carriages.

The High Speed Train, diesel-propelled expresses which travel at up to 125 m.p.h. over long distances is in the vanguard, with seven, eight and nine carriages. They are fully airconditioned, spaciously comfortable, carry either full restaurant or buffet (sometimes both) cars and are known as InterCity 125 expresses. No supplementary fares are required for travel in them.

They operate on the routes from London (Paddington) to Bristol, South Wales, Devon and Cornwall and from London (Kings Cross) to Leeds, York, Hull, Middlesbrough, Newcastle, Edinburgh, Dundee, Aberdeen and Inverness. To Newcastle for example, a distance of around 270 miles, on weekdays hourly 125s do the journey in a few minutes over three hours, including intermediate stops. To Edinburgh the famous *Flying Scotsman* express leaves Kings Cross at 10 A.M. every week-day and arrives in the Scottish capital 393 miles away at 2.30 P.M.

On the west-coast route to Glasgow (and also to Liverpool and Manchester) all trains are electrically hauled and again fully airconditioned, with long distances being run at speeds up to 110 m.p.h. The *Royal Scot,* another famous train, does the 404 miles between London (Euston) and Glasgow (Central) in just over five hours, with two stops en route.

On all other InterCity services the standards are high. On short distances, too, newer rolling stock ensures a comfortable ride with a high frequency of services such as those on the electric routes from London to Brighton and to Bournemouth; or in Scotland the fast (45 minutes for the 48 miles) line between Glasgow and Edinburgh with up to 24 trains each way daily.

London has a vast, mostly electrified, commuter network while cities like Liverpool and Manchester have similar but smaller systems. In Scotland a fully integrated rail, bus and ferry network centered on Glasgow now gives a second to none suburban transport system while the Metro—light rapid transit system —in Newcastle-upon-Tyne, does the same for that area.

For overnight travel most long-distance trains carry both 1st and 2nd class sleeping cars, some trains being sleepers only. The sleeping cars are of a standard design with full-size bed, hot and cold running water, soap, towel, footmat, adequate clothing hangers, several lights, individually-controlled heating and ventilation; each two cars share an attendant who provides drinks in your berth, and complimentary tea or coffee and biscuits in the morning. In 1st class there is one berth per compartment, in 2nd class two—an upper and a lower.

All sleeping cars are now of the latest Mark III design, fully airconditioned and giving a very comfortable ride. Supplements are £11 in 2nd class, £16 in 1st class on all routes, but there are combined "travel fare and sleeper" packages for some trips.

One thing must be stressed about rail travel from and to London. The city has no fewer than eight InterCity termini and several others handling suburban traffic. Be *quite certain* which one your train departs from or arrives at. All have Underground stations either on the premises or within a couple of minutes' walk; they are also served by many bus routes.

FARES. Although the standard fares on B.R. are comparatively high there are so many cost-cutting tickets available that you can keep your rail-travel budget surprisingly low. The range of these is formidable and they are constantly being added to, offering reductions of anything from 10% to as much as 60% off the standard fare. There are *Cheap Day* returns, *Saver* returns, *Merrymaker* special-day outings, and innumerable excursions of one kind or another.

For the keen sightseer we suggest buying the *BritRail Pass* which gives unlimited travel over the entire network (more than 11,000 route miles) including certain ferry routes in Scotland and also those from Portsmouth to the Isle of Wight. It is issued to overseas visitors *only,* and must be bought—from agents of BritRail International—before leaving their home country. Valid for 7, 14 or 21 days, or a month, it costs, respectively, $155, $230, $290, or $335, in 1st class, and $115, $175, $220, or $260, in Economy class (1985 rates).

British Rail will again be issuing for 1986 their popular *Railrover* rickets which give unlimited travel over either the whole of England or Wales or Scotland, or within specific regions such as the south-west of England, East Anglia, central Scotland or Northumbria. All of these are issued for seven days, some also for 14 days. Again, these are ideal for concentrated sightseeing in a limited time.

At peak-holiday periods and on popular routes we strongly recommend seat reservation for medium- and long-distance travel. On some trains—such as on Saturdays in mid-summer on expresses to Devon and Cornwall—seat reservation is obligatory. On other specified trains (e.g. the *Flying Scotsman* to Edinburgh and Aberdeen) seating is restricted and reservations are advisable at all times. The cost of reserving a seat (in 1st or 2nd class) is currently £1.

For the Disabled. An informative book, *Traveling with British Rail,* giving a wide range of information about rail travel for the disabled has been published jointly by British Rail and the *Royal Association for Disability and Rehabilitation*

(RADAR). Copies can be obtained by post from RADAR (£2 over counter, £2.80 inc. post/pack.), 25 Mortimer Street, London W1N 8AB. There is also a free leaflet available at principal stations. Another useful guide available from RADAR is *Access to the Underground* (95p, £1.20 inc. p./p.), published by London Regional Transport.

Rail Drive. One of the U.K.'s leading self-drive car companies, *Godfrey Davis-Europcar Ltd.* have self-drive cars available at most main line stations. You can make a reservation before you board the train and your car will be awaiting you on arrival. At very busy periods however it is advisable to book further in advance.

Rail Holidays. A highly successful part of B.R.'s marketing has been the *Golden Rail Holidays* scheme started over 15 years ago. These offer package deals in a score of cities, towns and holiday centers with rail travel as part of the deal. In each there is a wide range of hotel accommodations available. The holidays are usually for 7 or 8 days, but can be longer if you wish; they also offer the shorter *Golden Rail Short Breaks.* Prices obviously depend on destination and accommodations, but for example you can have 8 days touring Devon and the Cornish Riviera from £163 off-season, up to £230 in the summer months; or 8 days in the Scottish Highlands from £153 up to £230. Ask for the fully comprehensive brochure about these at any mainline station or Travel Center.

Another package deal is the one-day (a few are two-day) *Britainshrinker,* which is aimed particularly at overseas visitors with trips to places like Canterbury, Oxford, York, Plymouth and Edinburgh. Sightseeing and meals are included and also accommodation in the two-day programs. These cost between £29.60 (day trip to Cambridge) and £140 (2 days based in Edinburgh and staying at the Caledonian Hotel). A point to note is that Britrail Pass holders can get up to 45% reduction on these prices. To find out more, contact *Britainshrinkers,* 10 Queen Street, London W1 (tel. 499 5569). A full-color brochure gives all the details.

Further Information. British Rail have established a network of Travel Centers throughout the country based in main railway stations. These act as general information centers as well as booking offices where tickets can be bought and reservations may be made. In London they are to be found at the following termini—Kings Cross, Euston, Liverpool Street, Paddington, Waterloo, Victoria, London Bridge, Cannon Street, St. Pancras, and Charing Cross. In addition the British Rail Travel Center at 12 Lower Regent Street, S.W.1 (only two minutes' walk from Piccadilly Circus) and the B.R. offices at 407 Oxford St., W.1, 14 Kingsgate Parade, Victoria Street, SW1, 170b Strand, WC2, and 87 King William Street, EC4, are also full information and booking offices.

We strongly recommend that you use these Travel Centers for all rail travel plans.

North American Addresses: For all information on rail travel in the U.K. contact *BritRail Travel International Office,* 630 Third Ave., New York, N.Y. 10017, (212) 599–5400; 510 West Sixth St., Los Angeles, California 90014; 333 North Michigan Ave., Chicago, Illinois 60601; Plaza of the Americas, N. Tower, LB 356, Dallas, TX 75201. In Canada: 94 Cumberland St., Suite 601, Toronto M5R 1A3, Ontario; 409 Granville St., Vancouver V6C 1T2, British Columbia.

BY BUS. Although the U.S.A.'s *Greyhound Bus* organisation might dispute it, the United Kingdom has the world's most intensive network of bus and coach (this term is always used in England for long-distance bus services) routes. This has been greatly increased as a result of the 1980 Transport Act which broke the monopoly of the state-owned *National Bus Company.* Now private enterprise bus companies compete with the National Bus services on many routes.

Bus travel is not as fast as by train but with the use of motorways and fast dual-carriageways (divided highways) inter-city travel by bus is quite swift. For example, it is just over two hours to Bristol from London, a distance of 125 miles.

But what these services may lack in speed they certainly make up for in cost, with fares being roughly half those charged for the same distance by train. For example, London to Cardiff (in south Wales) can be as low as £11.50 return for off-peak services—not bad for 290 miles.

Bus and coach travel has become increasingly comfortable in recent years with long distance routes such as those linking London with Glasgow and Edinburgh being fully airconditioned.

London Crusader, the marketing arm of the National Bus Company, issue a BritExpress Card, covering a 30-day period and providing a discount of 33 1/3% on all National Express coaches throughout England, Scotland and Wales, also on the Flyteline service to Victoria Coach Station operating from Gatwick and Heathrow airports. Available in the U.K., it costs $10 if purchased in the States. The Explorer Pass, also from London Crusader, costs £2.50 (or £5 for family of four) and provides a varying discount on NBC transport—it all depends how much use you make of it; valid for one day only.

With the many local bus services it is fairly easy to get about the country without a car. Although many of these may only have one or two services a day, they do afford an excellent way to see the countryside and above all to meet local people. All local tourist information offices in England, Scotland, Wales and Northern Ireland have up to date timetables of local services.

For further information on National Bus routes and services, write to—or call in at—National Bus Information Office, Victoria Coach Station, Buckingham Palace Rd., London SW1 (tel. 730 0202).

For Green Line and London Country Bus, contact the office at Eccleston Bridge, Victoria, SW1 (tel. 834 6563). Information on the many private enterprise bus services can be obtained through various travel agents.

BY AIR. For a comparatively small country Britain does have an extensive network of internal air routes operated by about a dozen airlines with British Airways, the state-owned corporation, maintaining several of the main trunk routes. These include the Shuttle Services between London and Glasgow, Edinburgh, Belfast and Manchester. These are either hourly or every two hours, seven days a week. They are on a no reservations basis. Turn up and walk on with a guaranteed seat and back-up flights. Passengers can book in up to about half an hour before flight departure times.

British Caledonian Airways also fly to Glasgow, Edinburgh and Belfast from Gatwick. *British Midland* go to Teesside, Belfast, Liverpool, Glasgow, Edinburgh and the Isle of Man from London (mainly Heathrow), while *Dan Air* fly from Gatwick to Newcastle and Aberdeen and from Heathrow to Inverness (latter actually an *Aer Lingus* flight, handled by British Cal.), *Air UK* have an extensive system of internal routes, having taken over many formerly operated by BA, going to places like Leeds-Bradford, Southampton, Birmingham and Norwich.

Staying in London

SOURCES OF INFORMATION IN LONDON. The London Visitor and Convention Bureau operates the following information centers—*Victoria Station*, on forecourt, for information on London and England, sales of tours, tourist and theater tickets, comprehensive bookshop. Accommodation booking service, including *Book-a-Bed-Ahead* scheme. Open: 9–8.30 daily, including Sundays; extended hours in summer. *Heathrow Central Tube Station*, information and accommodation, tour bookings, etc. Open: 9–6 daily; Information Centers at *Harrods* (4th Floor); *Selfridges* (Ground Floor), and within the Tower of London. Their telephone information service is open 9–5.30, the number is 730 3488.

Apart from help from daily newspapers, magazines and publications like *London Planner* (available monthly from British Tourist Authority offices overseas), you can head the latest up to date information on an eclectic bundle of events and how to get to them, at the end of a telephone. This data is compiled by the B.T.A. at its London office, and available day and night. For a three minute recording of the day's goings-on in English, simply dial 01–246 8041 (if using a public call box, don't forget to have the correct coin(s) handy—see *Telephone,* p. 37). Don't worry if the message starts half-way through the recording—it's continuous and you'll soon hear it all over again. You'll also be told that information about cinema, theater and concert programs appears in the evening paper. Information on Children's London is available by dialing 01–246 8007. Remember that, if calling from the London area, you do not use the 01-prefix.

HOTELS AND RESTAURANTS. We feel that these two topics are so central to your visit to London, that we have set aside two separate chapters in which to discuss them. We would point out, though, in this Planning Section, that you can book your hotel well in advance of leaving home, and we heartily recommend that you do so. Naturally, if you are taking a package holiday, the hotel will be included.

TIPPING. Many large hotels and most of those belonging to chains automatically add a 10% to 15% service charge on your final bill. In this case you are *not* expected to tip, and any staff member who attempts to insinuate otherwise should be ignored, if not reported to the management. If you have received exceptional service from any member of staff, then you may of course tip accordingly. If you are *dissatisfied* with the service, then give your reasons and do not pay the service charge. You will be legally in the right.

If there is no service charge, then you may divide a sum equivalent to 10% of your total bill between those personnel who have been of service during your stay. This will generally include the chambermaid, porter and restaurant staff. In restaurants, tip 10–15% of the check. Bellhops and porters about 50p.

Taxi drivers should get 20p on fares up to £1.50, and 10% on fares higher than that. Beware however of those London Airport sob stories that frequently greet the traveler and concern waiting time! They are usually calculated to produce a bigger tip! You *should* pay about £16 exlcuding tip to central London from Heathrow Airport.

You do not tip while drinking at the bar in a pub, but you can offer the barman a drink if you are a habitué of the place. Do not tip cinema or theater ushers, nor elevator operators. Hairdressers and barbers are tipped 15% of the bill.

CLOSING TIMES. Legal holidays (Bank Holidays is the English term) are not uniform throughout Great Britain. In England the holidays are Jan. 1; Mar. 28, 31 (Easter); May 5; May 26 (Late Spring Holiday); Aug. 25 (Late Summer Holiday); Dec. 25, 26.

Usual shopping and business hours are 9 to 5 or 5.30 P.M. Banks open at 9.30 or 10 A.M., and close at 3.30 P.M. Mon.-Fri., closed Sat. Smaller shops may close on a variable half-day in the week. Best check locally. Big West End of London stores stay open until 7 or 8 P.M. one day a week, generally Wednesday or Thursday, and also open Saturday, though some of them only in the morning.

Drinking Hours. Approximately 11 A.M. to 10.30 or 11 P.M. with the exception of about 2½ hours in the afternoon, usually 3 to 5.30 P.M. depending on the area. On Sundays, hours are 12 noon to 2 P.M., and 7 to 10.30 P.M.

HISTORIC BUILDINGS AND GARDENS. Opening days and admission charges for houses, etc., are liable to change from season to season, especially as many are still privately owned and occupied. We therefore list only approximate days and times throughout this book. The National Tourist Information Office at Victoria Station (tel. 730 3488) can confirm the current times and charges if you are in doubt.

In our regional chapters we are able to list only a few of the outstanding stately homes, castles, and other properties that may be visited. An extremely useful publication, giving opening times and admission fees of many hundreds of houses and gardens open to the public, is *Historic Houses, Castles and Gardens in Great Britain and Ireland,* ABC Historic Publications, World Timetable Center, Church St., Dunstable, Beds. The entrance fee to most of the houses varies from 50p to £2.50, but is usually about £1.75–2.00.

Many houses belong to the National Trust, a privately funded organization, founded to help preserve the national heritage. An annual membership (£12.50) entitles you to visit free over 200 historic houses and 90 gardens; for information write *The National Trust,* 42 Queen Anne's Gate, London SW1.

For £8 (or £12 for a family) you can buy a year's membership from the Historic Buildings and Monuments Commission for England, entitling you to free entry to around 400 of England's most important historical sites, including Hampton Court and the Tower of London. Write to Room 32, Building 1, Vision Way, Victoria Road, South Ruislip, Middlesex HA4 0NZ, for further details.

SHOPPING—VALUE ADDED TAX. In addition to the details of shopping in London in the separate chapter, here is a very important point to keep in mind. To the eternal fury of Britain's shopkeepers, who struggle under cataracts of paperwork, Britain is afflicted with a 15% Value Added Tax. Foreign visitors, however, need not pay V.A.T. if they take advantage of the Personal Export Scheme.

To avoid V.A.T. there is an *Over-the-Counter* export scheme which enables shoppers to take possession of a purchase immediately. You may well have to ask if you wish to make use of the scheme, though most major stores will oblige. The sales clerk should fill out Form V.A.T. 407 and attach the invoice. The form and invoice, together with the goods, should be presented to the Customs officer at your point of departure from the U.K. (remember to leave yourself plenty of time at the airport for this, there's always a long line). Many stores provide a stamped addressed envelope, in which you must return the form to the store. Note that there is normally a minimum limit of £75, below which you cannot make use of the scheme for goods; and that you must have some proof of identity before the store will issue the form.

If you plan, instead, to send the goods home separately, then you have to use the *Direct Export* method. As with the Over-the-Counter scheme, you get Form V.A.T. 407 at the store; however, it must then be certified by the Customs or a notary public in the United States. Alternatively, any documentary evidence of payment in the U.S. of import duty or tax that identifies the goods may be provided. Once again, the form must be returned to the store of purchase. The refund will then be sent to you, minus a £2.50 service charge. The refund can take up to eight weeks to arrive.

The above two plans apply not only to the United States, but to all EEC countries, with the exception of France, where it is possible to receive your refund at the airport of port of departure.

Shopping Service. There are several firms offering shopping services to serious visiting shoppers. Among them is the whimsically-named *Spotted Dog*, run by Diana Scott Thorburn from 9 Cambridge St., SW1 (828 7921). She specializes in both tracking down items which might otherwise be difficult to find and in arranging shopping expeditions tailored to particular interests. Fee £35 for a half day, £60 a full day.

ELECTRICITY. If you're bringing electric shavers, irons, hair driers, etc., with you, it's best to check that they can be safely used on British voltages. The most general are 220 to 240 volts, AC., 50 cycles. Since most American appliances are designed to operate on 110 to 120 volts, 60 cycles, visitors from the United States will need transformers. Most hotels have special razor sockets which will take both voltages.

MAIL. *Inland:* letters and postcards up to 60 g, 13p (slow), 17p (fast). *To Europe:* letters up to 20 g, 22p, cards the same. Letters and cards go by air at these rates if this makes for earlier delivery, so there is no need to use airmail stickers, though lightweight paper will make for minimum postal rate. *To the U.S. and Canada:* letters and cards up to 10 g, 31p. Postcards 26p: airmail stickers should be used.

Telemessages. These replaced the much-missed internal telegram. The basic principle is the same—you book the message by phone—but delivery is with the following day's 1st class mail. Price is £3.50 *excluding* V.A.T. for up to 50 words, £1.75 per 50 words thereafter (exc. V.A.T.). You can still send overseas telegrams by phone to the U.S. *To the U.S.,* you can send either the normal telegram (£2, plus 32p per word), or a *Mailgram*—for which the rate is £5.75 the first 50 words and £2.50 per 50 thereafter (all excluding V.A.T.).

TELEPHONE. In much of central London, you will now find the familiar red phone box (which still accepts 5p and 10p coins) replaced by the press-button "Blue Pay-phone," which takes 2p, 5p, 10p, 20p, 50p and £1 coins. Instructions on how to use the new phone are clearly indicated within the kiosk. For making overseas calls, either call the operator or enquire at any post office. Or—go along to the Westminster Communications Centre (see below).

Dialing codes in the Greater London area: for general information 191; for London directory inquiries 142; for other inland directory inquiries 192; for inland long-distance calls 100; for continental calls 104 or 105; for overseas calls 107 or 108; cables 190 (inland), 193 (international).

In making overseas calls remember the difference in time zones. Thus, for most of the year 12 noon in London is 7 A.M. in New York, 6 A.M. in Chicago, etc.

For *emergency calls* (fire, police, ambulance) throughout the country dial 999.

Each large city or region has its own prefix (London's is 01) which is used when dialing from outside the city; when already in the city, the prefix is dropped and the seven figure number should be used.

Warning. You should not make long-distance calls from your hotel room without checking very carefully what the cost is likely to be. Hotels frequently add several *hundred* percent to such calls. This is an international practice and not just confined to Britain. It is worthwhile utilizing your telephone credit card for these calls to avoid the massive hotel surcharge and certain U.S. cards are valid in Europe for this purpose.

Useful Hint. Visitors to London—or anyone else for that matter—who wish to make overseas calls can avail themselves of the service offered at the *Westminster Communications Centre,* 1 The Broadway, SW1 (opposite the new buildings of Scotland Yard and right by St. James's underground station). It is open seven days a week from 9 until 7, and staff there will help you make a speedy connection.

Getting About London

BY BUS. The entire bus and Underground transport system in London is operated by London Regional Transport, successor to London Transport, and the largest undertaking of its kind in the western world.

The bus network is very intensive, most of the routes being operated by the familiar bright-red double-decker buses. On one or two routes for technical or logistic reasons there are single decker vehicles. Most are painted red.

On the front, side and rear they carry the route number, the ultimate destination of the bus and the principal stops on that route.

Many buses now have "one-man operation" whereby you pay as you enter. But the majority still carry a conductor who collects fares. You receive a ticket for this which you should retain until the end of the journey. The ticket is valid only for that journey and cannot be used on any other.

Buses stop only at the clearly indicated bus stops. There are two types of these. At main stops which have a plain white background and the London Regional Transport symbol in red on it, buses stop without any signaling being necessary. At other stops, which have a red background with the symbol in white and the word *Request* on it, the bus will only stop if intending passengers signal clearly by raising their hand as the vehicle approaches.

The pros and cons of travel by London bus are easily stated. In support are the facts that you can see so much of the town, perched high above most of the traffic, and see it at a reasonable cost, for the bus fares are lower than the underground ones. Against bus travel are the facts that London traffic slows the bus routes down so that you may find yourself waiting for twenty minutes for a bus, and then not be able to get on when it finally arrives. And, for the same reasons, it is almost impossible to time any journey; a trip that should take ten minutes might consume forty.

An absolute must for anyone wanting to travel a lot by London bus is the free bus map that London Regional Transport produce. With this in your hand it is almost possible to understand the convolutions of the routes.

BY UNDERGROUND. The Underground is equally extensive, with routes running out into the suburbs. All stations, both those on the surface and those below ground, are clearly marked with the London Underground roundel symbol and the word *Underground* on it. Trains are all one class and no smoking is permitted on them or at any station below ground level. There are nine basic lines, all of which have names, such as the Central, Piccadilly and Bakerloo, etc. But all except the Jubilee, Bakerloo, and Victoria lines have branches, so it is essential to know where you are going. Lighted signs on station platforms tell you the destination and route of the next train.

London Underground issue clear diagrammatic maps of the entire system. And on every platform there is at least one, generally two, of these maps on a larger scale. Each carriage also has the route map in it (as many as eight or ten of these) so it is easy to see where you are going. Station signs are very numerous.

The Underground on weekdays starts just after 5 A.M. and last trains leave the central London area between midnight and 12.30 A.M. On Sunday starting time is about two hours later (some services do start before that) and last trains leave roughly an hour earlier. The frequency of trains varies according to the time of day and the route—but you do not usually have to wait for more than a few minutes at any time other than in the very late evening.

After two or three years of expensive muddle, the ticket system for the Underground has at last settled down. London has been divided up into zones with simple unit fares. The central zone, which covers all the main inner area costs 40p; the central zone *plus* the next one costs 60p. Outside that there are other rates, but the two inner zones will cover most visitors' daily wants. Tickets can be bought from the ticket offices, or from automatic slot machines: they accept 10p, 20p, 50p and £1 coins. Remember always to collect your ticket when

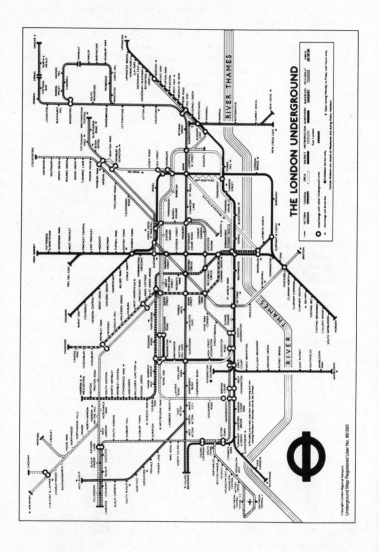

passing through automatic barriers, as it *must* be handed to the ticket collector at the end of your journey.

Decide on the line that you want, and follow the signs for the correct platform. When the train enters the platform, have a quick look at the front destination window to make sure that it's the line you want.

We should warn you that the simplicity of the system breaks down at one or two major interchange points, such as at King's Cross or Baker Street. These stations are, not to mince matters, frankly hell if you don't know them intimately. Follow the signs *very* carefully and, when in doubt, ask.

In the realm of semantics, two points—the Underground is called the "Tube" by almost everyone, from the fact that the deep-level tunnels in which the trains run are in reality steel tubes. A "subway" in Britain is a pedestrian tunnel, usually under a road and acting as an underpass from one corner to another.

SPECIAL FARES. For years London Transport had an unending number of special tickets which reduced the high cost of getting around the capital for the visitor. We suggest that you ask at a London Regional Transport Information Center for the latest advantageous scheme to help you navigate your way round the city at the lowest cost possible. Good value is the *Travel Card*, valid for a week or a month (starting any day) giving unlimited travel by Underground and bus. In the central and inner zones combined (covering the bulk of tourist London) the card costs £5.50 for a week as we went to press. *Cheap day returns* are also good buys (valid after 10 A.M. weekdays, and all weekend).

London Regional Transport also operate bus tours around the historic sights (and sites) throughout the year with a high frequency of departures in summer. There is a choice of two-hour circular tours, one with a guide the other without —the latter you can board or leave at several points including Baker Street, Victoria, near Marble Arch and near Piccadilly Circus. (See under *Sightseeing*.)

Information. London Regional Transport have a number of useful Travel Information Centers at the following Underground Stations—you can buy special fare tickets at these and also get up-to-date information: Oxford Circus (Mon.–Sat. 8.30–6, exc. Thurs. to 9.30; closed Sun.), Piccadilly Circus (Mon.–Sun. 8.30–9.30), Victoria (upstairs Mon.–Sun. 8.30–9.30, downstairs 8.30–6), King's Cross (Mon.–Sun. 8.30–6), Heathrow (Central Mon.–Sat. 7.30–9.30, Sun. 8.30–9.30; Terminal 1 Mon.–Sat. 8–9, Sun. 8.30–9; Term. 2 Mon.–Sat. 8–5, closed 11–12, closed Sun), and St. James' Park—which houses London Regional Transport headquarters (Mon.–Fri. 8.30–6). All these hours are A.M. to P.M.

For information on train times, costs etc. ring (01) 222 1234. This is a 24 hour service.

SUBURBAN RAILWAYS. All of London's 15 British Rail termini have suburban trains operating from them, some stations being exclusively for suburban traffic. All of these stations have enquiry offices where details of the services can be obtained. Note that Underground tickets are *not valid* on British Railways. But the *Capital Card,* valid for seven days, gives unlimited travel by Underground and suburban railway. Ask at any Underground or railway station for this.

BY TAXI. These unmistakable vehicles, with square bodies—no longer just black, they now come in a variety of colors—and the driver in a separate forward compartment, are liberally scattered throughout the streets of central and west London. If their flags are up, or a "for hire" sign is lighted on the top, just hail them. But you can rarely find an empty one between 5 P.M. and 7 P.M.—which is when you so often want one.

Taxi fares start at 80p when the flag falls; then, after 1,176 yards (or 4 minutes), the meter clicks up at the rate of 20p per 588 yards (or 2 mins.). This rate works up to six miles, after which it increases. Weekday nights, 8 P.M. to 12 midnight, and Saturdays up to 8 P.M. there is a 40p surcharge; weekdays midnight to 6 A.M., Saturday nights, Sundays and public holidays a 60p surcharge. Over Christmas and New Year's Eve, the surcharge is £2. Luggage carried in the driver's compartment and extra passengers also carry surcharges (10p, and 20p per person, respectively). If after reading all that you can bear to—tip the driver 10%.

A Handy Tip. Cab drivers now cruise, especially at night, with their "for hire" signs unlit. This is to enable them to choose their passengers and avoid those they think may cause trouble. If you see an unlit, passengerless cab, hail it, you may well be lucky.

BY CAR. Driving in London is not recommended for tourists. It is a very, very, big city, and whereas in New York, for example, there is some logic in the street planning, in London there is none. A minute grid system bequeathed to us by the Romans and extended in all directions in a crazily haphazard manner over roughly the last 2000 years, has in no way been clarified by the modern passion for one-way systems. Drivers who get lost and think to retrieve the situation by returning to base through a series of left-hand turns invariably find themselves quite somewhere else.

For those who must drive in London, however, the speed limit is 30 m.p.h. in the Royal parks as it is theoretically in all streets, unless you see the large 40 m.p.h. signs—and small repeater signs attached to lamp posts—found only in the suburbs. Pedestrians have total priority on "zebra" crossings. These have black and white stripes between two stiped beacon poles topped with orange bowls (that flash at night) and have zig-zag road markings on both sides. It is an offense to park within the zig-zag area on either side, or overtake another vehicle on the approach side. It will be seen that the British are meant to take their pedestrian crossings seriously, and mostly do. On other crossings pedestrians must give way to the traffic, but do take precedence over that turning left at controlled crossings, if they have the nerve.

The red, yellow and green traffic lights sometimes have arrow-style filter lights directing left- or right-hand turns. It is therefore important not to get into the turn lane if you mean to go straight on (if you can catch a glimpse of the road markings in time). The use of horns is prohibited in all built-up areas between 11.30 A.M. and 7 A.M. You can park at night in 30 m.p.h. limit zones provided that you are within 25 yards of a lit street lamp, but not within 15 yds of a road junction. To park on a bus route, side (parking) lights must be shown—but you'll probably be fined for obstruction. In the day time it is safest to believe that you can park nowhere but at a meter or in a garage. The cost of transgression is now £10, and you can't wheedle a traffic warden. If the car is towed away it could cost £45 (excluding ticket!) and a lot of tears and sweat to get it back, since the car pounds tend to be sited in the most out-of-the-way places imaginable. Another little official toy is called a Denver Boot, which clamps a wheel immovably and costs £29.50 (inc. the ticket) to get released. Note that it is now illegal to park on the sidewalk in London.

 BY CYCLE. A very good way of seeing London is by hiring a bicycle, by the day, by the week, or longer. Try *Savile's,* 97 Battersea Rise, SW11 (tel. 228 4279). Most will require a deposit and some form of identification— best bring your passport.From about £3 a day, and around £10 refundable deposit. Other addresses in Yellow Pages and business directories.

The really dedicated pedal-pusher should contact his or her local British Tourist Authority office, who will be able to supply details of companies hiring out bikes and tandems all over England, the Channel Islands, Scotland and Wales, together with prices, opening hours and other vital information. Alternatively, if already in London, go along to the new National Information Office at Victoria Station (run by London Visitor and Convention Bureau), who will also be able to help.

 BY RIVER. From Easter through to October, large motor launches operate on the Thames starting mainly from the piers at Westminster Bridge, Hungerford Railway Bridge (opposite the entrance to the Embankment Underground station) and the Tower of London. They go up river to Kew, Richmond and Hampton Court. Trips down river to the Tower and Greenwich operate all year round, from Westminster Pier. All have public address systems giving running commentaries on the passing scene.

Capital Cruises, based at Lamberth Pier and Tower Pier (tel. 870 7036 to book), offer two alternative ways of seeing the capital's landmarks with a disco cruise and a dinner-dance cruise.

The disco cruise, boarding at Tower Pier at 8 P.M. is £8.45 (£6.95 weekdays) for the 4-hour trip, including a two-course buffet; the dinner-dance cruise is £18.95, including a four-course dinner.

Full information on these river trips can be obtained from the information kiosks at the piers mentioned or from the London Visitor and Convention Bureau. The frequency of services depends on the time of year and often the weather conditions. The trip, say, from Westminster Pier to Greenwich takes about one hour, including stops en route.

BY CANAL. There is a variety of waterbus trips available on the Regent's Canal in summer months. Departures are usually from either Little Venice (nearest underground Warwick Avenue on Bakerloo Line) or Camden Lock (200 yards from Camden Town on Northern Line).

Canal Boat Cruises, 250 Camden High St., NW1 (tel. 485 4433/6210), ply the canal from Camden Lock to Little Venice Easter through Oct. in the *Jenny Wren.* Their fleet also includes the floating restaurant, *My Fair Lady,* on which you can have dinner for £14.95 (Mon.–Sat.) or Sunday lunch (£9.95). Operating out of Ladbroke Grove is *The Basin* (tel. 960 5456); no details of their sailings available at presstime—phone above number for latest position. The London Visitor and Convention Bureau can also provide information on what is available.

What to See and Do

SIGHTSEEING. By underground and bus. There are always new suggestions coming from London Regional Transport for money-saving tickets, so we suggest that you check with them (at one of their Information Centers) for the latest good news. Since the system, especially the Tube, will help you to get around very speedily, you will almost certainly find yourself using it a lot. You might just as well do it as cost effectively as possible. Full details and free bus and coach maps can be obtained from all railroad stations, most underground stations, and from London Regional Transport head office, 55 Broadway, SW1.

London Regional Transport also offers a 2-hour sightseeing tour of London by bus (some with an open top), covering 20 miles of the West End and City called the "Official London Sightseeing Tour." Most buses do not have a guide on board, so make sure you have a good map with you. No advance booking. Pick-up points are at Piccadilly Circus (Haymarket), Marble Arch (top of Park Lane, near Speakers' Corner), Grosvenor Gardens (close to Victoria Station) and Baker Street.

Complete tours of London by coach are offered by a number of operators, among them: *Evan Evans Ltd.,* 27 Cockspur St., SW1; *Frames Rickards Ltd.,*

11 Iterband St., WC1; *London Crusader,* 237–239 Oxford St., W1; and *Harrods,* who offer an up-market jaunt with a taped commentary in 8 languages.

Taxi Tours. One of the best and most easily accessible ways of getting a guided tour of London is to phone *Prestige Tours,* 3 Elystan St, SW3 (tel. 584 3118). These are normal London taxis, but driven by qualified guides. A day's notice is usually enough to lay on a really expert and comfortable tour around town (though for a straightforward trip, 30 minutes' notice is all they ask). £98 will pay for a full day's tour of London for four people; shorter trips also available such as half-days, costing £55, and 2-hour "Easy Riders" at £40. You can use the service for out-of-town trips too. Stratford and Oxford costs around £150. Although they are a bit expensive, the expertise, comfort and possibilities for a tailored-to-order tour make these guided trips excellent value.

Walking Tours. The City Corporation have laid out two walks around the City of London by means of directional studs. One, the Heritage Walk, takes in Bank, Leadenhall Market and Monument; you will find a map of the walk on the back cover of *A Visitor's Guide to the City of London* (available from the City Information Office opposite St. Paul's). The other is the Jubilee Walk, and this centers around St. Paul's and its environs. Further details about both from the City Information Office.

If you want to know more about Jack the Ripper, Samuel Pepys' London or ghosts in the city, join a walking tour organized by guides Alex and Peggy Cobban. They offer a variety of subjects (an intriguing new one is "Sir Winston Churchill"). Tickets are £1.75 for adults, £1.50 for students, and free for under 16s if accompanied by an adult; more details from *Discovering London,* 11 Pennyfields, Warley, Brentwood, Essex (tel. Brentwood 213704), or from L.V. & C.B. Another similar organization is *London Walks,* 139 Conway Road, N14 (tel. 882 2763). Prices here are £2.25 adults, £2 students, and again under 16s go free if with an adult. Our readers have found these excursions very informative and enjoyable; "they were well informed, interesting and friendly; and the lectures they presented in conjunction with the walks were well-prepared and covered a wide variety of topics," ran one of the letters we received. All of these walks take place year-round.

 MUSEUMS AND ART GALLERIES. London is one of the two or three most important centers of western civilization, and many of its museums are incomparable in their scope, variety and imaginative presentation. Here is a brief selection. Admission is free (unless otherwise indicated), and museums are usually open daily including Bank Holidays, except Good Friday, Christmas Eve, Christmas Day, Boxing Day and New Year's Day, and except where otherwise stated. The best times to visit are between 10 and 4, or Sunday afternoon. Information about public transport is included. Be sure to double check all opening times of museums and galleries on the spot. We have found that such times are liable to be changed with no notice at all, due to staff illness, strikes, fire and Acts of God, and you could easily make a trip only to find a locked door.

Note that we have given the popular name of each institution, the one you would use when asking for information. Some of them have official names which are slightly different.

Bethnal Green Museum, Cambridge Heath Rd., E2. Excellent collection of dolls, dolls' houses and toys. Daily 10–6 (closed Fri.), Sun. 2.30–6. Tube: Bethnal Green.

British Museum, Great Russell St., WC1. The single most important institution of its kind in the world. Among the various departments are prints and drawings; coins and medals; Egyptian and Assyrian antiquities; Greek, Roman, British, Medieval, Oriental antiquities; and The British Library. Try to find time to take in some of the excellent modern display techniques which have given new life to, e.g. the Parthenon Frieze and the Egyptian Collection. Weekdays, 10–5, Sun. 2.30–6. Tubes: Russell Square, Tottenham Court Road, Holborn (Kingsway).

British Museum/Museum of Mankind, Burlington Gardens, W1 (behind Royal Academy). Exhibits of tribal life and culture areas throughout the world, excitingly displayed. Same times as British Museum. Tubes: Piccadilly Circus, Green Park.

Cabinet War Rooms, Clive Steps, King Charles St., SW1, just behind Admiralty Arch in St. James's Park. Churchill's wartime bunker, ingeniously reborn at great cost but well worth seeing, for—among other things—the "toilet" that contained the hotline from Churchill to Ike. Admission £2. Tues.–Sun. 10–5.50. Tubes: Westminster, St. James's Park.

Costume Museum, Kensington Palace State Apartments, Kensington Gdns., W8. Newly opened 1984. Court dress from the 18th century onward, over 60 costumes in all, complete with appropriate accessories. Admission £2 (includes admission to State Apartments). Mon.–Sat. 9–5, Sun. 1–5. Tubes: Queensway, Kensington High St.

Courtauld Institute Gallery, Woburn Sq., WC1. Outstanding collection of French Impressionists, also varying modern collection. Recently enriched by the munificent bequest of the Prince's Gate collection of old masters. Eventually destined for Somerset House. Adult admission £1. Daily 10–5, Sun. 2–5. Tubes: Goodge St, Russell Square, Euston Square.

Dickens' House, 48 Doughty St., WC1. Occupied by the author from 1837 to 1839. On display are portraits, letters, first editions, furniture and autographs. Adult admission £1. Weekdays 10–5, closed Sun. Tube: Russell Square.

Dulwich Picture Gallery, College Rd., SE21. Newly-restored gallery with small but superb collection of paintings. Lies in attractive suburb. Adult admission 60p. Tues. to Sat., 10–5 (closed 1–2 for lunch), Sun. 2–5, closed Mon. Train: to West Dulwich or Sydenham Hill.

Geffrye Museum, Kingsland Rd., Shoreditch, E2. Furniture and furnishings arranged chronologically from 1600 on in attractive 18th-century almshouses. Daily 10–5, Sun. 2–5, closed Mondays. Tubes: Liverpool Street, Old Street.

Geological Museum, Exhibition Rd., SW7. Collections of gemstones and exhibitions of basic science and geology. Daily 10–6, Sun. 2.30–6. Tube: South Kensington.

Hayward Gallery (Arts Council of Great Britain), Belvedere Rd, South Bank, SE1. Open for specific exhibitions only. Hours and admission vary, depending on subject (latter up to about £2.50). Tube: Waterloo.

ICA Gallery (Institute of Contemporary Arts), Nash House, Carlton House Terrace, SW1. The latest "happenings" in art and art forms. Adult admission 50p unless member. Tues.–Sun., 12–9. Tube: Charing Cross.

Imperial Collection, Central Hall, Westminster, SW1. Subtitle "The Royal and The Imperial Crown Jewels and Regalia of the World" gives a general idea of what to expect of this new museum. Adult admission £2. Daily 10–6. Closed Sun. Tubes: Westminster, St. James's Park.

Imperial War Museum, Lambeth Rd., SE1. Comprehensive collection of the Commonwealth during two world wars, including an art collection and a library of films, photographs and books. Daily 10–5.50, Sun. 2–5.50. Tubes: Lambeth North, Elephant & Castle.

Jewish Museum, Woburn House, Upper Woburn Place, WC1. Fine collection of Jewish antiquities. Summer, Tues.–Fri., 10–4; winter, Tues.–Thurs., 10–4, Fri. 10–12.45; Sun. 10.30–12.45 all year. Euston, Euston Square.

Dr. Johnson's House, 17 Gough Sq., EC4. Home of the great lexicographer from 1748–1759. Adult admission £1. Daily 11–5.30 (11–5 in winter). Closed Sun. Tubes: St. Paul's, Chancery Lane, Blackfriars.

Keats' House and Museum, Keats Grove, NW3. The home of the poet during the most creative years of his brief life. Daily 10–6 (closed 1–2 for lunch), Sun. 2–5. Tube: Hampstead.

Kenwood House, Hampstead Lane, NW3. Fine paintings, Adam decoration. Daily Apr.–Sept. 10–7; check with Kenwood House for opening hours rest of year (tel. 348 1286). Tube: Archway or Golders Green, then bus 210.

London Dungeon, Tooley St., SE1. Authentic exhibitions of the Great Plague, Tyburn and other gruesome aspects of Britain's history. Adult admission £3.50. Daily 10–5.45, Oct.–March 10–4.30. Tube: London Bridge.

London Toy and Model Museum, 23 Craven Hill, W2. Opened 1982, this intriguing museum offers delights for children of all ages. Exhibits vary from year to year, but have included subjects ranging from dolls and model cars to Paddington Bear. Adult admission 1.80, children 50p. Tues.–Sat. 10–5.30, Sun. 11–5. Tube: Queensway.

London Transport Museum, Covent Garden, WC2. Relics from London Transport's better days. Doubtful value for the price (adult admission £2.20). Daily 10–6. Tube: Covent Garden.

Madame Tussaud's, Marylebone Rd., NW1. World's best-known wax-works of famous and infamous. Often crowded but the long lines move fast. Adult admission £3.30 Daily 10–6 (Apr.–Sept.), and 10–5.30 (Oct.–Mar.). Next door is the **Planetarium,** with its visual display of the night sky. There are regular star show presentations between 11 and 4.30 every day apart from Christmas. Adult admission £1.85. Most evenings laser light concerts are performed. Tel. 486 2242 for details. Adult admission £2.75. *Note.* There is a special Combined Ticket costing £4.45 which gives entry to both Madame Tussaud's and the Planetarium (not usable in the Planetarium in the evenings). Tube: Baker Street.

Maritime Trust, St. Katharine's Dock, E1 (481 0043). Collection of seven preserved historical ships, close by the Tower. Admission fee. Open 10–5, seven days a week, year round.

Museum of Garden History, St.-Mary-at-Lambeth, Lambeth Palace Rd., S.E.1. Interesting garden exhibits in old church next to Lambeth Palace; especially in spring and summer. Mon.-Fri. 11–3, Sun. 10.30–5, closed Sat. and Dec.-Mar. Tube: walk upriver from Westminster and over Lambeth Bridge.

Museum of London, London Wall, EC2. Devoted to the history of London, from prehistoric times to the present day. Based on the combined collections of the former Guildhall and London museums. Open Tues.-Sat. 10–6, Sun. 2–6. Tubes: St. Paul's, Barbican, Moorgate.

National Army Museum, Royal Hospital Rd., SW3. The story of the British Army from Tudor times up to 1914. Daily 10–5.30, Sun. 2–5.30. Tube: Sloane Square.

National Gallery, on Trafalgar Sq., WC2. Collection of Italian, Dutch, Flemish, Spanish, German and French paintings up to 1900, plus British painters from Hogarth to Turner; in effect there is at least one masterpiece by every major European painter of the last 600 years. Daily 10–6, Sun. 2–6. Tubes: Charing Cross or Leicester Square.

National Maritime Museum, Romney Rd., Greenwich, SE10. Superlative collection of ship models, navigational instruments, charts, uniforms, medals, portraits and paintings of naval scenes. Also some outstanding architecture to visit. Admission £1.50. Daily 10–6 (10–5 in winter), Sat. 10–5.30 all year, Sun. 2–5.30 (2–5 in winter). Train: Cannon Street, Charing Cross or Waterloo to Greenwich (change at London Bridge).

National Portrait Gallery, at St. Martin's Pl., Trafalgar Sq, WC2. Paintings, drawings, busts of famous British men and women from earliest times to the present. Adult admission charge to special exhibitions only (about £1.50). Open Mon.–Fri. 10–5, Sat. 10–6, Sun. 2–6. Tube: Charing Cross or Leicester Square.

National Postal Museum, King Edward St., EC1. Vast collection of stamps from all over the world. Open Mon.–Thurs. 10–4.30, Fri. 10–4. Tube: St. Paul's.

Natural History Museum, Cromwell Rd., SW7. Animals, plants, minerals, fossils (nearly 15,000,000 specimens). Rumors of impending admission charges at presstime. Daily 10–6, Sun. 2.30–6. Tube: South Kensington.

98A Boundary Road, Boundary Rd., NW8. Conceived from the considerable private collection of advertising supremo Charles Saatchi and his American-born writer–collector wife Doris (who are also the architects of the whole enterprise), this new (1985) gallery of contemporary international painting and sculpture features work by more than 50 artists—over half of them American, but who also include the Irish, Italians, British and Germans. Fri. and Sat. 12–6, Bank Hol. weekends excepted; otherwise by appointment. Tubes: Swiss Cottage, St. John's Wood.

Percival David Foundation of Chinese Art, 53 Gordon Sq., WC1. Chinese ceramics and a library of Chinese and other books. Mon. 2–5, Tues.–Fri. 10.30–5, Sat. 10.30–1. Tube: Goodge St. or Russell Sq.

Public Record Office Museum, Chancery Lane, WC2. Closed during 1985, the future of this museum was still uncertain as we went to press.

Queen's Gallery, adjoining Buckingham Palace, SW1. Paintings and masterpieces from the Royal Collection. Adult admission £1. Daily (except Mon.) 11–5, Sun. 2–5. Tubes: Green Park, Hyde Park Corner, Victoria.

Royal Academy, Burlington House, on Piccadilly, W1. The temple of traditional art. Mounts some of the largest exhibitions, including the annual summer one (May–Aug.) of works by living artists. Adult admission up to £ 3.50. Daily 10–6. Tubes: Piccadilly Circus, Green Park.

Science Museum, Exhibition Rd., SW7. Illustrates the development of mathematics, physics, chemistry, engineering, transport, mining, communications (an operating radio station), and industry as a whole. Originals of many famous locomotives, aircraft and cars. Many working displays; children's gallery. Open daily 10–6; Sun. 2.30–6. Tube: South Kensington.

Sir John Soane's Museum, 13 Lincoln's Inn Fields, WC2. Early 19th-century museum of art and antiquities. Tues. to Sat., 10–5. Tube: Holborn.

Tate Gallery, Millbank, SW1. An exciting collection of modern foreign paintings and sculpture, but primarily dedicated to British artists, especially Turner, Blake and the Pre-Raphaelites. Restaurant and café. Adult admission up to £2 to special exhibitions (gallery itself free). Daily 10–6, Sun. 2–6. Tube: Pimlico.

Victoria and Albert Museum, Cromwell Rd, SW7. Displays fine and applied arts of all countries and styles, British, European and Oriental; a magnificent collection. Daily (except Fri.) 10–5.50, Sun. 2.30–5.50. Tube: South Kensington.

Wallace Collection, in Hertford House, Manchester Sq., W1. Exceptionally fine works of Dutch, Flemish, French, Spanish, Italian and British painters together with sculpture, furniture, china, armor and gold. Daily 10–5, Sun. 2–5. Tubes: Baker St., Bond St.

Wellington Museum (Apsley House), Hyde Park Corner, W1. The London home (its address used to be "Number One, London"!) of the famous duke, containing uniforms, trophies and some paintings. Adult admission 60p. Daily 10–6 (closed Mon. and Fri.), Sun. 2.30–6. Tube: Hyde Park Corner.

Wesley's House, 47 City Rd., EC1. Shrine to John Wesley and museum of early Methodism. Adult admission 50p. Daily 10–4, Sun. 1–3. Next door to Wesley's Chapel which is also well worth visiting. Tube: Old Street.

Wimbledon Lawn Tennis Museum, The All England Club, Church Rd., SW19. A must for tennis buffs, this truly unique museum chronicles the history of lawn tennis and the games that preceded it. A library and audio-visual theater are included. Adult admission £1.50. Open during the All England Championships; for rest of year, tel. 946 6131. Train: Victoria or Blackfriars to Wimbledon.

 PLACES OF INTEREST. Although there is inevitably a certain amount of overlapping between the previous list of Museums and Galleries and this listing of Places of Interest, the intention was to separate the buildings and areas that are interesting for themselves, from the buildings which are more interesting for the collections that they house. Most of the places below are given a more extended treatment in the chapter, Exploring Central London.

Banqueting House, Whitehall, SW1. Only remains of the old Whitehall Palace. Designed by Inigo Jones (1619). The painted ceiling by Rubens was commissioned by King Charles I, who in 1649 was executed on a scaffold outside this building. Open to the public when not in use for official functions. Phone 930 4179 to check whether open. Adult admission 50p. Daily 10–5 (closed Mon.), Sun. 2–5. Tubes: Charing Cross or Westminster.

Buckingham Palace, The Mall, SW1. With its surrounding parks, the official royal residence is appropriately majestic and beautifully situated. Best approached down the Mall from Trafalgar Square. The statue of Queen Victoria in front provides a good vantage point for Changing of the Guard. Not open to the public, though the Queen's Gallery to one side is. Tubes: Green Park, Hyde Park Corner or Victoria.

Chelsea Physic Garden, 66 Royal Hospital Rd., SW3. Entry from Swan Walk. Founded 1673, with many rare plants. Admission fee. Open Mid-April–mid-Oct., Sun., Wed. and Bank Hols., 2–5. Chelsea Flower Show week, Tues.–Fri., 12–5.

Chelsea Royal Hospital, Royal Hospital Rd., SW3. Charming home for old soldiers ("pensioners"), founded by Charles II and designed by Wren. Daily 10–12 and 2–4; Sun. 2–4 all year. Tube: Sloane Square.

Chiswick House, Burlington Lane, W4. Lovely restored Palladian villa. Admission 50p. Mid-Mar–mid-Oct., 9.30–6.30; mid-Oct.–mid-Mar., 9.30–4; closed Mon. and Tues. all year. Tube: Hammersmith then 290 bus to the gate.

The Commonwealth Institute, Kensington High St., W8, is the building that took the place of the old Imperial Institute as a national memorial for Queen Victoria's Jubilee in 1887. There is a modern exhibition hall with permanent displays for all Commonwealth countries. Other features include an art gallery, cinema, library and information center. Daily 10–5.30, Sun. 2–5. Tube: High Street, Kensington.

Covent Garden Market, The Piazza, Covent Garden, SW2. Beautifully restored 19th-century building, former home of London's fruit and vegetable market. Now bustles with some of the capital's trendiest shops. Tube: Covent Garden.

Cutty Sark, Greenwich Pier, SE10. Last of the famous tea clippers. Nearby is *Gypsy Moth IV,* Sir Francis Chichester's round-the-world yacht. Adult admission £1. Daily 10.30–5 (to 6 in summer), Sun. 2.30–5 (12–6 in summer). By boat from Westminster, Charing Cross or Tower Piers, or by train to Maze Hill (from Charing Cross).

Guildhall, King Street, Cheapside EC2. The 15th-century council hall of the City, scene of civic functions. It has an extensive medieval crypt. The whole is beautifully restored, and there is plenty of historic interest. Daily, 9.30–5, closed Sun. (Nov.–April) and 3 or 4 days before and after any special function. There is also the **Museum of the Worshipful Company of Clockmakers,** housed in the same building. Mon.–Fri. 9.30–4.45. Closed Sat. and Sun. Tubes: Bank, Moorgate, St. Paul's.

Hampton Court Palace, Hampton Court, East Molesey. The former residence of Cardinal Wolsey and Henry VIII. Staterooms, tapestries and pictures. Set in beautiful grounds with the famous maze. Adult admission £2 (in summer), £1 (in winter). Open Apr.–Sept., weekdays 9.30–6, Sun. 11–6; hours vary rest of year–best to check. Easily reached by boat from Westminster Pier (summer) or train (from Waterloo).

Houses of Parliament, Westminster, SW1. The House of Commons sits at 2.30 P.M. Mon. to Thurs. and 9.30 A.M. on Fri. Visitors wishing to watch the proceedings from the Strangers' Gallery of either House should join the public queue outside St. Stephen's Entrance, and seek further directions from the police there. The head of the public queue is not normally admitted until 4.30 P.M. (9.30 A.M. on Fri.). Overseas visitors may obtain Cards of Introduction from their Embassy or High Commission in London. In addition, visitors may apply for tickets well in advance to a Member of Parliament. Parliament does not sit during Recesses which are at the Christmas, Easter and Spring Bank Holidays and in the summer (usually August and September).

The House of Lords sits at 2.30 P.M. on Tues., Wed. and some Mon., at 3 P.M. on Thurs., and occasionally at 11 A.M. on Fri. Procedure for admission to the Strangers' Gallery is the same as for the Commons, or by application in advance to a peer.

The Palace of Westminster, including Westminster Hall, is no longer open for guided tours on Saturdays. The only tours available are those which have been pre-arranged through a Member of Parliament, and these are allowed on Mon.–Thurs. mornings. Tube: Westminster.

Kensington Palace State Apartments, Kensington Gdns., W8. The official residence of the Royal Family before Buckingham Palace. Paintings from Royal Collections, early Georgian and Victorian furniture and objets d'art. Adult admission £2 (inc. admission to Costume Museum). Daily 9–5, Sunday 1–5. Tube: Queensway or Kensington High Street.

Kew, Royal Botanic Gardens, one of the oldest and loveliest botanical gardens anywhere. Admission 25p. Within the gardens are **Kew Palace** (once known as the Dutch House and open Apr.–Sept., Mon.–Sun., 11–5.30; admission 60p) and **Queen Charlotte's Cottage** (Apr.–Sept., Sat., Sun. and Bank Hols. only, 11–5.30; admission 30p). Tube: Kew Gardens.

Law Courts, Strand, WC2. The legal enclave called the Temple at the entrance to Fleet Street comprises the Inns of Court or Courts of Law. The whole area down to the Thames is worth your careful contemplation; Old London at its most charming. The public is no longer admitted to the galleries for security reasons, but seating is usually available in the back two rows of the well of the court; sessions at 10.30–1, 2–4, Mon. to Fri., except during Law Vacations. Tubes: Chancery Lane, Temple.

The Monument, Fish St. Hill, EC3. Commemorates the Great Fire of 1666, which broke out in Pudding Lane 202 ft. from the monument—its height. The upper gallery is open Mon.–Sat. (April–Sept.) 9–6, (Oct.–Mar.) 9–4. Sun. (May–Sept. only) 2–6. Admission 50p. Tube: Monument.

Old Bailey, Old Bailey, EC4. Central Criminal Court. (More what you would expect if you get a kick out of watching a trial, than is offered by the Law Courts.) To attend session: Public Gallery opens 10.30–1 and 2–4. Line up at door in Newgate St. Tube: St. Paul's.

St. Paul's Cathedral, EC4. The masterpiece of Sir Christopher Wren, built after the Great Fire of London. Contains memorial chapel to the American forces in Britain. Tours of the Cathedral (at about £2.50) take place at 11, 11.30, 2 and 2.30, Mon.–Sat. Admission charges to some areas (40–75p). Open daily. Tube: St Paul's.

Southwark Cathedral, Borough High St, SE1. Across the river from St. Paul's, and several centuries older, Southwark Cathedral is one of the finest Gothic buildings in London. Also includes the Harvard Chapel, damaged during the war and restored through the generosity of Harvard Alumni in the U.S. Open daily. Tube: London Bridge.

Thames Barrier, Eastmoor St., off Woolwich Rd., SE7. Opened 1984, and not to be missed for a unique view of the river. Audio-visual and other displays. Open daily 10.30–5 (to 6.30 Apr.–Oct.).

Tower of London, Tower Hill, EC3. Outstanding collection of armor, uniforms, historic relics; and Crown Jewels are in the Jewel House. Also of considerable interest is the new Heralds Museum in the Waterloo Building. Admission charge (quite expensive—as much as £3 for an adult in high summer —with an extra 80p to see the jewels). Daily 9.30–5 (9.30–4 Nov.–Feb.), Sun. 2–5 (closed Sun. in winter). The Jewel House closes for the whole of Feb. for cleaning purposes. The Tower gets very crowded so try to avoid mid-day and weekends. Tube: Tower Hill. Buses: 35 or 40 to Monument, then walk, or 23 to Tower Hill. **Tower Bridge** is open to view, 10–6.30 (in summer), 10–4.45 (in winter), 7 days a week. Adults £2, children £1 in winter; £3 and £1.50 in summer.

Trafalgar Square a well-known landmark, with Nelson's Column, the fountains and pigeons—there is an excellent view of the area from the steps of the National Gallery. A huge tree is erected each Christmas, and crowds gather on New Year's Eve to celebrate en masse. Tube: Charing Cross.

Westminster Abbey, Broad Sanctuary, SW1. Nave open daily, 8–6. Royal Chapels open weekdays 9–4.45, last tickets at 4; Sat. 9–2.45 (last tickets 2) and 3.45–5.45, last tickets 5. Adult admission £1.40 (free Wed. 6–7.45). Tube: Westminster or St James's Park.

Westminster Cathedral, Ashley Pl., SW1. Most important Roman Catholic church in England. Daily 7 A.M.–8 P.M. View London from 284 ft tower, open 10–4 daily (April to Sept.); closed at dusk other months. (*Note:* It might be advisable to check whether tower is still open if you are planning a visit, as it is not in the best of health at present.) Adult admission 70p. Tube: Victoria.

Zoo. Situated in Regent's Park, NW1, the huge London Zoo (The Gardens of the Zoological Society of London) contains one of the world's largest collections of animals, reptiles, and birds. Children's Zoo shows farm animals and offers pony and donkey rides. Daily, 10–5 in winter (10–4 in darkest winter), 9–6 in summer (9–7 Sun.). Adult admission £3.20. Charges have been stabilized but it can still be expensive for a large family! Tubes: Baker Street then 74 bus, or Camden Town, then 74 bus or walk.

 CHANGING OF THE GUARD. This colorful ritual takes place in two ceremonies—*Queen's Life Guard,* daily at 11 A.M. (10 on Sunday) lasts for 20 minutes and is held at the Horse Guards, Whitehall. *Queen's Guard,*

daily at 11.30 A.M., Apr.–Sept.; every other day at 11.30, Oct.–Mar. This lasts for 30 minutes, and is held at Buckingham Palace. Unfortunately it is subject to cancellation without notice. Tube for Whitehall is Charing Cross. Buses: 3, 12, 53, 77, 88, 159. Tubes for Buckingham Palace, Victoria, Green Park or Hyde Park Corner.

 PARKS AND GARDENS. Londoners are proud of their precious green breathing spaces. First come all the squares and private gardens with which London teems, turning it into one of the greenest cities on earth. Then come the chains of public parks that can be found throughout the capital. They are popular for picnics, riding, or just walking the dog. You can also listen to music or do almost anything except pick the flowers.

Battersea Park, SW11, owned by the Greater London Council, covers 200 acres, with lake. Borders the Thames.

Blackheath, SE3. A big sweep of open common covering 268 acres, is an open space where fairs are staged, also cricket matches.

Dulwich Park, SE21 (72 acres). Famous for its rhododendrons and azaleas. The western gate leads into semi-rural Dulwich Village, and the superb Dulwich Picture Gallery, London's first public art gallery.

Green Park, smallest (53 acres) of the Royal Parks, between Piccadilly and St. James's Park.

Greenwich Park (which adjoins Blackheath—see above) is a Royal Park of 200 acres beside the river, containing Royal Naval College, and Maritime Museum.

Hampstead Heath, a GLC park, covers 800 acres. North London's favorite Bank Holiday spot, with fun fairs and openair displays. Also Kenwood House, Bull & Bush, Jack Straw's Castle and the old Spaniards Inn.

Holland Park, W8 (off Kensington High St.). 55 acres, once the private grounds of old Holland House, this lovely area contains part of the Elizabethan mansion, now a youth hostel and an orangery. Charming gardens, with 3,000 species of British trees and plants, as well as peacocks, and openair theater and concerts in summer. Excellent chic restaurant.

Hyde Park, W1. Most famous of the Royal Parks, 340 acres stretching from Park Lane to Kensington Gardens. Swimming and boating in the Serpentine lake, Rotten Row for horse-riding, Apsley House. Famous also for "Speakers' Corner" near Marble Arch.

Kensington Gardens, W2. A 275-acre Royal Park adjoining Hyde Park and extending to Kensington Palace. Contains the Albert Memorial and Round Pond (famous for model yacht sailing), and part of the Serpentine. Carefully-tended flower-beds are a picture in summer (along the south edge).

Parliament Hill, NW3. 271 acres adjoining Hampstead Heath, with swimming lakes. Popular with kite-flyers.

Regent's Park, NW1. Royal Park stretching from the Marylebone Road to Primrose Hill, covers 464 acres, and dates from the days of the Prince Regent. Surrounded by beautiful houses. Contains the Zoo, Regent's Canal, lake, Queen Mary's Rose Garden (a wonderful sight when the roses are in bloom), and an openair theater with Shakespearean productions.

Richmond Park, Richmond. Largest (2,470 acres) of the Royal Parks, with many deer as well as fine trees, ponds and mansions.

St. James's Park, SW1. Small (93 acres), but most attractive and oldest of the Royal Parks. Lake with many ducks and pelicans. Fine view of Buckingham Palace and the towers and spires of Whitehall from the bridge over the lake. Ideal for an after-theater summer stroll.

Syon Park, near Kew Gardens. Contains Syon House, historic home of the Duke of Northumberland, who created in 1968 a national Gardening Center. (Small admission charge.) Its 55 acres include 10,000 roses and a lake area with the largest collection of water lilies in the country. Excellent restaurant in grounds. Admission 85p, House 80p, combined £1.50. Apr.–Oct., daily, 10–6, Nov.–Mar. 10–5.30. (House opening times differ, so do check).

Waterlow Park, N6. A small park of 26 acres on the southern slopes of Highgate Hill, containing Lauderdale House, formerly occupied by Nell Gwynn. Visitors to the Park have included Julius Caesar. Open-air concerts.

You can visit private gardens in London through the National Gardens Scheme, 57 Lower Belgrave St., SW1 (730 0359).

SPORTS

CRICKET is the traditional summer game, played daily all over the country. The first-class matches in the London area are those played at the Oval ground, where Surrey have their headquarters, and at Lord's, the Middlesex ground at

St John's Wood. The best way to get a taste of cricket without being bored to tears is to attend a one-day match of the NatWest Trophy, the Benson and Hedges Cup or the John Player League. Other matches worth seeing are the Test Matches between England and overseas teams, or the Eton v. Harrow public schools game at Lord's in July—the latter for crowd watching too.

If you can, watch village cricket, played every weekend in all areas around London, which is often more fun.

FOOTBALL (Rugby Union) is played between October and the end of March. Big matches are staged at the Twickenham ground, within easy reach of Waterloo station, about six times during the season. Otherwise, rugby matches are club ones in the London area.

FOOTBALL (Soccer) is the leading British winter game—though as we write, it is becoming increasingly marred by the ugly spectacle of crowd violence, which can make it safer to stay at home. Best first-class matches, held on Saturday afternoons in the London area, are to be seen at Chelsea, West Ham, Tottenham, and Highbury.

At the end of May the Cup Final is played at Wembley Stadium when thousands of fans watch the last two survivors of an 8-month-long knock-out competition battle for honors. Tickets for this popular event are virtually unobtainable at short notice, but it is fully televised on British networks.

GOLF. Although most golf clubs in the Greater London area are private, visitors are often able to play on them by payment of a green fee, which varies widely according to the course. It is best, especially with private courses, to telephone in advance to find out what the fee is and the restrictions (if any) for visitors. A letter of introduction from your own course at home is always valuable.

For a complete run-down of all of the area courses (as well as those throughout England), we suggest that you refer to the *Golf Course Guide* which costs £4.95 (£5.50 by post) and is available from the Sunday Telegraph Bookshop, 130 Fleet St., London E.C.4 (tel. 353–4242). Some of London's larger bookstores may carry the guide, too.

RACING. You can watch speedway racing at Wimbledon Stadium on occasion, cycle racing at Herne Hill Stadium (under some threat of closure as we write), and motor racing—both cycle and car—at Brands Hatch which is 30 minutes from Victoria to Swanley by British Rail, though easiest reached by car.

HORSE AND DOG RACING. Several horse and greyhound racing tracks are to be found in the London area, where you'll find both tote and bookmaker betting. Visitors will have no trouble placing bets for horse races or dog races (as greyhound races are called). Betting shops are on every other corner, almost as common as pubs.

Horse Racing

For information about racing fixtures, phone the Jockey Club, on 486 4921.

Ascot Flat and jump racing. Reached by Southern Region electric trains from Waterloo (28 miles) or by Green Line bus. Royal Ascot is the very fashionable meeting attended by the Queen during the third week in June. Ascot course stages 1-day, 2-day and 3-day meetings each season. For information phone Ascot 22211.

Epsom Flat racing only. Scene of the Derby, held first week in June. Reached by electric trains from Victoria to Epsom Downs or Charing Cross to Tattenham Corner in about 35 minutes (21 miles), 3 days in April, 4-day Derby and Oaks meeting in June, 2-day meeting in August.

Kempton Park Steeplechasing and flat racing. At Sunbury-on-Thames, railway station is Kempton Park, reached by electric train from Waterloo in 35 minutes. Four winter 2-day steeplechase meetings; five summer 2-day flat meetings, including popular evening meetings.

Sandown Park Steeplechasing and flat racing. Train to Esher station, Surrey, from Waterloo, in 21 minutes. Six winter 2-day steeplechase meetings; five summer flat meetings of 1–2 days.

Windsor Steeplechasing and flat racing. A mile west of Windsor. Four steeplechase and six flat meetings each year, including popular evening meetings.

Dog Tracks

Most tracks stage meetings twice weekly, not conflicting with each other if possible, such as Tuesday and Friday, Wednesday and Saturday. On Saturday, when tracks in various parts of London hold meetings, some will start at 2.45 p.m. others at 5 p.m. or 7.30 p.m.; occasional morning meets; there's usually at least one meeting every evening, year round, at the London tracks.

Main tracks are: *White City, Wimbledon, Catford, Wembley, Hackney Wick, Romford, Walthamstow,* and *Watford.*

HORSE RIDING in Hyde Park, Richmond Park or Wimbledon Common is a lovely experience, and there are still a number of stables from which you can hire horses. *Lilo Blum,* 32a Grosvenor Crescent Mews, SW1 (tel. 235 6846).

If you just want to watch other riders in action, the *Royal International Horse Show* is at Wembley each July, a major event for the world's top riders; another is the *Royal Windsor Horse Show* at Ascot, in May.

ROWING. You can row on the Serpentine, Regent's Park, and on the Thames from Kew and other places.

For more formal rowing, the four-day *Henley Royal Regatta* is a colorful occasion held at Henley-on-Thames in July. The regatta is over 130 years old and world famous.

Another well-known event is the annual boat race between Oxford and Cambridge Universities, which takes place on the Thames, from Putney to Mortlake, in March.

SKATING (Ice and Roller). Rinks usually have two sessions during the day including weekends. Check with the rinks for the hours and charges for the day you wish to go. The nearest to central London is *Queen's Ice Skating Club,* Queensway, W2 (tel. 229 0172). Tubes: Queensway and Bayswater.

Streatham Ice Rink, 386 Streatham High Rd., SW16 (tel. 769 7771). Best is the main line Southern Region to Streatham or Streatham Common.

SWIMMING. London's Lido is the Serpentine, in Hyde Park. Among the municipal pools are: the Oasis, 32 Endell St, Holborn, WC2; Great Smith Street Baths (near Westminster Abbey); and Swiss Cottage Baths, Winchester Road, NW3. Openair swimming is also possible at Parliament Hill Fields, on the edge of Hampstead Heath. Or contact the Amateur Swimming Association at Harold Fern House, Derby Square, Loughborough, Leic. (tel. Loughborough 230431).

TENNIS headquarters for not only London but the world is Wimbledon. This is a large suburban center reached by train from Waterloo in 12–15 minutes or by District Line underground from Kensington and Earls Court. Many tennis clubs exist all over London, and thousands of public courts are available in the parks by the hour for modest fees.

The tennis tournament season in Britain starts early in April on hard courts and changes to grass toward the end of May. The Surrey Championships are held at Surbiton, 12 miles from Waterloo, and the Kent Championships at Beckenham, 10 miles from Victoria. The London Championships are held at Queen's Club, West Kensington, immediately before the All-England Championships at Wimbledon in late June. Obtaining tickets for Wimbledon is a matter of luck and perseverance. Write to the *All England Lawn Tennis Club,* Church Rd, SW19, enclosing a stamped addressed envelope, any time from Oct. 1 in the year preceding the championships you wish to visit, uptil the end of the following January; you will be sent an application form, but tickets are finally allocated by ballot once all applications have been received. Reserved tickets are from £6 to £17. If you can't get tickets for any of the show courts, then you can always just turn up, pay your £4 entrance fee (£3 the second week, £2 after 5 p.m.) and wander around the outside courts where you will often find some really excellent games and plenty of big names, especially during the first week. However, it can get extremely crowded and unfortunately many of the subsidiary attractions are both increasingly expensive and tawdry.

For the really keen there are also a number of standing places available on the center court every day. However, these are issued on a first come first served basis and as the demand is incredible you must be prepared to arrive very early in the morning and stand in line for a very considerable time.

Useful Addresses

AIRLINES. Phone numbers for reservations: *Air Canada,* 759 2636; *British Airways,* 897 4000; *PanAm,* 409 0688; *TWA,* 636 4090; *United,* 997 0179.

CLUBS. The *English-Speaking Union,* 37 Charles St., W1 (tel. 629 0104), is a meeting-place for the people of Britain, the Commonwealth, and the Americas. Although it is open to members only, it is accessible to all American (and other visiting) E.S.U. members and their guests.

American Chamber of Commerce in London, 75 Brook St., W1 (tel. 493 0381). *YMCA,* 112 Great Russell St., WC1 (tel. 637 1333) and the *YWCA,* 16 Great Russell St., WC1 (tel. 636 7512).

A Cut Above the Rest. Reciprocal arrangements have been made between some clubs in London and those abroad so that overseas visitors may be able to experience the genteel life in exclusive—and usually only men's—clubs: The Savile with the Players and Coffee House in New York, the Cosmos in Washington, the Tavern in Boston; Brooks' with the Knickerbocker in New York; The Garrick with the Century, the Players, and the Lotos in New York, St Botolph's in Boston; The Travellers' with the Cosmos and Georgetown in Washington, the Harvard Club of Boston, the Rittenhouse in Philadelphia; Boodle's with the Somerset in Boston and the Knickerbocker in New York.

Reciprocal arrangements usually need a letter of introduction from the home club and allow entrance to the reciprocating club for up to nine months.

EMBASSIES. *American Embassy,* 24 Grosvenor Sq., W1; *Canadian High Commission,* Canada House, Trafalgar Sq., SW1.

LOST PROPERTY. Anything found in the street should be handed to the police. Items lost in trains, tubes and buses should be inquired for at the London Transport Lost Property Office, 200 Baker St., London NW1. Office hours are 9.30–2 Mondays through Fridays. For property lost in taxi-cabs check with the Public Carriage Office, 15 Penton St., N1 (tel. 278 1744), open 9–4 Mon.–Fri.

RELIGIOUS SERVICES. There are hundreds of churches in London; check national daily or Sunday newspapers for details. Here are just a few of the famous, or conveniently located ones. Church of England centers, with Holy Communion service at 8 a.m., morning service at 10 or 10.30 a.m., are: *St. Paul's Cathedral,* City EC4. *Westminster Abbey,* SW1. *St. Martin-in-the-Fields,* Trafalgar Sq., WC2. *St. George's,* Hanover Square, W1. *Southwark Cathedral,* SE1. Telephone 222 9011, for more information.

Leading Roman Catholic churches, with weekday and Sunday Mass, are: *Westminster Cathedral,* Ashley Gardens, Victoria St, SW1 (tel. 834 7452). *Brompton Oratory,* Brompton Road, SW3 (tel. 589 4811).

Among the leading synagogues are: *Central Synagogue,* Great Portland St., W1; *Marble Arch Synagogue,* 32 Great Cumberland Place, W1; *West London Synagogue* (Conservative), 34 Upper Berkeley St., W1; *The Liberal Jewish Synagogue* (Reform), 28 St. John's Wood Rd., NW8. Also the *Spanish and Portuguese Synagogue* (Bevis Marks Hall), the oldest still in use in London, 2–4 Heneage Lane, EC3. Information on other London synagogues on 289 2573.

TRAVEL. *American Express* has offices at: 6 Haymarket, SW1 (tel. 930 4411) and 89 Mount St., W1 (tel. 499 4436). *Diners Club* at 176 Tottenham Court Rd., W1 (tel. 580 0437). *Thomas Cook* offices at: 45 Berkeley St., Piccadilly, W1; Marble Arch, 11 Great Cumberland Pl., W1; 378 Strand, WC2; St. Pancras Station forecourt, Euston Rd., NW1; Ludgate Circus, 108 Fleet St., EC4; and many others.

USEFUL LONDON TELEPHONE NUMBERS

Dial
123	for the correct time.
142	London directory inquiries.
192	Directory inquiries outside London.
246 8041	*Teletourist Service* giving information on the principal events of the day. (If from a call box refer to the instruction notice!)
353 4242	*Daily Telegraph* general information service.
246 8091	for the local weather report.
246 8021	for road conditions within 50 miles of London.
246 8026	*Financial Times* Index and Business News Summary.
222 1234	*London Regional Transport* travel inquiries.
283 3400	Samaritans' emergency number.
387 7070	Euston/St Pancras railway stations for train information.
278 2477	King's Cross railway station train information.
283 7171	Liverpool St railway station train information.
262 6767	Paddington railway station train information.
928 5100	Victoria/Waterloo railway station train information.

HELP!

Real Emergencies are taken care of by dialing 999 (fire, police or ambulance). But what about other situations which seem like emergencies—when you want a meal at 5 a.m. or to buy aspirin at midnight? Well, here's a little helpful miscellany.

Emergency Casualty. The following hospitals have 24-hour casualty departments: Guys, Middlesex, St Bartholomew's, St Thomas's, University College, Westminster.

Chemists (Drug Stores). *Bliss Chemist,* 50–56 Willesden Lane, NW6 (624 8000), is open 24 hours a day, seven days a week, while the branch at 5 Marble Arch, W1, opens 9 a.m. to midnight (again, seven days a week).

Jab Center. If you have urgent need of an inoculation for travel, go to 75 Regent St., W.1, where *British Airways* have a complete service. For appointments and information call 439 9584.

Money. Banks are the best bet for changing money, as they charge least commission. However, when they are shut there are change bureaux at main hotels, airports and air terminals. Also: *Thomas Cook* (Exchange) at Victoria railway station (tel. 828 4442), open until 10 p.m., seven days a week. There are also many branches of *BCCI* (27 in all, most open Mon.–Sat. during business hours) and *Cheque Point* (16 in all, three open 24 hours a day, seven days a week; the others open 8.30 a.m. to midnight) in Central London.

Leaving Britain

 CUSTOMS GOING HOME. If you propose to take on your holiday any *foreign-made* articles, such as cameras, binoculars, expensive timepieces and the like, it is wise to put with your travel documents the receipt from the retailer or some other evidence that the item was bought in your home country. If you bought the article on a previous holiday abroad and have already paid duty on it, carry with you the receipt for this. Otherwise, on returning home, you may be charged duty again.

Americans who are out of the United States at least 48 hours and have claimed no exemption during the previous 30 days are entitled to bring in duty-free up to $400 worth of articles for bona fide gifts or for their own personal use. For the next $1,000 of goods beyond the first $400, inspectors will assess a flat 10% duty. Remember that *already used* does not exempt an item. If you buy clothing abroad and wear it during your trip it is nonetheless dutiable when you return. The value of each item is based on the retail value of the goods in the country where acquired (so save your receipts). Every member of a family is entitled to this same exemption, regardless of age, and the allowance can be pooled. Infants and children get the same exemptions as adults except for alcohol and tobacco.

Not more than 100 cigars, 200 cigarettes, (one carton), may be included in your duty-free exemption, nor more than a liter (33.8 fl. oz) of wine or liquor (none at all if your passport indicates you are from a "dry" state or under 21 years old). Only one bottle of perfume that is trademarked in the U.S. may be brought in, plus a reasonable quantity of other brands.

Do not bring home foreign meats, fruits, plants, soil, or other agricultural items when you return to the United States. To do so will delay you at the port of entry. It is illegal to bring in foreign agricultural items without permission, because they can spread destructive plant pests and diseases. For more information, read the pamphlet *Customs Hints,* or write to: Quarantines, U.S. Department of Agriculture, Federal Building, Hyattsville, Md. 20782 for Program Aid No. 1083 *Travelers' Tips.*

Antiques are defined, for customs purposes, as articles manufactured over 100 years ago and are admitted duty-free. If there's any question of age, you may be asked to supply proof. The U.S. Embassy in London has a special customs adviser in case you have any questions about this or any other customs matter.

Smaller gifts may be mailed to friends (but not more than one package to one address). There should be written notation on the package "unsolicited Gift (nature of gift) value under $50." Duty-free packages, however, cannot include perfumes, tobacco or liquor.

If your purchases exceed your exemption, list the most expensive items that are subject to duty under your exemption and pay duty on the cheaper items. Any article you fail to declare cannot later be claimed under your exemption.

A foreign-made automobile that was ordered before your departure is subject to tax (10% of its "dutiable value"), even though delivered abroad. This same rule applies to any purchase initiated in advance of your trip.

Canada. After at least 48 hours abroad, residents of Canada may bring back $10 of duty-free articles. After at least 7 days aboard you may, upon written declaration, claim an exemption of $300 in Canadian funds for each calendar year, or $50 for every calendar quarter, and an allowance of 40 ounces of alcohol, 50 cigars, 200 cigarettes, and 2 lbs of manufactured tobacco. Restrictions on agricultural produce and meat apply, as for the US. For personal gifts the rules are the same as for the U.S.—"unsolicited Gift (nature of Gift), value under $40." For details ask for the Canada Customs brochure *I Declare.*

DUTY FREE is not what it once was. You may not be paying tax on your bottle of whiskey or perfume, but you are certainly contributing to somebody's profits. Duty free shops are big business these days and mark ups are often around 100 to 200%. So don't be seduced by the idea that because it's duty free it's a bargain. Very often prices are not much different from your local discount store and in the case of perfume or jewelry they can be even higher.

As a general rule of thumb, duty free stores on the ground offer better value than buying in the air. Also, if you buy duty free goods on a plane, remember that the range is likely to be limited and that if you are paying in a currency different from that of the airline, their rate of exchange often bears only a passing resemblance to the official one.

Tabarde Inn. 1390

LONDON HOTELS

Homes Away from Home

London's hotels have become of late among the most expensive in Europe. This trend may ease off in the next year or so as hoteliers become increasingly concerned about the effect high prices are having on their business. They are already making the right noises, and some of them—though not enough—are introducing budget schemes. Needless to say, you should make sure you know exactly what your room will cost before you check in. In common with most other European countries, British hotels are obliged to display a tariff on the reception desk. Study it carefully. Remember also that rates in June, July and August can be higher than in slacker seasons.

The general custom is for rates to be quoted for both bed and breakfast. But more and more London hotels, especially the top-class ones, have begun to give rates for room only. Again, check if this applies in your case. The prices we quote are inclusive of both VAT and service and are based on those of mid-1985.

Because of the upsurge in tourism, especially from the States, due to the favorable rates of exchange, you had best be sure to book in advance. Seasonal events, trade shows or royal occasions can fill hotel rooms for sudden, brief periods. If you haven't booked your hotel before you arrive, the following organizations can help you find a room:

Hotel Bookings International, Kingsgate House, Kingsgate Place, London NW6 (tel. 328 1790).

Hotel Reservation Center (tel. 828 2425), and the *London Tourist Board,* both at Victoria Station, SW1. The latter cannot make bookings over the phone.

After the words of warning, a small measure of cheer; London's hotels, especially in the lower-priced range, can still represent good value for money. And if you are prepared to face the price tags in the higher ranges, you'll find the more famous hotels are still as gracious and comfortable as ever.

LUXURY

(Double Room £110 and up)

Athenaeum, 116 Piccadilly, W1 (tel. 499 3464). Renovated, with a strong dash of originality and managerial flair. Rooms are first class and well positioned at the "right end" of Piccadilly. Their malt-whisky bar has become a favored haunt.

Berkeley, Wilton Pl., SW1 (tel. 235 6000). An English hotel experience akin to staying in the finest country house; impeccable décor, service and fairy-tale banqueting facilities. No one will ever afford to build like this again. *Le Perroquet* restaurant with background evening mood music, discotheque later, and superb cuisine, has everything for the ideal celebratory evening. Tops every list.

Blakes, 33 Roland Gardens, SW7 (tel. 370 6701). Chic and trendy, mainly show business clientele. Book ahead.

Churchill, Portman Sq., W1 (tel. 486 5800). A success ever since they opened the doors to that large regency style lobby and those splendidly comfortable bedrooms. A good management team helps, but the position is very convenient.

Claridge's, Brook St., W1 (tel. 629 8860). Don't be discouraged by the usual clichés. True—this hotel is the home of dignity, royal or otherwise, but the staff are friendly and not in the least condescending while the rooms are luxurious. A living hotel legend.

Dorchester, Park Lane, W1 (tel 629 8888). The traditional luxury standards are still intact at this bastion of good living, with the famous *Terrace Restaurant* deserving its reputation. Now owned by the Sultan of Brunei and in process of being transformed into "the most luxurious hotel in the world," which could clearly mean some interruption in normal service.

Dukes, 35 St James's Pl., SW1 (tel. 491 4840). Quietly, but centrally located in a small backwater reeking of old London. An excellent choice, for those who relish small-scale, sedate accommodation backed by friendly service.

Europa, Grosvenor Sq., W1 (tel. 493 1232). Overlooking the square and convenient for Mayfair shopping.

Grosvenor House, Park Lane, W1 (tel. 499 6363). Completely renovated as well-appointed conference hotel with hardly a trace of former Grosvenor style. New restaurants include the luxurious *Ninety Park Lane*.

Hilton, 22 Park Lane, W1 (tel. 493 8000). Not the best of the chain, but keeps the Hilton flag flying. Fine views and plenty of variety in bars and restaurants.

Howard Hotel, Temple Pl., WC2 (tel. 836 3555). Convenient for both City and West End. Opulent bedrooms with fine reproduction pieces.

Hyatt Carlton Tower, Cadogan Pl., SW1 (tel. 235 5411). Convenient for town and Chelsea. Elegant accommodation suited particularly to guests who like a touch of Bohemia nearby. The *Chelsea Room* is an excellent restaurant for serious gourmets, while the *Chinoiserie* foyer is a delightfully elegant spot for tea that won't ruin your budget.

Hyde Park, 66 Knightsbridge, SW1 (tel. 235 2000). Facing Knightsbridge for shopping and backing onto Hyde Park for relaxation. Fairly sumptuous in a distinctly Victorian way, with marble and chandeliers.

Inn on The Park, Hamilton Pl., Park Lane, W1 (tel. 499 0888). An opulent interior, eminent situation and high standards have spelt success for this member of the Park Lane family. The rooms are all beautifully furnished and ultracomfortable.

Inter-Continental, Hyde Park Corner, W1 (tel. 409 3131). Cool and modern with flawless rooms and service—fantastic views straight over Hyde Park Corner. *Le Soufflé* is elegant but over-priced.

Lowndes, 21 Lowndes St., SW1 (tel. 235 6020). Deep within the residential heart of Knightsbridge. Adamesque decor and picturesque people.

Montcalm Hotel, Great Cumberland Place, W1 (tel. 402 4288). Encased in an elegant Georgian crescent and centrally placed. An extremely civilized house, admirably suited to those of sybaritic tastes. Highly recommended.

Portman, 22 Portman Sq., W1 (tel. 486 5844). Older brother of the Inter-Continental, this hotel has quietly established and maintained a high reputation.

Ritz, Piccadilly, W1 (tel. 493 8181). César Ritz's elegant landmark provides sumptuous décor and fine service. Cunard ownership has refurbished public rooms to their former splendor. The Ritz restaurant is once more making gastronomic news.

Savoy, Strand, WC2 (tel. 836 4343). Synonymous with old-fashioned luxury, yet pleasurable also for those small corners of happy informality. A grand hotel of brilliant contrasts, personalities and mood, though competition from other refurbished hotels emphasizes the serious need for modernization.

Sheraton Park Tower, 101 Knightsbridge, SW1 (tel. 235 8050). Luxury bedrooms sport fine views from this circular tower, now part of Knightsbridge scene. Casino.

Stafford, 16 St. James's Pl., SW1 (Tel. 493 0111). In a secluded courtyard complete with gaslights, yet only five minutes from Piccadilly. Excellent choice for small-hotel fans; attentive service and pleasing décor.

EXPENSIVE

(Double Room £80–110)

Britannia, Grosvenor Sq., W1 (tel. 629 9400). Top marks for a modern hotel facade blending unobtrusively with the Square. Inside, restrained decor and comfort. Central location, friendly service.

Browns, Dover St., W1 (tel. 493 6020). Very British, very Victorian (though showing signs of its now being part of a major chain), with moderately modern comfort. Try their afternoon tea, before a stroll down Dover St., but don't forget their excellent restaurant afterwards. Bedroom sizes vary.

Cadogan, 75 Sloane St., SW1 (tel. 235 7141). This rejuvenated hotel has original Adam ceilings in the bar. Before it became a hotel, Lillie Langtry lived here. Bedroom standards and amenities are variable.

Capital, 22 Basil St., SW3 (tel. 589 5171). Small, tasteful and near Harrods. Excellent personal service and décor. *Les Trois Canards* restaurant highly recommended for moderate cost and friendly service. Book well ahead. Highly recommended.

Cavendish, Jermyn St., SW1 (tel. 930 2111). Centrally located for St. James's shopping and theaters; functional hotel in spite of its 'Duchess of Duke Street' past. 24-hour coffee shop.

Clifton Ford, Welbeck St., W1 (tel. 486 6600). Pedigree situation at reasonable prices. Popular with tours.

Connaught, Carlos Pl., W1 (tel. 499 7070). With only 90 superb rooms and a world-wide reputation, here is true quiet luxury. One of the best hotel bases for touring London. Their famous kitchen is splendidly dominated by one of the world's best chefs.

Gloucester, 4 Harrington Gdns, SW7 (tel. 373 6030). Modern hotel close to hectic Gloucester Road and tube station.

Goring, 15 Beeston Place, Grosvenor Gdns., SW1 (tel. 834 8211). The Goring family provide personal, friendly service in this modernized Edwardian hotel. Very hospitable.

Holiday Inn, Marble Arch, 134 George St., W1 (tel. 723 1277). Recently refurbished bedrooms in this centrally located chain member.

Holiday Inn, Mayfair, Berkeley St., SW1 (tel. 493 8282). Well-situated close to Bond St. In spite of the very modern exterior, this is a lavishly comfortable place with a markedly French decor. Good service. Easy parking.

Holiday Inn, Swiss Cottage, 128 King Henry's Rd., NW3 (tel. 722 7711). Well-appointed and handy for north London, but a bit far from the center. Very reasonable indeed for (E) category. Also at **Chelsea,** Sloane St., (tel. 235 4377). Both reliable and well managed; indoor pools.

Kensington Hilton, 179 Holland Park Ave., W11 (tel. 603 3355). The utility-style Hilton in West London; makes for transport problems.

London Marriott, Duke St., W1 (tel. 439 0281). Extensively refurbished in 1984. With all facilities; airconditioning, some double-glazing. Diplomat Restaurant.

May Fair, Stratton St., W1 (tel. 629 7777). Animated lobby reflects Mayfair bustle outside. Has undergone massive refurbishment program to emerge with every conceivable luxury facility. Still retains its tiny theater and even smaller cinema.

New Berners, 10 Berners St., W1 (tel. 636 1629). Many original architectural features in the busy, well-run hotel off Oxford Street.

Park Lane, Piccadilly, W1 (tel. 499 6321). Most rooms upgraded during 1985 but hotel retains its original character, with Victoriana throughout.

Royal Garden, Kensington High St., W8 (tel. 937 8000). Crisp modern hotel convenient for this good shopping street; some rooms with stunning views of the Park.

Royal Lancaster, Lancaster Terrace, W2 (tel. 262 6737). Excellent views from a well-decorated hotel with everything for an enjoyable stay.

St. James, Buckingham Gate, SW1 (tel. 834 2360). Most rooms with bath; large grey hotel set in interesting little streets.

Selfridge, Orchard St., W1 (tel. 408 2080). Attached to the famous store for obvious shopping expedition possibilities. Modern and attractively-conceived with well-fitted bedrooms and willing staff.

7 Down Street, 7 Down St., W1 (tel. 493 3364). Recent addition to the London scene, comprising just six double suites, each with its own theme. For example there's an Indian Room, a Blue Room (with original Tudor four-poster), and Kalahari Room. Unusual.

Westbury, New Bond St., W1 (tel. 629 7755). The first of the American-style hotels in London is now under British ownership. The bar's the coolest place in London on a hot summer's day. Rooms are good and the location very handy, but the hotel is beginning to show its age.

White House, Albany St., NW1 (tel. 378 1200). A large hotel overlooking Regent's Park, with a solid reputation for comfort. Good value.

MODERATE

(Double Room £50–80)

Alexander, 9 Summer Place, SW7 (tel. 581 1591). Comfortable bedrooms in an attractive establishment.

Basil Street, SW3 (tel. 581 3311). Traditional style and elegance—an ideal spot for the well-heeled single woman.

Charing Cross, Strand, WC2 (tel. 839 7282). Gaunt exterior but friendly heart, beside theaterland with excellent restaurant and interesting architectural features preserved. Rooms are comfortable.

Clive, Primrose Hill Rd., NW3 (tel. 586 2233). Quiet Hampstead location with great views.

Cumberland, Marble Arch, W1 (tel. 262 1234). Massive central evergreen offers good value.

Ebury Court, 26 Ebury St., SW1 (tel. 730 8147). A fine example of value for money in the escalating prices of London hotels. Considerable genteel charm and courteous, friendly staff. Good restaurant and elegant Belgravia location. Book well in advance.

Gore, 189 Queen's Gate, SW7 (tel. 584 6601). Personally-run, with a friendly atmosphere.

Grafton, 129 Tottenham Court Rd., W1 (tel. 388 4131). A member of the Edwardian Group, who re-opened it in 1982 after a multimillion pound refurbishment program. Above-average for the Moderate range.

Great Western, Praed St., W2 (tel. 723 8064). Huge bedrooms and lofty ceilings remain in this imposing and well-modernized Victorian hotel, joined to Paddington Station.

Kensington Close, Wrights Lane, W8 (tel. 937 8170). Facilities include two squash courts and swimming pool.

London Embassy, 150 Bayswater Rd., W2 (tel. 229 1212). Handy for Hyde Park and the colorful Greek Queensway scene.

London International, 147 Cromwell Rd., SW5 (tel. 370 4200). Functional and a bit anonymous, but handy for the museums and the exhibition centers. Bedrooms have been refurbished; airy coffee shop.

London Metropole, Edgware Rd., W2 (tel. 402 4141). Reasonably priced for the amenities provided, but in dull area. However, it is reasonably comfortable, and the service is efficient.

London Tara, Wrights Lane, W8 (tel. 937 7211). Good value accommodation on 12 stories—factory style but competently run. Just off Kensington High Street.

Londoner, Welbeck St., W1 (tel. 935 4442). A well-placed, small hotel within strolling distance of shops, pubs and quiet residential London.

Mount Royal, Bryanston St., W1 (tel. 629 8040). Big and central, beside Marble Arch; reasonable rooms and good value steak bar and coffee shop. Their English breakfast is topnotch.

Norfolk, Harrington Rd., SW7 (tel. 581 0601). Closed for renovation during 1985. In popular bedsit area.

Number 16, 16 Sumner Pl., SW7 (tel. 589 5232). 32-room hotel in South Ken., winner of an award for excellence in the 1984 Good Hotel Guide.

Portobello Hotel, 22 Stanley Gdns., W11 (tel. 727 2777): An unconventional and enjoyable small hotel; potted palms and military furniture in "antique land." Recommended.

Royal Court, Sloane Sq., SW1 (tel. 730 9191). Well-located and highly convenient for Chelsea sorties.

Royal Horseguards, 2 Whitehall Ct., SW1 (tel. 839 3400). Variable room standards and functional public areas in a good "historical" situation for touring town.

Royal Trafalgar, Whitcombe St., WC2 (tel. 930 4477). Very handy for Nelson's column and almost everywhere else.

Royal Westminster, Buckingham Palace Rd., SW1 (tel. 834 1302). Well-located modern hotel, highly recommended by our readers. Bedrooms especially comfortable.

Rubens, Buckingham Palace Rd., SW1 (tel. 834 6600). Proximate to Palace and refurbished.

Russell, Russell Sq., WC1 (tel. 837 6470). Handy for the British Museum; a good choice, if you don't mind the décor on the ground floor.

St. George's, Langham Place, W1 (tel. 580 0111). Near Oxford Circus, this hotel occupies the top floors of a tower block and was largely designed for the business man. Right beside the BBC.

Strand Palace, Strand, WC2 (tel. 836 8080). Comfortable and good value without fuss or frills.

Tower, St. Katherine's Way, E1 (tel. 481 2575). A vast modern hotel beside the Tower with suitable riverside ambience. Nearest tube is Tower Hill, then a five-minute walk—not very convenient.

Vanderbilt, 76 Cromwell Rd., SW7 (tel. 584 0491). Another member of the Edwardian chain, with all that entails in terms of facilities, and service.

Waldorf, Aldwych, WC2 (tel. 836 2400). Midway between theaterland and the City, with a blended atmosphere of both, plus a touch of Edwardiana.

Westmoreland Hotel, 18 Lodge Rd., NW8 (tel. 722 7722). Overlooking Lords and popular with our readers for its friendly staff, good rooms, and value for money.

Whites, Lancaster Gate, W2 (tel. 262 2711). Old building overlooking Hyde Park. Very friendly staff.

INEXPENSIVE

The following selection includes only a few of London's dozens of guest houses and smaller private hotels, offering reasonable accommodation. Most of them are converted 19th-century terrace houses. Double rooms up to £50, though many of the following have rooms well under that. A good budget chain is Ladbrokes (tel. 221 2626).

Apollo, 18 Lexham Gdns., W8 (tel. 373 3236)
Arlanda, 17 Longridge Rd., SW5 (tel. 370 5220)
Barkston, 36 Barkston Gdns., SW5 (tel. 373 7851).
Bedford 83 Southampton Row, WC1 (tel. 636 7822).
Bloomsbury Crest, Coram St., WC1 (tel. 837 1200).
Chesham House, 64–66 Ebury St., SW1 (tel. 730 8513).
Colonnade, 2 Warrington Cres., W9 (tel. 289 2167).
Concord, 157 Cromwell Rd., SW5 (tel. 370 4151)
Durrants, George St., W1 (tel. 935 8131).
Eden House, 111 Old Church St., SW3 (tel. 352 3403)
Eden Plaza, 68 Queen's Gate, SW7 (tel. 370 6111).
Elizabeth, 37 Eccleston Sq., SW1 (tel. 828 6812)
Elizabetta, 162 Cromwell Rd., SW7 (tel. 370 5096).

George, 58 Cartwright Gdns., WC1 (tel. 387 1528)
Jenkins, 45 Cartwright Gdns., WC1 (tel. 387 2067)
Leicester Court, 41 Queen's Gate Gdns., SW7 (tel. 584 0512)
Leinster Towers, 25 Leinster Gdns., W2 (tel. 262 4591).
London Ryan, 10–12 Gwynne Pl., WC1 (tel. 278 2480).
Manor Court, 35 Courtfield Gdns., SW5 (tel. 373 8585).
Mornington Lancaster, 12 Lancaster Gate, W2 (tel. 262 7361).
Pembridge Court, 34 Pembridge Gdns., W2 (tel. 299 9977).
Regent Palace, Piccadilly Circus, W1 (tel. 734 7000).
Ruskin, 23 Montague St., WC1 (tel. 636 7388)
Tudor Court, 58 Cromwell Rd., SW7 (tel. 584 8273)
Wilbraham, Wilbraham Pl., SW1 (tel. 730 8296).
Willett House, 32 Sloane Gdns., SW1 (tel. 730 0634).

LONDON AIRPORT (HEATHROW)

Expensive (E), £80–110; Moderate (M), £50–80

All of these have bus services to get you into the airport without hassle.

Ariel (M), Harlington Corner, Bath Rd., Hayes (tel. 739 2552). Unusual circular hotel with well-maintained bedrooms for an overnight airport stopover.

Excelsior (M), Bath Rd., West Drayton (tel. 759 6611). Located at the north entrance to airport, with a businesslike atmosphere for stopovers.

Heathrow Penta (M), Bath Rd., Hounslow (tel. 897 6363). Luxury hotel actually within the airport borders and filled with every jet-set facility; getting known for good eating—their Continental food festivals are worthwhile.

Holiday Inn (M), Stockley Rd., West Drayton (tel. 089–544 5555). Handy version of the standard chain facilities.

Post House (M), Sipson Rd., West Drayton (tel. 759 2323). Comfortable, though some of the facilities are a bit on the small side. Good food. At lower end of price range.

Sheraton Heathrow (M), Colnbrook Bypass, Longford, West Drayton (tel. 759 2424). Quite adequate for the one-night stopover. Downstairs can be good for drinks and dining, prior to catching the next flight.

Sheraton Skyline (E), Bath Rd., Hayes (tel. 759 2535). The really bright airport spot with lovely bedrooms and lively entertainment. Heated patio guarantees easy Caribbean acclimatization. Has a very good, if slightly overdressed, restaurant.

Skyway (M), Bath Rd., Hayes (tel. 759 6311).

APARTMENTS

Many people prefer the liberty and convenience of having a service flat rather than living in a hotel when on holiday. It frequently works out cheaper, too. So we would like to suggest a few excellent possibilities from among the many available. Please note that prices were those obtaining as we went to press (mid-1985) and that you would be well advised to check the latest rates (phone numbers given below).

Dolphin Square, Dolphin Square, SW1 (tel. 834 9134). A huge spread of apartments and a familiar fixture on the London scene for decades. Sites close to the Thames, in Pimlico. Much of the Square is permanently let, but Rodney House has several types of apartment available. Weekly rental from £228 for a single, and £552 for a 2 twin-bedded apartment.

Embassy Apartments, 24 Queensborough Terr., SW7 (tel. 584 7222). Five apartments. Well decorated and equipped. Maid service. £45 to £75 nightly rate, depending on apartment.

Lambs Service Flats, 21 Egerton Gdns., SW3 (tel. 589 6297). In quiet, elegant houses only a couple of hundred yards from Harrods and other Knightsbridge Aladdin's caves. All apartments have complete maid service. Weekly rates £249.55 to £354.20 (suites £499.10).

One Carlos Place, 1 Carlos Place, W1 (tel. 491 4165). Absolutely exclusive and better value than most hotel suites. Beautifully decorated; with two penthouse suites available, too. £125 up to £325 per day (not including VAT).

Regency Suites, 130 Queen's Gate, SW7 (tel. 370 4242). A good selection of apartments (52 in all) in four converted old terrace houses. Plenty of facilities available (including a babysitting service). Seasonal rates vary, but average out from £339.25 up to £1955 per week (latter rate for suite with 3 twin-bedded rooms.

Rutland Court, 21–23 Draycott Pl., SW3 (tel. 589 9691). Charmingly decorated and equipped flats with all mod cons. 10 units, from small to quite large (taking six people). £205 to £645.

LONDON RESTAURANTS

International Cookery—and the British Pub

Once upon a time, when the world was young, eating in London was an experience to be endured rather than enjoyed. Things are very different now. There are restaurants offering cuisine from all over the world—and even, be it said in reverent tones, from Britain itself. There have always been Italian and French restaurants, some dating back for fifty years or more; solid reliable places, with solid reliable menus. But now there are literally dozens of possibilities with exciting, adventurous cooking served in intriguing surroundings with, high on the list of un-English activities, the farouche joys of the wine bar.

It is difficult to say what brought about this *volte face*. One of the more obvious reasons is the great influx into Britain in the last decade of new citizens who have brought their own cooking with them. That might explain the opening of what seems like endless chains of Tan-

73

doori restaurants, but in no way deals with the fact that, on almost every level of society, Britons are becoming more conscious of what they eat.

And not just conscious but downright pernickety. The *Good Food Guide* (that opinionated, invaluable gastronomic bible) has developed over the years of its existence into a kind of public diary in which contributors can record their dissatisfaction with the amount of vinegar in a sauce or the callousness of a waiter. That they *do* write in, by the thousand apparently, shows that food is now taken very seriously in Britain, and such high-seriousness can only benefit the visitor to the country. Whatever your taste, it is likely to find satisfaction in London.

The same cannot necessarily be said for your purse, which might well not be so happy. The London tourist boom has brought on a rash of smart looking restaurants that charge grossly inflated prices for mediocre food at tables set much too close together and with service that gives amateurism a bad name. Even the older establishments have had to increase their rates, forced into an ever-rising spiral by high rents and taxes.

The result has inevitably been that fewer and fewer Londoners are able to eat out with any regularity, unless they are on expense accounts or celebrating their golden wedding anniversaries. It has also meant that restaurants which have reasonable prices and still give value-for-money and courteous service are treasured as rubies beyond price.

Most restaurants post their menus outside, so that the wary passerby can check before committing himself. Unless you are traveling on an expense account, we strongly suggest you look before you eat.

What Will it Cost?

We have divided our main listings here by price, rather than by culinary type. All the grades cover an approximate price for a dinner for two, including wine and V.A.T. (The wine in Budget is carafe.)

Luxury, £60 and way up—you could find yourself faced with a £100 check for two in the upper reaches of this grade; Expensive, £40–£60; Moderate, £20–£40; Budget, £20 and below.

There are some serious defects still to eating in London. The main one is that it is difficult to do so on Sunday or late at night. You should always check if a restaurant is open on Sundays; it could save you a wasted journey. You will find a list at the end of the *Facts at Your Fingertips* section of some restaurants open until a late hour.

Another point to remember is that not all restaurants accept credit cards. One kindly owner remarked, when asked if he accepted plastic money, "No. We take only cash, checks and hostages."

A law obliges all U.K. restaurants to display their prices, *including* V.A.T., outside their establishments. Not all restaurants conform to this sensible piece of consumer legislation but most do, and if you are on a very tight budget, it's wise to read them carefully. Look for the hidden extras such as service, cover and minimum charge which are usually at the bottom of the menu and make sure the menu inside is the same!

LUXURY—£60 and way, way up

À l'Écu de France, 111 Jermyn St., SW1 (930 2837). Elegant and well-established near Piccadilly Circus, with wide-ranging menu and notable wine list. Close Sat. lunch and Sun.

Athenaeum Hotel Restaurant, 116 Piccadilly, W1 (499 3464). Reliable, with excellent wine list. Outstanding business lunch.

Berkeley Hotel Restaurant, Wilton Place, SW1 (235 6000). Superb classical cuisine perfectly served by friendly professional and predominately British staff, in elegant surroundings to complete a memorable experience. Closed Sat. **Berkeley Buttery** offers popular lunchtime buffet, and an evening change of mood to serious dining and music. Both consistently good. Closed Sun.

Café Royal, 68 Regent St., W1 (437 9090). Lavishly painted ceilings and memories of Oscar Wilde in the "grill." Next door **Nicols Restaurant** is open throughout the day for breakfast, snacks, teas and set table d'hôte.

Capital Hotel Restaurant, 22–24 Basil St., SW3 (589 5171). It's wise to book and wiser to take the food seriously here. Dedication to the highest standards becomes instantly apparent to both palate and the eye. The limited menu helps to boost confidence.

Cecconi's, 5a Burlington Gdns., W1 (434 1500). An elegant Italian locale which attracts a chic set. Closed Sat. and Sun.

Claridges Hotel, Brook St., W1 (629 8860). The **Causerie** is one of the best buys in town, with a mouthwatering lunch or dinner buffet. **Claridges Restaurant** is very dependent upon people to create the right ambiance. Food similarly can be dull, but generally well worth a visit.

Connaught Hotel Restaurant, Carlos Place, W1 (499 7070). London's current gastronomic temple presided over by high priest Michel Bourdin and, befitting its status, it has more than a touch of hierarchical tradition. The range of dishes is vast and their wine selection extremely good value. But don't forget this is in the *very* expensive category, even so you must book.

Dorchester Grill and Terrace Restaurant, Park Lane, W1 (629 8888). **The Grill** combines fine British food, service and wine, with more than a dash of style and these days has a very mixed clientele. The elegant and beautifully-decorated **Terrace** is a shrine to *nouvelle cuisine* with one of its best exponents, Anton Mosimann, in charge; now also serving his new *cuisine naturelle* for the health conscious.

Le Gavroche, 43 Upper Brook St., W1 (408 0881). Not the place for business discussions or têtes à têtes; superb food reigns supreme in elegant new surroundings, strictly conforming to the classical French ideas of cuisine and service. Priced at the top of the range, but the meal will be superb. Closed Sat. and Sun.

Grosvenor House Hotel, Ninety Park Lane, 90 Park Lane, W1 (499 6363). A grand luxury restaurant with English/French menu and a fine wine list. Closed Sat. lunch and Sun.

Hyatt-Carlton Tower Hotel, Chelsea Room, Cadogan Place, SW1 (235 5411). Dining room has delightful views across Cadogan Square. Soigné French cooking and agreeable service. Try **The Chinoiserie** for an unusually elegant tea.

Hyde Park Hotel, Grill Room, 66 Knightsbridge, SW1 (235 2000). A hold-over from the palmy days of Edwardian London with its marble and plush well-maintained. Popular lunchtime buffet. Closed Sat.

Inigo Jones, 14 Garrick St., WC2 (836 6456). Close to gaslights and the Bow Street Runners' narrow street, this Covent Garden venue offers original bare brick and stained glass decor and an original version of *nouvelle cuisine.* A fine spot for a reasonable lunch or an expensive dinner. Must book ahead. Closed Sat. lunch and Sun.

Inn on the Park Hotel, Four Seasons, Hamilton Place, Park Lane, W1 (499 0888). An expensive restaurant, but one with imaginative cooking and pleasant service. The **Lanes** is much less pricey, but maintains the same high and attractive standards, with a *prix fixe* lunchtime menu, including wine.

Intercontinental Hotel, Le Soufflé, 1 Hamilton Place, Hyde Park Corner, W1 (409 3131). '20s décor is a backcloth here to first-class food, expertly served, but a bit overpriced. Despite the name, there are many dishes to surpass their soufflés. For the budget-minded there is a set-price lunch.

Interlude de Tabaillau, 7 Bow St., WC2 (379 6473). *Prix fixe* excellence immediately beside Covent Garden Opera House. Fairly new to the scene, but it caught on immediately. Excellent cuisine with a Gavroche background. Must book as the prices are still quite reasonable for the quality and the locale ideal.

Keats, 3 Downshire Hill, NW3 (435 3544). Superb French food includes their special 12-course gourmet dinners, on set dates by reservation only. Wise to book on ordinary days, too. Dinner only. Closed Sun.

Leith's, 92 Kensington Park Rd., W11 (229 4481). Prudence Leith is also a well-known writer on food, a teacher and fine cook herself. As you'd expect the food here is interesting and usually successful. You might possibly find it expensive for what is on offer, but it is at least worth trying once. Dinner only, 7 days a week.

Maxim's, 13 Panton St., Haymarket, WC2 (839 4809). For once the advance publicity didn't lie—this is a mirror image of the Paris version. Interesting menu in opulent surroundings. Dress up for dinner, and be prepared for anything up to £100 on the check. Dancing possible. Closed Sun.

Mirabelle, 56 Curzon St., W1 (499 4636). This is *the* place for a celebration—followed by bankruptcy. The atmosphere is attractively 50s. Legendary wine list. Closed Sun.

Le Poulbot, 45 Cheapside, EC2 (236 4379). This is *the* elegant City venue for businessmen with taste. French food at its peak; run by chef/owners of **Le Gavroche.** Opens for lunch only and is closed both Sat. and Sun. French food at its height.

Rue St. Jacques, 5 Charlotte St., W1 (637 0222). The winning combination of Carrier's ex-chef, the ex-manager of Boulestin and three high-style different-mood dining rooms make this London's most attractive newcomer. Expect rich food and a fittingly serious wine list. Look out for the set lunch.

Savoy Hotel, Grill Room and **Restaurant,** Strand, WC2 (836 4343). A well-founded reputation for classic French cooking and impeccable service at this ornate restaurant overlooking the river. More for the view and atmosphere than the food, and so ideal for a special occasion.

Scott's, 20 Mount St., W1 (629 5248). Masculine (high expense account) ambiance with well-cooked traditional food, with a distinct flair for fish.

La Tante Claire, 68 Royal Hospital Rd, SW3 (352 6045). Forget the decor and the crowded tables, for here is the temple of *Cuisine Minceur* and similar chic food. Lunch is excellent value. Must book well ahead as it's extremely popular. Closed Sat. and Sun.

Trader Vic, Hilton Hotel, Park Lane, W1 (493 7586). Still one of London's best spots for a touch of the exotic at those difficult hours between 6 and 8 P.M.; they continue into the small hours, of course. Menu large and variable.

Waltons, 121 Walton St., SW3 (584 0204). One of the small band of newish excellent restaurants. Service superb, food consistent but expensive. Book ahead.

Wiltons, 55 Jermyn St., SW1 (629 9955). In new premises, Wiltons retains its original Edwardian charm, discreetly efficient staff, and a menu of British dishes with seafood and seasonal game specialties. Closed Sat. and Sun.

EXPENSIVE—£40–£60

Alcove, 17 Kensington High St, W8 (937 1443). Good fresh quality fish is best sampled here unadorned (branch of Wheeler's). Closed Sun.

Baron of Beef, Gutter Lane, Gresham St., EC2 (606 9415). A popular lunchtime venue for traditional English fare. Fine wine list. Closed Sat. and Sun.

Belvedere, Holland Park (behind Commonwealth Institute), W8 (602 1238). Now called the *Fisherman's Wharf at the Belvedere*—the latest of a series of manifestations—this one run by Lyons. Concentrates on fish dishes with a Scottish accent. Very pretty decor and views, though best in summer. The Scottish theme extends to a selection of 91 Malt Whiskies!

Bentley's, 11 Swallow St, W1 (734 6210). Traditional seafood restaurant upstairs with a downstairs oyster bar. A classic spot. Closed Sun.

Bewicks, 87 Walton St., SW3 (584 6711). An intimate restaurant with mainly French food and an interesting wine list. Closed lunch Sat. and Sun.

Braganza—see *Wheeler's*

Capability Brown, 351 West End Lane, NW6 (794 3234). A small bistro-like restaurant, whose interesting menu is occasionally overambitious and a little overpriced. Excellent presentation and service.

Chez Nico, 129 Queenstown Rd., SW8 (720 6960). Consistently high standards at this Gallic restaurant, as the raw materials used are first class.

Ciboure, 21 Eccleston St., SW1 (730 2505). Delightfully cool spot with fine *nouvelle cuisine* and friendly service. Between Victoria and Sloane Square. Closed Sat. lunch and Sun.

English House, 3 Milner St., SW3 (584 3002). Lovers of traditional English food can enjoy a taste of the past in this charming dining room. Booking essential.

L'Etoile, 30 Charlotte St., W1 (636 7189). Small and tasteful French place with the true touch of Paris. Super wine list and generally good to know.

Frederick's, Camden Passage, N1 (359 2888). An imaginative menu served beneath high ceilings with a lovely conservatory too.

Greenhouse, 27a Hays Mews, W1 (499 3331). Airy setting for interesting range of dishes in this smart restaurant tucked away behind Grosvenor Sq.

Hilaire, 68 Old Brompton Rd., SW7 (584 8993). The latest "in" spot for top-quality *cuisine electique* from a very talented chef who was once an inspector for Egon Ronay!

Langan's Brasserie, Stratton St., W1 (493 6437). Best for after-theater dining when the "30s" mood, background jazz and celebrities complement good food and fast service. So trendy it's like a 3-D version of Who's Who. Must book.

Leoni's Quo Vadis, 26 Dean St., W1 (437 9585). Heart-of-Soho, long-established and very reliable. Fine Italian cooking. Karl Marx lived upstairs. Closed for lunch Sat. and Sun.

Lichfield's, Lichfield Ter., Sheen Rd., Richmond, Surrey (940 5236). Worth the trip to Richmond, don't be put off by the unpromising exterior—Stephen Bull's food is a fine example of imaginative modern French cooking. Excellent set lunch. Closed lunch Sat. and Sun.

Locket's, Marsham Court, Marsham St., SW1 (834 9552). Close to the House of Commons; traditional English cooking. Closed Sat. and Sun.

Ma Cuisine, 113 Walton St., SW3 (584 7585). Currently among London's most popular for excellent cooking, especially lunch. Book well in advance as it's extremely difficult to get in. Closed Sat. and Sun.

Ménage à Trois, 15 Beauchamp Pl., SW3 (589 4252). The befores-and-afters restaurant ("no inter-course" says chef/patron Antony Worral-Thompson) made famous by a visit from Princess Diana. Closed Sat. and Sun.

Mijanou, 143 Ebury St., SW1 (730 4099). Fine delicate French cooking— among the best. Closed Sat. and Sun.

Mr Chow, 151 Knightsbridge, SW1 (589 7347). Chinese for Westerners, with prices to match.

Mr Kai of Mayfair, 65 South Audley St., W1 (493 8988). Not a hairdressers, but a modern, stylish restaurant on two levels—lots of mock flowering trees. Fine cooking and exotic Chinese service.

Neal Street Restaurant, 26 Neal St., WC2 (836 8368). Prized spot for that business lunch or dinner. Trendy but cool Conran decor. Closed Sat. and Sun.

Odins, 27 Devonshire St., W1 (935 7296). Unusual and original food with a good wine list. Must book. Closed Sat. lunch and Sun.

L'Olivier, 116 Finborough Rd., SW10 (370 4183). South-of-France inspired and decorated restaurant as famous for its plain roast meats as it is for its French shellfish and simply but superbly prepared fish dishes. Related to top fish restaurant **Le Suquet.**

L'Opera, 32 Great Queen St., Covent Garden, WC2 (405 9020). Convenient for eating post-theater. Reliable French food from a well-established restaurant. Closed Sat. lunch and Sun. all day.

Oslo Court Restaurant, Prince Albert Rd., NW8 (722 8795). Balkan and Greek dishes ranging from the simple to the sophisticated, prepared with skill.

Pomegranates, 94 Grosvenor Rd., SW1 (828 6560). An international culinary extravaganza. The food ranges from Scandinavian to Chinese.

Read's, 152 Old Brompton Rd., SW5 (373 2445). Charming and very pretty small restaurant, offering superb value, quality French inspired food from a young, British, female chef. Well-explained wine list. Traditional British Sunday lunch is one of the best in town. Closed Sun. dinner.

Ritz Hotel, Louis XVI Restaurant, Piccadilly, W1 (493 8181). Good food and an excellent wine list in magnificent surroundings, recently restored to their original glory.

Rules, 35 Maiden Lane, WC2 (836 5314). Since 1798, they have been serving truly English food here in great style, though it's now beginning to show its age a little. Wise to book.

St. Quentin, 243 Brompton Rd., SW3 (589 8005). Brightly-lit, popular eatery with well-prepared food and a bright clientele, too.

Sheekey's, 28–32 St. Martin's Court, WC2 (240 2565). Traditional haunt for good pre-theater fish meals of large proportions. Also excellent oyster bar.

Simpsons, 100 Strand, WC2 (836 9112). An English Institution for roast beef or saddle of mutton; go for the rather staid atmosphere—not the food.

Le Suquet, 104 Draycott Ave., SW3 (581 1785). The last word for fish—including take-away! Definitely in the lower end of the price range.

Tai Pan, 8 Egerton Garden Mews, SW3 (589 8287). Colonial-style basement, serving high-quality regional Chinese food. Discreet service; haunt of the famous.

Trattoo, 2 Abingdon Rd., W8 (937 4448). Friendly service for well-cooked Italian dishes in this bustling appealing restaurant. Consistently good, with obliging staff.

Wheelers, 12A Duke of York St., SW1 (930 2460), 19 Old Compton St., W1 (437 2706) and others, inc. the **Braganza,** 56 Frith St., W1 (437 5412). An excellent, long-established seafood chain, with interesting atmosphere—especially the Duke of York St. one, in a tall narrow house. See also **The Alcove.**

Wind in the Willows, 4 Elliot Rd., W4 (995 2406). Tiny, intimate restaurant in Chiswick with interesting and unusual menu. Must reserve.

MODERATE—£20-ᶠ40

Ajimura, 51 Shelton St., WC2 (240 0178). Certainly not elegant, but simple, excellent Japanese food at very reasonable prices. The *tonkatsu* is especially good. Handy for Covent Garden area. Closed Sat. lunch and Sun.

Anna's Place, 90 Mildmay Park, N1 (249 9379). Charming, small restaurant with unusual and excellent menu. Closed Sun. and Mon.

L'Artiste Assoiffé, 122 Kensington Park Rd, W11 (727 4714). This purposely "Bohemian" restaurant near the Portobello Road is always entertaining and good value. Summer dining outside. Closed Sun.

Ashoka Tandoori, 181 Fulham Rd, SW3 (352 3301). Varied Tandoori cooking with intriguing decor. A long established favorite.

Aunties, 126 Cleveland Street, W1 (387 3226). Small restaurant serving English pies, cutlets, etc., in friendly style.

Al Ben Accolto, 58 Fulham Rd., SW3 (589 0876). Good pedigree ownership assures quality fare of mingled French and English antecedents. Friendly service to younger clientele.

Le Bistroquet, 255 Camden High St., NW1 (485 9607). Large and delightfully decorated brasserie-style restaurant with a short regional menu, afternoon tea and regional French wines. Small terrace for al fresco dining. Popular Sunday brunch, booking advised.

Bombay Brasserie, Courtfield Close, Courtfield Rd., SW7 (370 4040). Large and stunningly decorated in colonial style, with a pretty conservatory room available for party bookings. At lunch there is a hot buffet and, like the à la carte, offers a varied menu of regional Indian food.

La Brasserie, 272 Brompton Rd., SW3 (584 1668). Authentically Gallic with onion soup, etc., 8.30 in the morning (Sat. 11, Sun. 11.30) to midnight.

Bubbs, 329 Central Market, EC1 (236 2435). Characteristic French restaurant, small selection, but excellent quality. Next to Smithfield meat market.

Bunny's, 7 Pond St., NW3 (435 1541). Informal, French-style cooking, with a frequently changing menu in an excellent Hampstead spot. Budget Fondue upstairs.

Camden Brasserie, 216 Camden High St., NW1 (482. 2114). Unpretentious and reliably good French cafe where everything is homemade and they cater as much for meat lovers as for vegetarians. Sunday brunch is popular; booking advised.

Le Caprice, Arlington House, Arlington St. (just behind the Ritz), SW1 (629 2239). Stylish and stylishly-run haunt of media, successful artists et al. Short menu of fashionable French food and an equally good Sunday brunch menu. Do book. Closed Sat. lunch and Sun. dinner.

La Capannina, 24 Romilly St., W1 (437 2473). Good Italian restaurant. Closed Sat. lunch and Sun.

Cellier du Midi, 28 Church Row, NW3 (435 9998). Open evenings only, and worth traveling out to Hampstead, a delightful part of London. Provençal cooking.

Le Chef, 41 Connaught St., W2 (262 5945). Small, maybe even too intimate, but unpretentious and very French (they even close in August—very Parisian!). Book in advance. Closed Sun. and Mon.

Chelsea Rendezvous, 4 Sydney St, SW3 (352 9519). Very popular for prodigious Chinese cooking with high prices. Open 7 days a week.

Chez Gerard, 8 Charlotte St., W1 (636 4975). French steakhouse with both atmosphere and quality. North Soho. Closed Sat. lunch.

Chez Solange, 35 Cranbourne St., WC2 (836 0542). Satisfactory basic French cooking and character.

Chez Victor, 45 Wardour St., W1 (437 6523). Relic of former Soho days. Small and genuinely French. Closed Sat. evening and Sun.

Como Lario, 22 Holbein Pl., SW1 (730 2954). All the family works to run a very happy restaurant, with a particularly good *zabaglione.* Closed Sun.

La Cucaracha, 12 Greek St., W1 (734 2253). Mexican food in a delightfully atmospheric vaulted cellar. Guitar music completes the mood-Mexicana. Closed Sat. lunch and Sun.

Dan's, 119 Sydney St., SW3 (352 2718). Good example of the U.K. version of the new, lighter French cooking techniques. Closed Sat. and Sun.

Drakes, 2a Pond Place, Fulham Rd., SW3 (584 4555). Atmospheric cellar with wine-bottle decor. Well recommended for high standards verging on excellence.

The English Garden, 10 Lincoln St., SW3 (584 7272). A very pretty restaurant, designed like a conservatory and decorated in white and pink with lots of plants. Open every day for lunch and dinner.

Fagin's Kitchen, 82 High St., NW3 (435 3608). Good solid food and friendly service in the heart of Hampstead.

Gavvers, 61 Lower Sloane St., SW1 (730 5983). Related to the famous Le Gavroche, they serve expertly cooked French food. There is a useful fixed price menu, which is altered daily. Closed at lunchtime and on Sunday.

Gay Hussar, 2 Greek St., W1 (437 0973). A long-standing favorite with an atmosphere that's always dynamic. Hungarian cooking at reasonable prices. Book well in advance.

Good Earth, 91 King's Rd., SW3 (352 9231). Cantonese and Pekinese dishes, with delicate flavors.

Hostaria Romana, 70 Dean St., W1 (734 2869). Typically good and old-fashioned Soho Italian restaurant. Plenty of ebullience and big helpings. Closed Sun.

Au Jardin des Gourmets, 5 Greek St., W1 (437 1816). Art nouveau makes this elegant restaurant, with sound cooking. Closed Sat. lunch and Sun.

Kalamaras, 66 Inverness Mews, W2 (727 9122), and 76/78 Inverness Mews, W2 (727 9122). Relaxed and informal Greek restaurants, with imaginative house specialties. Closed Sun.

Ken Lo's Memories of China, 67 Ebury St., SW1 (730 7734). An elegant, modern spot with reputation as a leading Chinese eatery.

Ley Ons, 56 Wardour St., W1 (437 6465). Long established and still serving excellent standard Chinese. Especially good for a Dim-Sum meal.

Maggie Jones, 6 Old Court Place, W8 (937 6462). Extraordinarily haphazard decor and extremely well-cooked food in this bistro-style spot just off Kensington Church St. (bottom end). Fine value, but must book.

Magno's Brasserie, 65A Long Acre, Covent Garden, WC2 (838 6077). One of the few places calling themselves "Brasserie" with real reason. Gallic atmosphere and exactly the right bistro food. Usually crowded, though, so be sure to book. Lunch Mon. to Fri., dinner Mon. to Sat. Closed Sun.

Manzi's, 1 Leicester St., WC2 (734 0224). A happy fish spot; value is good and the helpings generous. Very central and always crowded to the gunwales, so be sure to book.

Mon Plaisir, 21 Monmouth St., WC2 (836 7243). A bustling French bistro in the heart of theaterland. Their cheeseboard is among the best in London and the Gallic ambiance is hard to beat. Must book. Closed Saturday and Sunday.

New World, 1 Gerrard Pl., W1 (734 0677). Huge, bright and modern cafe, related to its popular neighbor, Chuen Cheng Ku. Dim sum at lunch, or choose from long and explained à la carte.

Le Papillon, 57 Greenwich Church St., SE10 (858 2668). Small and excellent Greenwich restaurant. Book ahead. Closed Sat. lunch and Sun.

Plexi's, St. Christopher's Pl., W1 (935 1047). Has an intimate candlelit basement. Upstairs does a good lunch trade, too.

Pontevecchio, 256 Old Brompton Rd., SW5 (373 9082). Busy Italian restaurant.

La Provençal, 8 Mays Court, WC2 (836 9180). Small and friendly spot in lane beside the Coliseum; handy for pre- and post-theater meals. Closed Sat. lunch and Sun.

Rodos, 59 St. Giles High St., WC2 (836 3177). In the shadow of Centrepoint this small family-run Greek cafe serves the best *mezedakia* (eight courses) in town. Everything is cooked to order before your eyes.

The Rossetti, 23 Queen's Grove, NW8 (722 7141). This hybrid pub trattoria near St. John's Wood tube is known for its hors d'oeuvres table and excellent food. Good for summertime dining. Must book.

RSJ, 13a Coin St., SE1 (928 4554). Useful and reliably good modern French restaurant south of the river. Closed Sun.

St. Moritz Restaurant, 161 Wardour St., W1 (734 3324). Close by Oxford Street for genuine Swiss food at reasonable prices. Closed Sat lunch and Sun.

San Frediano, 62 Fulham Rd., SW3 (584 8375). Basic Italian, good and fast service and excellent specialties especially the homemade pasta.

Soho Brasserie, 23 Old Compton St., W1 (439 9301). Snack at the bar, or dine on fine examples of *nouvelle-cuisine*—inspired food at this well executed pub conversion. Short but well-chosen wine list. Closed Sun.

South of the Border, 8 Joan St., SE1 (928 6374). Convenient for the National Theater to dine in this converted factory. Closed Sun.

Surprise, 12 Great Marlborough St., W1 (434 2666). Imaginative, New York style eating house with emphasis on American food. Ideally placed just behind Liberty's for shoppers and theater-goers. Book ahead.

Sweetings, 39 Victoria St, EC4 (248 3062). Small, 150-year-old fish restaurant with a charming atmosphere. Drinks from a good short winelist; or be adventurous with Black Velvet. Lunches only, Mon. to Fri.

Swiss Centre, 2 New Coventry St., W1 (734 1291). A very handy place to meet friends. Has four restaurants, all with a different Swiss accent, so you can take your pick—the price range varies too. All have straightforward mass Swiss catering, but good value.

Throgmorton Restaurant, 27 Throgmorton St, EC2 (588 5165). Beside the Stock Exchange; excellent value for traditional English beef, pies and fish. A city institution. Mon. to Fri., lunch only.

Le Tire Bouchon, 6 Upper James St., W1 (437 2320). Good-value brasserie spot just off Golden Sq. Simple menu. Closed weekends.

Viceroy of India, 3 Glentworth St., NW1 (486 3515). Something special in the way of Indian restaurants. Imaginative elegance in the decor, subtly spiced food, discreet service.

Wild Thyme, 96 Felsham Rd., SW15 (789 3323). Here is a tiny place with enthusiastic food and friendly service, just south of Putney Bridge. Highly original menu.

BUDGET—£20 and under

London has many hundreds of budget eating places, which often do better than their expensive relations. We can only list a few, so please use your nose and your judgement for the others. Remember that pubs can provide an excellent cheap midday meal, while the West End is chock-a-block with sandwich shops for that light picnic in one of the parks or squares.

Agra, 135 Whitfield St., W1 (387 4828). Good solid Indian fuel-food, washed down by excellent draught Pilsner. Extremely reasonable.

Cafe des Amis du Vin, 11–14 Hanover Place, WC2 (379 3444). Right by the side of Covent Garden Opera House. An excellent spot with a geniunely French feel to it. Cold platters are often better than the hot dishes—but, naturally, the wine is great. Breakfast till 11.30 a.m. Closed Sun.

Anemos, 32 Charlotte St., W1 (580 5907). Greek informality, taverna atmosphere.

Ark, 122 Palace Gdns. Terr., W8 (229 4024). Unbeatable for excellent value and really good cooking. Wise to book. Closed Sunday lunch. Highly recommended.

Bistro Vino, 303 Brompton Rd., SW3 (589 7898). Good value at this busy bistro. Under vivacious new management.

Blooms, 90 Whitechapel High St., (247 6001). Jewish restaurant particularly popular for that East End Sunday excursion, but excellent anytime. Enormous portions, reasonable service; takeaway also. Totally Kosher.

Brasserie des Amis, 27 Basil St., SW3 (584 9012). Light and cheerful brasserie, with popular French dishes.

Bumbles, 16 Buckingham Palace Rd., SW1 (828 2903). Original cooking at reasonable prices; self-service also available at lunchtimes.

Byblos, 262 Kensington High St., W8 (603 4422). Lebanese food geniunely prepared and priced.

Cafe du Jardin, 28 Wellington St., WC2 (836 8769). Bright and cheerful brasserie-style restaurant with a large conservatory-type basement. Excellent value pre-theater meals. Closed lunch Sat. and Sun.

Cafe Fish des Amis du Vin, 39 Panton St., SW1 (930 3999). French and English shellfish and fish served French-cafe-style with basement wine bar. Open from 11.30 A.M.–midnight, Mon. to Sat.

Cafe Pelican, 45 St. Martin's Lane, WC2 (379 0309). Along with **La Brasserie,** London's closest equivalent of a French brasserie, serving breakfast, bar snacks, set meals, and tea at the bar. Superb modern French cooking from a talented chef in the back restaurant. Late and daily.

Caravan Serai, 50 Paddington St., W1 (935 1208). Afghan specialties in a comfortable, modern restaurant.

Columbina, 4–5 Duke of York St., SW1 (930 8279). Reasonable prices for good standard Italian fare. Closed Sun.

Chicago Pizza Pie Factory, 17 Hanover Sq., W1 (629 2669). Hectic and crowded, purveying the "deep" pizza species to enthusiastic customers.

Chicago Rib Shack, 2 Raphael St., SW7 (581 5595). Barbecued ribs, club sandwiches, pecan pie. Good service, and lots of towels to make up for the lack of cutlery. Closed Sunday.

Chuen Cheng Ku, 17 Wardour St., WC2 (437 1398). Excellent Cantonese-style at very reasonable prices.

Cranks, 11 Covent Garden Market, WC2 (379 6508). Vegetarian and whole-food served in rustic setting. Three other branches in W1—at 8 Marshall St. and at 214 Oxford St., (in Peter Robinson's by Oxford Circus).

Daquise, 20 Thurloe St., SW7 (589 6117). Haunt of mid-European emigrés, this restaurant serves specialties such as stuffed cabbage and goulash.

Dukes, 55 Duke St., W1 (499 5000). Hardly an apt name for budget-dining, but good value nevertheless; handy for shopping.

Elephants and Butterflies, 67 Charlotte St., W1 (580 1732). Functional, large basement with imaginative daily-changing menu of essentially vegetarian hot and cold food. Good salads and puddings. Closed Sat. and Sun.

Etoile Bistro, 41 Bridge Rd., Hampton Court (979 2309). Excellent value bistro-type restaurant; home cooking at its best and very friendly service. A real find.

Food for Thought, 31 Neal St., WC2 (836 0239). Menu changes twice daily in this simple, whitewashed health locale. Wildly popular with lunchtime lines.

Fountain Restaurant, Fortnum and Mason, 181 Piccadilly, W1 (734 4938). Delicious food and ice-cream sodas, in an unhurried atmosphere. Best for light snacks. The restaurant is open until 11.30 P.M., closed Sunday.

Hard Rock Café, 150 Old Park Lane, W1 (629 0382). A loud-rocking favorite with burgers and juke box. Unfortunately, there's always a line.

Joe Allen's, 13 Exeter St., WC2 (836 0651). Not so much the food as the people, piano, and theatrical flavor of this basement haunt. Particularly good late night, but highly recommended for value and atmosphere at any time.

Joy King Lau, 3 Leicester Sq., WC2 (437 1133). Authentic Cantonese—full of Chinese at lunchtime and early evening.

Justin de Blank, 54 Duke St., Grosvenor Square, W1 (629 3174). Delicious food, mainly of the salad type with a different range of hot dishes every day. Mouthwatering desserts. A takeaway service is available. Closed Saturday evening and Sundays. Justin de Blank also runs the restaurant in the *General Trading Co.* store at the bottom end of Sloane St. (no. 144). Light lunches and great teas at normal store hours. Good for shopping in the King's Rd. area.

Khans, 13/15 Westbourne Grove, W2 (727 5420). Crowded, noisy Indian restaurant. Extremely good value. Very popular so book ahead.

Last Days of the Raj, 22 Drury Lane, WC2 (836 1628). A popular 'new' Indian restaurant with the best of North Indian dishes.

Light of India, 284 King St., W6 (748 2579). Well-chosen flavors provide good basic Indian food.

L.S. Grunt's Pizza Pie Factory, 12 Maiden Lane, WC2 (379 7722). A lively Covent Garden pizza joint.

Luba's Bistro, 6 Yeomans Row, SW3 (589 2950). Russian Bistrovitch with a long-established reputation for good portions. No license—so bring your own bottle. Cramped but fun. Closed Sun.

Luigi's, 15 Tavistock St., WC2 (240 1795). This Italian bistro on 3 floors is well worth a visit before—or after—the opera. Closed Sun.

Melange, 59 Endell St., WC2 (240 8077). Interesting, inexpensive Frenchish food, served by a young team in their own designed '50s-style tabac (downstairs) and restaurant (upstairs). Closed Sat. lunch and Sun.

Michel, 343 Kensington High St., W8 (603 3613). Though it looks like an Italian trat, you'll find excellent quality and reasonably-priced French food here. The set lunch is outstanding value.

Mykonos, 17 Frith St., W1 (437 3603). Reasonably-priced Greek food in the right surroundings. Try the Mykonos Mixed plate, which gives you a taste of all the grilled specialties.

Payton Plaice, 96 Charing Cross Rd., WC2 (379 3277). Nautical extravaganza serving crab claws, deep-fry fish and strips (chips with the skin on), salads and wonderful American puddings. Seating for 300. Hollywood muzak. Late and daily.

Palms on the Piazza, 39 King St., Covent Garden, WC2 (240 2939); **Palms on the Hill,** 2/3 Campden Hill Rd., W8 (938 1830). Two huge premises cleverly decorated with Italian newsprint and tall, frondy palms; serving an essentially pasta menu. Cheap, filling and a pleasant place to be. Late and daily.

Pollyanna's Bistro, 2 Battersea Rise, SW11 (228 0316). Extremely reasonable and well-run with friendly service and atmosphere. Their wine bar around the corner makes a suitable rendezvous.

Pooh Corner, 246 Battersea Park Rd., SW11 (228 9609). Wide range of well-cooked food; bistro ambiance.

Poons, 4 Leicester St., WC2 (437 1528). Authentic Chinatown restaurant for cooking rather than comfort. The expensive branch in King St, WC2 (tel. 240 1743) has the reverse order of priorities. Closed Sun.

Porters, 17 Henrietta St., WC2 (836 6466). Another welcome budget spot in the new Covent Garden area. Pies and other goodies with wrap-around sound. Run by Viscount Newport. Open Sunday, too.

Surinder's Cafe, 43 Hereford Rd., W2 (221 9192). Almost a brasserie, serving breakfast, cheap daily dishes and modestly-priced three-course set dinner. Closed Sun. and Mon. evening.

Texas Lone Star Saloon, 154 Gloucester Rd., SW7 (370 5625) Packed with American artefacts and live Tex/Mex music every night; go here for authentic enchiladas, tacos, nachos and hot-dog or steak sandwiches. Late and daily.

Tuttons, 11 Russell St., WC2 (836 1167). Popular, trendy eating house beside the restored Covent Garden Market. Slightly more expensive downstairs, but quieter. Open 7 days a week, noon to 11.30.

WINE BARS

Wine bars provide a slightly raffish way of having a bite to eat and a glass or two of wine in crowded, often noisy, sometimes highly priced surroundings. These atmospheric establishments are a fairly recent phenomenon on the London scene, at least in their present proliferation, though there have always been one or two of them about. But in the last few years they have sprung to life whenever an area gains popularity, however transient. The most outstanding example of this is the Covent Garden Market neighborhood, where seemingly dozens of wine bars have appeared overnight, like mushrooms in the dewy grass.

They sometimes open up in former shops, often in old cellars and basements, sometimes in closed pubs. Usually the proprietors choose a site that has some character to it ("character," of course, is the property agent's euphemism for decrepitude), and they turn the "character" to their advantage. We can thoroughly recommend the burgeoning wine bars for their atmosphere, sometimes for the variety of their wines, often for the food they dispense, quiches and salads and such— but we should warn you again that they are not always budget spots, and one or two of them are very pricey indeed.

Archduke, Arch 153, Concert Hall Approach, SE1 (928 9370). Attractive decor, good food with international sausage specialties. Occupies two of the railway arches just beside the Festival Hall (near Waterloo Station) and so is very handy for after a concert or a visit to the National Theater.

L'Artiste Musclé, 1 Shepherd Market, W1 (493 6150). A typical French bistro bar with tables on the pavement. Good food and excellent house wines. Closed Sun. lunch.

Bill Bentley's Wine and Oyster Bar, 31 Beauchamp Pl., SW3 (589 5080). Excellent seafood restaurant upstairs with fluent service, or enjoy the crowded main bar and cellar below. Closed Sun.

Blushes, 52 King's Rd., SW3 (589 6640). French-cafe style singles bar. Mirrored interior with a profusion of palms and potted plants.

Bouzy Rouge, 221 Kings Road, SW3 (351 1607). Below the similarly named wine shop, it offers live jazz at night, and a choice of over 60 wines.

Bow Wine Vaults, 10 Bow Churchyard, EC4 (248 1121). Sandwiches and excellent set lunches frenetically available. Located just behind Bow Church.

Brahms and Liszt, 19 Russell St., WC2 (240 3661). Very good value food supported by funky decor and very loud music. The odd name is Cockney rhyming slang for . . . well, drunk. Closed Sun. evening.

Charco's, 1 Bray Pl., off Anderson St., SW3 (584 0765). Their peerless buffet presents a superabundance of delicacies, complemented by a solid wine selection; just off the King's Road. Tables outside are pleasant in warm weather.

Chez Solange, 11 St. Martin's Court, WC2 (240 0245). In the lane beside Wyndhams Theater, this wine bar is an extension of the same-name restaurant. Relaxed spot for good food, better wine and congregating.

Cork and Bottle, 44 Cranbourne St., WC2 (734 7807). A welcome civilized downstairs oasis, sandwiched between sex shops and the dubious delights of Leicester Square.

Crusting Pipe, 27 The Market, Covent Garden, WC2 (836 1415). Good spot to refresh yourself after a visit to the new market at Covent Garden. On the expensive side.

Daly's, 210 The Strand, WC2 (583 4476). Frequented by lawyers, it's right opposite the law courts; excellent food.

Downs, 5 Down St., W1 (491 3810). Top-drawer bar for huge portions and excellent wines, especially from the Loire. Convenient for Park Lane and Mayfair.

Draycott's, 114 Draycott Ave., SW3 (584 5359). Smart, elegant bar, full of bright young things. Small selection of good food at lunchtime and in the evening. Closed Sun. evening.

Ebury Wine Bar, 139 Ebury St., SW1 (730 5447). Wise to wait patiently for their excellent food and wines.

El Vino, 47 Fleet St., EC4 (353 6786). Famous watering hole for journalists, lawyers, and press barons—a discriminating and expert clientele. They don't serve women at the bar, a rule which has made them the subject of frequent (so far unsuccessful) court cases. Closed Sun.

Fino's Wine Cellar, 123 Mount St., W1 (492 1640). The discreet Mayfair address conceals a vaulted cellar for candlelit dining. Good also as a friendly meeting spot. Also at 37 Duke St, W1 (tel. 935 9459), 12 North Row, W1 (491 7261) and 104 Charing Cross Rd., WC2 (836 1077). Quieter and more relaxed.

Hobson's, 20 Upper St. Martin's Lane, WC2 (836 5849). Victorian-style wine bar under a pub in the theater district. Generous food. Closed for lunch Sat. and Sun.

Jimmy's Wine Bar, Kensington Church St., W8 (937 9988). This converted section of the barracks becomes more enjoyable as the evening lengthens, particularly when guitar music is featured.

Julie's, 137 Portland Rd., W11 (727 7985). Good food in the cellars of no. 135, or wander with wine upstairs; atmosphere abounds.

The Loose Box, 136 Brompton Rd., SW3 (584 9280). This large wine bar on two levels is usually bustling, often with shoppers from Harrods. A modest selection of wines and good choice of food. Closed Sun.

Le Metro, 28 Basil St., SW3 (589 6286). The menu is overseen by the chef of next-door Capital Hotel, and it's more like brasserie food; expect sophisticated salads, smoked meats and ripe cheeses, plus a dish or two of the day. Cruover machine and good wine list.

Mother Bunch's Wine House, Arches F & G, Old Seacoal Lane, EC4 (236 5317). Worth the search underneath the arches for the Victorian charm plus good wines. Service can be erratic. Book for a lunchtime table.

Reams, 34 Store St., WC1 (631 4918). Outstandingly good food is served here; game in season, home-made sausages and fresh fish daily.

Russkies, 6 Wellington Terr., W2 (229 9128). Situated opposite the Russian Embassy, this is a small cellar-bar with elegant Victorian decor. An international wine list and excellent hot *plats du jour* as well as cold buffet.

Whittington's Wine Bar, 21 College Hill, EC4 (248 5855). Vaulted cellar reputed to have been owned by Dick Whittington. Buffet food at the bar or you can lunch in their small restaurant. No food in the evening.

PUBS

The pub is a unique British institution. And, like many British institutions, it is both admirable and rather eccentric. The first quirk that strikes many visitors is how frequently pubs are closed. There are quite large parts of the day when it is practically impossible to buy an alcoholic drink at all. This puritanical oddity stems from World War I when, in a burst of misplaced patriotic fervor it was felt that many potential fighting-men were more tempted by afternoon drinking sessions than by their duty to King and Country. Thus were the licensing laws born.

There are many hundreds of pubs in London and every Londoner will have his own "regular." You will find the most surprisingly attractive pubs in the most squalid surroundings, frequently because they are survivals from a more opulent age. There has been a regrettable tendency on the part of the brewers who own most of the pubs to modernize them and turn what was the equivalent of a Victorian parlor into a comfortless, shiny, space-age speakeasy. But most of the pubs we list below have preserved their own special aura.

Various efforts have been made to bring Britain into line with the rest of the world and allow pubs to stay open all day, and even allow children inside. But somehow or other, you get the feeling that it is a losing battle and that, in a curious way, the British are rather fond of this daft habit. The dreaded licensing hours in London are from 11 to 3 and from 5.30 or 6 to 11, and, on Sundays, from 12 to 2 and from 7 to 10.30.

A number of other points can trap the unsuspecting visitor. One is the increasingly arbitrary distinction between the Saloon Bar and the Public Bar. As the names imply, this is a hangover from the class war. The Public Bar was for the working class and the Saloon Bar for the middle class. Though some pubs still have this social barrier, it is not unusual today to go through the door marked Saloon Bar and find it leads to exactly the same part of the pub as that marked Public Bar.

Another point to remember is the unusual system of drink measurements. Those for spirits are self-explanatory—though Americans may find the measures small—but beer comes in two "sizes"; pints and half pints. If you're feeling curious about British beer, but nothing more, have a half. If you feel more than curiosity, have a pint.

While on the subject of beer, one healthy feature of London pub life is the return of real ale. Over the last five years, there has been an increasing reaction against the insipid offerings of the big brewers (who own most London pubs). As a result, the smaller brewers, who produce stronger and more traditional beer, have grown in popularity and more and more good beer has become available. But it can be strong, so be careful.

You will also find that many pubs provide reasonable lunches; sandwiches, steak-and-kidney pie, shepherds pie and other English staples. If you are looking for a quick budget meal, these can be a very good idea. However, very few pubs have food in the evening, unless you don't mind the lunchtime leftovers. You'll find these can become surprisingly stale in the course of an afternoon.

A final point to bear in mind is that children under fourteen are not allowed in pubs. If they go in, they will certainly be asked to leave. Those under 18 may not order, or consume, alcohol.

The Anchor, 1 Bankside, SE1. Shakespeare drank in the original. Excellent restaurant and good views of St. Paul's.

Antelope, 22 Eaton Terrace, SW1. Popular watering hole with good food and beer.

Black Friar, 174 Queen Victoria St., EC4 (right beside Blackfriars tube). A different pub-esthetic experience. The grotto at the back of the Black Friar is a refurbished, dazzling Art Nouveau masterpiece.

City Barge, Strand-on-the-Green, W4. Very popular for Thames tow-path drinking.

Dickens Inn, East Smithfield, E1. In the middle of what was dockland, but is now a yachting marina, St. Katharine's Dock, not far beyond the Tower. Good atmosphere and food.

The Dove, Upper Mall, Hammersmith, W6. Old and small, with Thames views as painted by Turner and Brangwyn. Excellent beer, but it's very strong.

The Flask, South Grove, N6. Highgate side of Hampstead Heath area. Loads of character (the place was rebuilt in 1767) and a great draw for locals and visitors alike. Large courtyard for exterior slurping.

The George Inn, 77 Borough High St., SE1 (407 2056). Originally a Victorian coaching inn, they have now added a wine bar serving food. Excellent food is also available upstairs; in a restaurant complete with beamed ceiling, leaded windows, and hunting prints.

The George & Vulture, Castle Court, EC3, off Cornhill, was in existence in 1175 as a tavern called The George. Chaucer and Daniel Defoe were regular visitors, and Charles Dickens wrote part of *Pickwick Papers* while staying there. Reputed to be the oldest tavern in the world, it has re-opened after a £40,000 facelift.

Lamb, 94 Lambs Conduit St., WC1. Small, atmospheric and popular. Recommended, but crowded at lunchtime.

Lamb and Flag, 33 Rose St., WC2 (down a tiny alleyway). Home-made game pie and good beer in this tiny, enjoyable haunt near Covent Garden.

Mayflower, Rotherhithe St., SE16. Where the Pilgrims allegedly stepped on to the boat for Holland; a new pub on site of an old one, blitzed during the war. (Passenger manifest on the walls.)

Nag's Head, James St., WC2. Next to the Royal Opera House and a favorite spot with the theater crowd.

Olde Cheshire Cheese, Fleet St., EC4. Once a favorite with all the literary lights—Congreve, Thackeray, Dickens, Conan Doyle and just possibly Dr. Johnson himself. Close to the newspapers and law courts, so it's still well frequented, especially by tourists. Steak-and-kidney pie a specialty.

Prospect of Whitby, 75 Wapping Wall, E1. Right on the riverside and named after an old sailing ship. Full of character; good for lunch, but not easy to get to.

The Red Lion. 2 Duke of York St., SW1. Victoriana at its very best. A small pub in the heart of St. James'—no room but lashings of period charm.

The Salisbury, St. Martin's Lane, WC2. Fine Victoriana, excellent cold food and lots of actors. A gay haunt.

Scarsdale Arms, 23 Edwardes Sq., W8. Lively and attractive Kensington pub in an elegant 19th-century square. Good beer; can be crowded.

The Spaniards, Spaniards Rd., Hampstead Heath, NW3. Just the spot for allaying the dust after walking on the Heath and viewing London from afar. Lots of atmosphere.

Star, Belgrave Mews, SW1. Good beer and plenty of atmosphere in this small mews pub.

Steam Packet, Strand-on-the-Green, W4. A warm friendly pub with huge helpings of home-cooked food at reasonable prices and fine beer.

Sun in Splendour, 7 Portobello Rd., W11. Small, attractive pub with good beer and excellent food. Tiny garden at the back. Close to the market.

Surprise, 6 Christchurch Terrace, SW3. Small, lots of character and strong beer. Just round the corner from where Oscar Wilde lived.

Windsor Castle, Campden Hill Rd., W8. A large paved garden makes this smart but friendly spot perfect for a relaxed summertime drink. Can get very crowded.

ENTERTAINMENT IN LONDON

All the World's Stage

The West End of London, theaterland, is once more on the up and up. Gone are the depressing predictions of doom and disaster which ran like wildfire through the gossipy haunts of theaterfolk a couple of years back. As we go to press, there is not one theater "dark"—that euphemism for shut—and indeed most of the West End venues are doing excellent business. And it is not just revivals of Broadway musicals that are packing them in, as it was once upon a time. British musicals, too, are going great guns and straight drama continues to play to full houses.

While *On Your Toes* and *42nd Street* enchant the West End theatergoer just as they do on Broadway, the home-grown article continues to defy the aging process. *Evita* staggered into its seventh year in 1985, while *Cats,* another musical from the pen of Andrew Lloyd-Webber and directed by one of the Royal Shakespeare stalwarts, continues to entrance its audiences. As the first of their spectaculars which needed a theater converted to house the production it has one of our favorite sentences from any theater advertisement—"Latecomers not admitted while the auditorium is in motion, please be prompt."

Yet another ground-breaking hit from the same team, *Starlight Express,* opened early in 1984 and is still playing to delirious audiences as we write. As one critic said "the show is a millionaire's folly, which happens to be open to the public." But he and all the other critics seem to have had a ball, and the younger they were, the bigger the ball. *Cats* and *Starlight Express* have both created a totally new theatrical art form, based entirely on brilliant staging, with the music coming a long way second and the storyline nowhere in sight. They are triumphs of visual imagination, and they are British!

But the occasional pyrotechnical display by a theatrical impresario of genius does not mean that the London theater is out of the financial wood. Times are still straitened, and everyone, in both the commercial and the state-subsidized theater, watches the box office like a hawk. In a way, the present wobbly finances of the theater have brought these two means of financing into sharper focus. Both are under threat—the commercial side from public taste, the state theater from cuts in the Arts Council budgets—and the interesting thing is to see the way both sides try to tackle their problems.

The West End

Theatrical London rotates around Shaftesbury Avenue. There, or nearby, are the majority of theaters. The West End cannot be quite equated with New York's Broadway, since London has never really managed to shine in the field of the indigenous musical (Andrew Lloyd Webber always excepted), but it has very much the same attraction to a fledgling actor who wants to see his name in lights. The entirely commercial West End has two powerful rivals in the heavily subsidized Royal Shakespeare Company and the National Theater. As we will see, both these repertory companies constitute a major alternative to all the other theaters combined.

The staple fare that the West End offers to its patrons—about 30 percent of whom are tourists, a figure that hardly varies all the year round, though often a theater can be virtually sold out to US visiting tours—tends to be light, well-made comedies varied by a healthy admixture of leading actors or actresses showing their paces in a not-too-indigestible diet of lightweight classics. The commercial theater is exactly that, commercial, and tries to provide what the vast bulk of the theater-going public want to see and are prepared to pay for.

But Britain's theater is a strange amalgam of government subsidy and commercial enterprise living cheek by jowl. For example, it never fails to amaze anyone who has any knowledge of theater at all, that the *Mousetrap* by Agatha Christie has been running as long as it has—it has nearly reached its 40th birthday. It *seems* to have been going since the time when Sherlock Holmes was a boy. But the play, in its now mediocre production, is a classic example of what so many people want to see. It is commercial theater raised to the status of Fort Knox.

On the other hand several plays from the state subsidized companies have been transferred to the West End over the years and played there to tremendous acclaim (*Educating Rita* and *Poppy* from the RSC, and, from the National, *Equus, No Man's Land* and, above all, *Amadeus,* which has had a huge success not only in the West End, but also on Broadway, both times in the National production). To the layman, that the subsidized theaters are allowed to transfer their successes to the commercial zone, thereby managing to rake in some more shekels for their depleted coffers, seems strangely at odds with the tenets of private enterprise. But then, so does the punitive levying of Value Added Tax on theater tickets.

Broadly speaking, the London theater can be divided into three main camps: the strictly commercial West End managements, the State repertories and the experimental companies. Of the fifty or so theaters that are in business, the strictly commercial ones set their sights on the bullseye of a hit show. The managements of the State repertories do not aim mainly at commercial success, although, over and over again, they hit that bullseye slap in the middle. The experimental companies, like experimental companies the world over, are above such mundane considerations. All three poach regularly on each others' preserves. It can be very confusing.

Most of the theaters are to be found within walking distance of one another, between Piccadilly Circus in the west, Aldwych in the east and Tottenham Court Road in the north. The oldest of present-day theaters is the Theater Royal, at Drury Lane, which was opened in 1663 and has been reconstructed several times since. The existing theater was finished in 1812, and although the auditorium was completely reconstructed in 1922, the foyer, rotunda and staircase are original and are the only remaining example of Georgian theater architecture left in London. Drury Lane was for long the home of spectacular dramas and pantomimes, but in recent years it has housed some successful and some not so successful musicals. It was launched on this pattern by the success of *Oklahoma* several decades ago. Its last hit was *Pirates of Penzance.* In fact, most theaters usually maintain a tradition as to the type of production staged.

Most of the West End theater buildings are late-Victorian or Edwardian, with a sprinkling which date from the '30s. They are all privately owned by managements who rent them out to producers. This system shows serious signs of being grossly uneconomic, since the owners of the property would make much more by selling the sites for redevelopment, which has indeed already happened in several cases.

The RSC at the Barbican Center

Productions of serious drama, especially of classical drama, are generally limited to the two main repertory companies; the National Theater Company which has its home at the National Theater on the South Bank, with three auditoria, the Lyttelton, Cottesloe and Olivier—and the RSC, which has now moved to its brand-new home in the Barbican Center. Both of these major companies transfer commercial successes, as we have seen, to the West End, where they enter into direct competition with the commercial theater.

The RSC, which has its home base in Stratford-upon-Avon, where Shakespeare is naturally the order of the day, has always used its London outpost to perform a great variety of plays, with a bias towards socially improving Russian sub-classics, and a strong line in hugely enjoyable revivals of box-office successes of grandfather's day (or, indeed great-grandfather's) such as *Saratoga* and *Peter Pan*. They also bring the best of their Stratford Shakespeare productions to town to provide a backbone to their London seasons.

The RSC has been through several sticky patches in recent years, but a few seasons ago suddenly surfaced from its latest quicksand and began a hugely successful and enjoyable series of productions. The chemistry that produces such theatrical experiences is hard to define, made up as it is of actors', directors' and designers' talents, all bubbling together in the crucible. But however difficult it is to estimate the causes, there can be no doubt that theatergoing both at Stratford and in the RSC's two London auditoria is unrivalled in the world today.

In May, 1982, the RSC finally opened in its new home in the Barbican, leaving the Aldwych Theater after a couple of decades and with mixed feelings. The theater in the Barbican Center was tailormade for the company, who had planned its construction for a long time, trying to create the perfect acting space as well as the best possible conditions for their audiences.

As we write the company has been in its new quarters long enough for it to be clear that they have a winner on their hands. The auditorium of the main theater—there is also a small studio auditorium called The Pit—is so arranged that everyone is fairly close to the stage. The seats in the two top circles are most certainly not for anyone who doesn't have a head for heights—they are almost like ledges on a cliff—but all the rest of the house is comfortable and the sightlines are good even in the tucked away corners. The sound has a clean immediacy to it, voices reaching easily to all parts of the house.

It is early days, yet, to say if the stage facilities are as successful as those of the auditorium. Certainly the company has avoided the wide desolate spaces that afflict at least one of the National Theater's stages, and they have all the most modern technical advances to rely on.

A worry to devotees of the RSC is the fact that the company seems almost lost in the middle of the Barbican Center's vast bulk. For years the RSC were a highly idiosyncratic presence in their own quirky theater in the West End, turning the severe disadvantages of the Aldwych stage into positive virtues. All the followers of the RSC bade farewell to that strangely grim auditorium with regret—although the thought of more comfortable seats, better sightlines and more luxurious front-of-house facilities beckoned like the mirage of a distant oasis.

While the new Barbican RSC theater seems to have justified all the expense and long years of delay, the same cannot really be said about the Center in general. It is the victim of several factors—it was originally designed in the 1960s; it is said that by the time the incurred debt has been paid off in 60 years time it will have cost £200 million, as against the original estimate of £19 million, and even that was supposed to have allowed for inflation; and it is situated in the middle of an area which, although it is quite accessible to the City, is not easily reached from the rest of London.

The Center has the feel of an air terminal run by well-heeled, conservative cave dwellers. Only three of the eight levels are actually below ground but, as there are very few windows, the whole place has a subterranean atmosphere to it. The interlocking stairs and terraces seem to lead even deeper into the bowels of the earth, with the combination of hammered concrete walls, soft carpets and massive girders—used decoratively as well as structurally—combining with strangely low ceilings to give a sensation of a troglodyte empire.

The Center has been planned as a complete arts complex—and the stress is most definitely on the word complex, since it will take several visits even to begin to feel that you know your way round. Apart from the concert hall and the RSC theater, there are two cinemas, exhibition areas, a public library, a conservatory on the roof (the only place in the whole building where there is a feeling of space and light), a restaurant which works on the carvery method and is decorated in a hectic mixture of menopausal purple, red and pink, a cafeteria with very poor food, and, outside, a terrace lying beside a large reflecting pool with a view across to the carefully preserved church of St. Giles.

Undoubtedly one of the chief functions of the new Center is to act as a conference venue. It has clearly been created with that in mind as much as its arts role, and such a function is probably needed in the City. For this is a creation of the City, of the country's financial heart, and of the gnomes of London who have financed it and supported it entirely on their own. The great question is—the City of London may want it, but does London as a whole need it? For no one can pretend that London is under-supplied with theaters, nor is it poor in concert venues —indeed the Festival Hall complex is finding it difficult to fill its programs with drawing performances.

One of the worst features of the Center is its desperately confusing layout. Even the Administrator, after years of a fixed public-relations smile, admitted that "If I were to do it again I'd shoot all the architects. They built a building that wasn't workable."

The National Theater

The National Theater has been open for several years now and its vices and virtues are no longer an unknown quality. There is one thing that must be said immediately about the National, loud and clear—go there! It is one of the more exciting modern theatrical conceptions, flawed but fascinating. Also built of concrete, it has much more sense of space and light to it than the Barbican Center, with high cathedral-like windows looking out onto the Thames. Like the Barbican, the foyer areas are incredibly complicated. It seems that modern designers are unable to create public sections of arts centers which allow for simple, easy traffic flow. The three auditoria are very mixed in their stage facilities. The Olivier has wide intractable spaces that tend to swamp the plays that are staged in them, the Lyttelton is more manage-able while the smaller studio-type Cottesloe provides some of the National's best work.

The National's policy is much more flexible than the RSC's in terms of the company that works there. The RSC has created a very close, almost family sense of artistic co-operation; the National's players come and go, with a cadre remaining to act as a backbone. The National is, in many ways, a latterday Comédie Française, staging classics from all over the world, scoring the occasional triumph with some very unlikely material. "Classics" is interpreted in the widest sense—one of the most recent hits has been *Guys and Dolls,* given in a production which would not disgrace Broadway. The company also produces some exciting new plays, most notably those of Peter Shaffer; *Royal Hunt of the Sun, Equus* and *Amadeus* were all premiered by the National. Some rather obscure classics, also, have found success under the National banner. *On the Razzle,* Tom Stoppard's reworking of a play by the

Austrian playwright Nestroy, provided a popular success for a play which had already been the original for Thornton Wilder's *Merchant of Yonkers* and the musical *Hello Dolly.* The one strange failing in the National's work has been their productions of Shakespeare, some of the worst Shakespeare seen in London of recent years has been on the South Bank. It is an odd streak in such a vital and talented company that they should not be able to cope with the national playwright.

In a way Britain has two National Theaters, the original product and the RSC. They fulfill two quite different roles in the nation's theatrical life and have developed along quite dissimilar lines. There is a touch of *folie de grandeur* about the National, a magnificent grandiosity which seems to lie a little uncomfortably with an organization crippled by the expense of maintaining its huge premises. The RSC, too, has enormous financial problems, but its days of grandiose schemes are past. It now has what is probably the highest ticket sales of any theatrical set-up anywhere in the world, and it husbands its resources to the utmost to ensure that it can continue to operate in an inimical financial climate. Both of these companies have huge Arts Council subventions, but the general feeling is that the RSC gives the public more value for its money.

Some Less Establishment Establishments

While there is nothing strictly comparable to "off-Broadway" theaters in London, there are a number of theaters well worth visiting outside the West End, though they are usually quite tricky to find.

Upstairs at the Royal Court in Sloane Square is a small theater-in-the-round with an enviable list of successes. The Royal Court itself, which heralded the revival of theater in Britain with its production of *Look Back in Anger,* has fallen on hard times artistically and frequently suffers from a stridently-voiced social conscience.

Several other theatrical experiences for stage buffs are just waiting to be sought out. Regent's Park Open Air Theater is ideal for a summer's night. With its new, semi-permanent auditorium, it is the best possible way to relax and let the joy of Shakespeare in at every pore.

A few blocks south of the National Theater stands the Old Vic. It was the original home of the National and, before that, of the mightily prestigious Old Vic Company, which saw its heyday under Olivier and Richardson. The theater was originally a Victorian gin palace, rescued by a very eccentric lady called Lilian Baylis and converted into a haven for working-class culture vultures. The building was closed down for a while, a couple of years ago, before being purchased by Ed Mirvish, a Canadian millionaire with both courage and taste. He tore out a lot of the internal accretions of decades and restored the attractive building to its original elegant splendor. He is currently running it on a system which is unusual in London these days, as a venue for visiting companies, and as we go to press his initiative seems to be paying off. For anyone who loves theater history, this is a visit not to miss.

If you feel more adventurous still, there are several excellent theater clubs, which produce plays on almost every subject. Most important is the Hampstead Theater Club, at Swiss Cottage. You must, however, be a member, but this is easily arranged over the telephone and for a low cost. If you would like to spend an evening at a real Edwardian music hall, then you should apply for temporary membership of the Players, which is built into the railway arches just below Charing Cross Station (Villiers Street). With all clubs there is a statutory period before membership becomes valid, but this can be waived.

There are also several lunch- and dinner-time operations like the King's Head in Upper Street, Islington, which is a pub theater. The King's Head has an enviable reputation for coming up with hits that have transferred to more central locations, and also attracts top talent who seem to enjoy working in such close contact with audiences.

Out on the western fringes at Shepherd's Bush, is the tiny theater club The Bush (membership 50p on night). In a large room over a pub, this is the nearest to off-Broadway that London gets, and stages imaginative modern works that have little general public appeal, but are often of a very high standard. Nearest Tube, Shepherd's Bush. Only 100 seats so phone ahead (743 3388).

A final note of hope is struck by the Lyric Theater, Hammersmith. This was a very pretty old theater which was due for demolition. Theater-lovers with foresight, not to say inspiration, managed to salvage all the intricate plasterwork and, when the big new concrete block of offices was finally erected, encased in its depths, like the crysalis of a butterfly deep in its cocoon, there was a brand new theater, built to the exact dimensions of the old one, and flaunting all the old interior decoration. It is now a very lively neighborhood theater, doing fine work and drawing crowds. If you are a theater buff, this is one for your collection. It also has a small studio auditorium, which, though tiny, has attracted star names to its productions.

For details of the enormously useful *Fringe Box Office,* see page 105.

Music

London's principal concert center is the Royal Festival Hall complex on the South Bank, near Waterloo Station. The first building went up for the 1951 Festival of Britain and there have been extensive additions over the years. The largest of the three halls is the Festival Hall, used for major symphony concerts, ballet performances and allied events.

The Queen Elizabeth Hall houses smaller chamber orchestras and solo recitals primarily; and the little Purcell Room, intimate recitals, folk music and lectures.

The splendid acoustics and comfort of the whole complex, added to its superb position on the bank of the Thames, attracts musicians from all over the world and capacity audiences to enjoy their work. There is a selection of restaurants and bars overlooking the river where you may drink, dine or simply relax.

In 1982 the concert hall of the Barbican Center opened its doors to a very mixed reception. (We have already talked about the building itself and about the RSC's theater.) Undoubtedly, the concert hall is an interesting addition to London's facilities, but it is not entirely clear yet—and probably won't be for some years to come—quite how this auditorium will fit into the pattern of London's musical life. The rather brash woodwork of the walls around the platform and the deep factory-type roofspace is only patchily successful where acoustics are concerned. No doubt it will be tuned to a more satisfactory evenness of tone.

One of the most important facets of this new set-up is that it provides a permanent home for one of London's major orchestras, the London Symphony. It is the first London orchestra to have such a permanent base and it may well be that a new pattern has been woven here that other orchestras will copy. Although the London Symphony plays for only three months a year at the Barbican, the very concept of having such a home base is of enormous psychological value.

One of the most lovely spots anywhere to hear music is St. John's, Smith Square, close to the Houses of Parliament. This church, which was rescued from the wreckers and converted into a concert hall, houses mainly chamber music, especially the lunch-time concerts sponsored by the BBC. It is well worth visiting, for a chance to hear delightful music in elegant surroundings.

Wigmore Hall, in Wigmore Street, run by the Arts Council in the heart of the West End, is comparable to New York's Town Hall. Here, virtually every new soloist or singer makes his professional debut. An appearance at the Wigmore Hall is a sort of audition before London's severe and powerful music critics.

During the spring and summer, various London boroughs hold arts festivals, the largest of which is the Camden Arts Festival, whose music program always embraces a wide range, from wayout operas to top-rank soloists.

An essential part of the London music scene are the Promenade Concerts at the Albert Hall (July to September). Founded by Sir Henry Wood, a favorite conductor in the first decades of this century, they will celebrate their 92nd season in 1986. They are called "promenade" because it is possible to stand in the large arena and listen to the music. The cost of the prom ticket is low and, as you would expect, most of the promenaders are young students. The last night of the proms, if you are lucky enough to obtain a ticket, is a unique spectacle, in which patriotism or just plain sentiment (with the audience traditionally singing *Rule Britannia*) frequently silences satire.

During the summer there are frequent open-air concerts at Kenwood House and Holland Park, details of which can be obtained from County Hall (633 1707). And, of course, there are brass band concerts in all the major parks whenever the weather permits, and often when it doesn't! This is the chance to hear some of the best military bands in the world, as well as some of the most unlikely ones, but always dressed in fancy uniforms.

One final point on the music scene. For centuries Britain has been famed for its church music, usually more for performance than for the creation of new works. Several of London's churches have fine choirs and dedicated organists, whose work is well worth going a long way to hear. Among them are: Brompton Oratory; St. Paul's, Knightsbridge; St. Peter's, Eaton Square; Westminster Cathedral (Roman Catholic, near Victoria station); Westminster Abbey; St. Paul's Cathedral; Temple Church and Southwark Cathedral. The Sunday papers usually carry details of any special event at these churches, but even their normal, run-of-the-mill services are of an extremely high musical caliber.

Opera

Dr. Samuel Johnson accused opera of being an exotic and irrational entertainment. It has always been a slight oddity on the British scene. Sir Thomas Beecham spent most of his life fulminating against the lack of interest that the British showed in opera. Unfortunately he did not live quite long enough to see the current upsurge of popularity that the art is enjoying.

Of course opera *is* irrational. It was born in the royal and ducal courts of Europe, where expense had no meaning. All efforts to circumscribe the form within the belt of economic rule are doomed to failure. It is essentially a spectacular and extravagant entertainment. There are small scale, chamber works, that catch the imagination and fulfill the ideal of music drama, but they have never had really wide public appeal. It is the grandiose, throat-catching works, *Aida, The Ring, Turandot,* and (though not so grandiose, of course) the works of Mozart, that the public at large want to see, and it is those works that any opera house worth its salt eventually has to stage.

Britain is lucky to have five major opera companies, presenting a vast range of operas. In London there are the Royal Opera at Covent Garden, and the English National Opera at the Coliseum; in Wales there is the Welsh National Opera; and in Scotland the Scottish National Opera has its home in Glasgow. The latest addition to the family is the English National Opera's northern company, working in Leeds.

The Royal Opera was conceived in 1946 as a deliberate attempt to create an internationally valid company in one of the world's loveliest and most inconvenient theaters. It staggered through the first years, but gradually took hold and is now recognized, alongside such old hands as the Met and La Scala, as one of the leading opera companies of the world. It stages a limited range of works, usually in their original language and with casts drawn from all over the globe. Ticket prices here are high—up to £40 a seat for some performances and the standards of performance do not always justify the cost. But as an exercise in gracious living it takes a lot of beating—especially if you enjoy watching audience one-up-manship rampant.

The English National Opera used to be the Sadler's Wells Opera, an offshoot of the Old Vic, in a rebuilt theater in Islington. In the early days they performed Wagner with an orchestra of twenty, and used *Hamlet*'s cardboard scenery for *Il Trovatore*. The company slowly developed over the decades, sometimes performing as many as thirty-six operas in a season, all in English translations, and earning the undying gratitude of generations of opera-goers who learned their opera through the Wells' simple, faithful productions.

Time passed and though the costs grew, the auditorium at Sadler's Wells did not. To be able to play to larger audiences, the company moved to the rather barn-like Coliseum in St. Martin's Lane, where they set up shop and continued to thrive.

The ENO was directed for over 16 years by the Earl of Harewood, the Queen's cousin, who transformed what had been a good, solid, almost provincial, company into one of the most exciting in Europe. He assembled a young cadre of directors and conductors and injected a healthy element of risk into the repertory. With productions that can be provocative, to say the least, a musical standard that sometimes ranks with the best that can be heard internationally, and seats that are much cheaper than at Covent Garden, the ENO is a company treasured by London operagoers. If it has one defect it is that the acoustics of the Coliseum sometimes overtax the vocal resources that the company can assemble. But the imagination is almost always stimulated, and the vernacular versions that the company uses make for an immediacy that fancy companies cannot give.

Unique in the world is the Glyndebourne Festival Opera, which is also one of the highlights of the English summer season. Evening dress is advisable, and the operas are given in two parts, with a long interval, during which the audience walks in the superb grounds of the house and picnics by the cool lakes and woodland pools or dines in the restaurants; if picnicking, bring your own hamper and wines. It is perhaps worth mentioning that Glyndebourne is very much a social occasion and many of the audience attend no other opera performances. Tickets are only available direct, and are still difficult to obtain even in these days of economic belt-tightening. Although the car park is always packed with Rolls-Royces and Bentleys, do not be deterred as there is an excellent train service that leaves Victoria Station mid-afternoon, connecting with a bus at Lewes; the return to London is accomplished by midnight. Count on spending at least £60–70 per person for tickets, train and dinner—though if you go by car and take a picnic it will be less—but not by much. Phone (0273) 812411 for program and booking details.

Ballet

Dr. Johnson may have called opera an exotic and irrational entertainment, but there is something even more exotic and irrational about ballet. Also, one would have thought that it was essentially un-British. The miracle is that it has not only become a British art form, but that it has, for several decades, taken such deep root in the country that missionaries have gone out into all lands, preaching the gospel according to de Valois, Rambert and Ashton.

Ballet in Britain can be dated almost exactly from 1911 when the great Diaghilev brought his Ballet Russes to London. Somehow, against all possible expectation, those first seasons caught the public imagination and started a series of passionate vogues, not only for the dance, but also for the imaginative and richly colored style of decoration that the productions gloried in. There were some English dancers in the company, who went on to found British ballet.

Like so much that is of any worth in British cultural life, ballet struggled very slowly up the ladder from near-amateur beginnings to the massive structures of today's companies. The Royal Ballet, which shares Covent Garden with the Royal Opera, and provides more than its share of the box-office receipts, began tentatively as the dancing interludes in Sadler's Wells' operas. It moved to Covent Garden after the Second World War and never looked back. Which is not entirely true, for the smaller company of the Royal Ballet, which tours Britain and manages to do some of the experiments that the parent company is too unwieldy to encompass, re-established a home base at Sadler's Wells during the fall of 1976, and now works out of this theater for its tours of Britain and abroad.

The Royal Ballet now represents the Establishment of British dance. It could be argued very seriously that the eminence it has attained has brought with it a hardening of the arteries, perhaps not too surprising in a body half-a-century old. Certainly in its fifty years of existence it has imperceptibly placed more and more reliance on the established classical favorites which bring money into the box office, and has been less willing to experiment with new forms. The company is currently having some of the worst press notices of its long career—but, however much the critics carp, a visit to Covent Garden can still be an evening to remember.

The Ballet Rambert, which is well into its second half century, is roughly the contemporary of the Royal Ballet, but, because it has remained a small company, and has always reflected the dedication of its founder Dame Marie Rambert to the cause of experiment, it has also remained youthful and vibrant. Like many of the country's smaller companies, it is always on the move, and visitors to Britain are as likely to catch it performing in a small town as they are to see it in London.

The other major company is the Festival Ballet, which is currently directed by yet another graduate from the Royal Ballet. Although it does have its London seasons, the policy of the Festival Company is to bring all the major works of the ballet repertory to the country at large. It has a few near-experimental works, but its staple diet is the same, basically, as Diaghilev's. Indeed, the company has revived one or two of his ballets, such as *Sheherazade,* which would not otherwise be seen here.

The ballet scene in Britain is not so rich in fringe companies as is drama, but there are a fair number. The New London Ballet, the London Contemporary Dance Theater, the Scottish Ballet are just a few of the groups which have taken wing and are now bringing dance in all its forms to the country at large. They and other visiting companies bring their works to the Coliseum, Covent Garden, the Festival Hall and Sadler's Wells.

Theater and Concert Hall Details

To find out what is on in the entertainment world in London, consult *What's On in London, Time Out,* or *City Limits,* which is better for the fringe events. The evening paper, *The Standard,* carries listings, as do the major Sunday papers.

Most of the theaters have a matinee twice a week (Wed. or Thurs. and Sat. usually), and an evening performance which begins at 7.30 or 8. Sunday drama performances are very rare in London still, though there is a movement towards them.

Prices for seats vary a lot, but you should expect to pay within a range from £4.50 for a seat way up in the ceiling to around £12.50 for a good one in the stalls or dress circle (British for mezzanine). For opera the prices will be higher—up to £34 a head for the best Covent Garden can offer, and from £3.50 to £19.50 at the Coliseum. Concert tickets are still very moderate, ranging from £2.50 to about £9.50, though a visiting celebrity such as von Karajan can command much higher prices. Most theaters accept credit cards at the box office.

A really excellent bargain in theater tickets can be found in the Leicester Square ticket booth, established by the Society of West End Theater, which sells tickets for 45 London theaters at half price, plus 75p service charge, on the day of performance subject to availability. Open Monday—Saturday 12–2 for matinee performances and 2.30–6.30 for evening performances.

One of London's local radio stations, Capital, runs a very valuable ticket service for fringe theaters. The *Fringe Box Office* is located in the Duke of York's Theatre in St. Martin's Lane, WC2 (tel. 379 6002). The box office handles an average of 40 fringe theaters at a time and can provide information as well as booking services. By phoning in or visiting the Duke of York's you can save yourself a trip out to the backwoods where most of the fringe theaters are located. Credit cards are accepted. Open 10–6, Mon. to Sat. The helpful staff will also answer inquiries from abroad.

There are many theatrical ticket agencies, of which *Keith Prowse* is probably the leader with around a dozen branches around the West End (look under *Keith* in the phone book—not *Prowse*). If you are coming from the States and want to book seats in advance, Keith Prowse have a New York branch—234 West 44th St., Suite 902, New York, N.Y. 10036, (212) 398-1430, (800) 223-4446.

All the big hotels have desks at which you can book for an entertainment, staffed by well-informed personnel. Naturally, you will have to pay a service charge, and, if you intend to do a lot of theatergoing, you would be better advised to go to the box offices in person.

Warning. Be very careful of scalpers outside theaters and concert halls. They have been known to charge £200 or more for a ticket for a sought-after event. Not only is the practice one to be discouraged— you could easily get caught with a forged ticket!

Here are the main London theaters and concert halls—the box office phone numbers are in brackets following the addresses:

Adelphi, Strand, WC2 (836 7611)
Albery, St. Martin's Lane, WC2 (836 3878)
Aldwych, Aldwych, WC2 (836 6404)

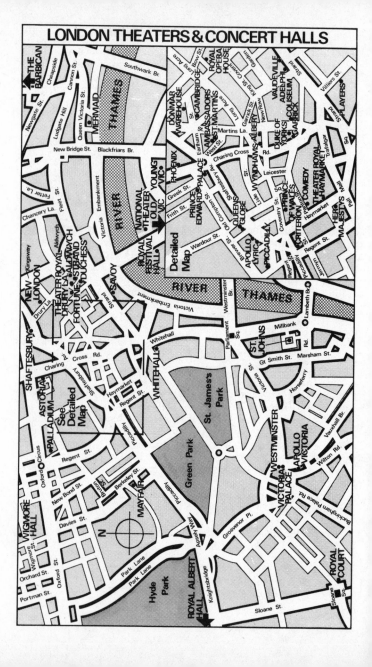

Ambassadors, West St., WC2 (836 1171)
Apollo, Shaftesbury Ave., W1 (437 2663)
Apollo Victoria, Wilton Rd., SW1 (828 8665)
Barbican Center, Silk St., EC2 (Concerts and Royal Shakespeare Company, 628 8795, 628 2295)
Cambridge, Earlham St., WC2 (836 6056)
Coliseum, St. Martin's Lane, WC2 (836 3161)
Comedy, Panton St., SW1 (930 2578)
Covent Garden (see Royal Opera House)
Criterion, Piccadilly, W1 (930 3216)
Donmar Warehouse, 39 Earlham St., WC2 (379 6565)
Drury Lane (Theatre Royal), Catherine St., WC2 (836 8108)
Duchess, Catherine St., WC2 (836 8243)
Duke of York's, St. Martin's Lane, WC2 (836 5122)
Fortune, Russell St., WC2 (836 2238)
Garrick, Charing Cross Rd., WC2 (836 4601)
Globe, Shaftesbury Ave., W1 (437 1592)
Haymarket, Haymarket, SW1 (930 9832)
Her Majesty's, Haymarket, SW1 (930 6606)
Lyric, Shaftesbury Ave., W1 (437 3686)
Lyric Hammersmith, King St, Hammersmith W6 (741 3211)
Mayfair, Stratton St., W1 (629 3036)
Mermaid, Puddle Dock EC4 (236 5568)
National Theatre, (Cottesloe, Lyttelton and Olivier), South Bank Arts Centre, SE1 (928 2252)
New London, Drury Lane, WC2 (405 0072)
Old Vic, Waterloo Road, SE1 (928 7616)
Palace, Shaftesbury Ave., W1 (437 6834)
Palladium, 8 Argyll St., W1 (437 7373)
Phoenix, Charing Cross Rd., WC2 (836 2294)
Piccadilly, Denman St., W1 (437 4506)
Players, 173 Hungerford Arches, Villiers St., WC2 (839 1134)
Prince Edward, Old Compton St., W1 (437 6877)
Prince of Wales, 31 Coventry St., W1 (930 8681)
Queens', 51 Shaftesbury Ave., W1 (734 1166)
Regents Park (Open Air), Inner Circle, Regents Park, NW1 (935 5884, 486 2431)
Riverside Studios, Crisp Rd., Hammersmith W6 (741 2251)
Royal Court, Sloane Square, SW1 (730 1745); **Theatre Upstairs** (730 2554)
Royal Albert Hall, Kensington Gore, SW7 (589 8212)
Royal Festival Hall, South Bank, SE1 (928 3002) (Queen Elizabeth Hall and Purcell Room)
Royal Opera House, Covent Garden, WC2 (240 1066)
Sadler's Wells, Rosebery Ave., EC1 (278 8916)
St. George's, 49 Tufnell Park Rd., N7 (607 1128)
St. John's, Smith Square, SW1 (222 1061)

St. Martin's, West St., WC2 (836 1443)
Savoy, Strand, WC2 (836 8888)
Shaftesbury Theatre, Shaftesbury Ave., WC2 (379 5399)
Strand, Aldwych, WC2 (836 2660)
Theatre Upstairs, Royal Court Theatre, Sloane Square, SW1 (730 2554)
Theatre Workshop, Stratford, E15 (534 0310)
Vaudeville, Strand, WC2 (836 9988)
Victoria Palace, Victoria St., SW1 (834 1317)
Westminster, 12 Palace St., SW1 (834 0283)
Whitehall, 14 Whitehall, SW1 (930 6692/7765/6)
Wigmore Hall, 36 Wigmore St., W1 (935 2141)
Wyndham's, Charing Cross Rd., WC2 (836 3028)
Young Vic, 66 The Cut, SE1 (928 6363)

Defensive Fortification

Every London theater, and most of the cinemas in the West End, has its own bar, serving a wide variety of drinks at fairly reasonable prices. Most open half-an-hour before the performance starts. During the intervals they get very crowded, so if you want refreshment then it is worth ordering it in advance, before the show starts. Do this at the bar, and your order will be placed on a table or ledge with a ticket attached, ready for the break. It is often possible to follow the same procedure with bar snacks.

Most theaters provide some sort of food, usually sandwiches. But some of them have rather more inspired catering: all the South Bank spots—National Theatre, Festival Hall etc.—have counters with quiches and salads; Covent Garden and the Coliseum do more exciting versions of sandwiches, smoked salmon and so forth; Sadler's Wells can provide salad plates on request; the Lyric at Hammersmith has a cafeteria which is open all day long as well as during performances; the Mermaid and ICA also have cafeteria setups . . . in fact if you want to fortify the inner person to cope with a hard evening's work you shouldn't have much problem. Unfortunately, keeping to a diet is not so easy.

Nightclubs and Dinner-Dance

In London, nightclubs usually put more emphasis on cuisine than elsewhere. They are really clubs, and most people join them for the exclusive atmosphere, for the floor shows, and for an opportunity to dance way into the small hours. To join a nightclub, telephone the secretary, then take your passport along to be shown at the door. Most Americans will be made temporary members for a nominal subscription fee right on the spot. Commonwealth or foreign visitors resident in London will have to join normally, and annual subscriptions vary from one to ten pounds. Establishments requiring membership are indicated by "sub" after the name.

Nightclubs come—and they go—so we list only a few well-established ones, together with some good dinner-dance spots. Evening dress is optional in most, desirable in a few.

The most famous—and most expensive—clubs are **Annabel's, Legends, Tramp,** and **Wedgies;** each of which can look like a 3-D version of Who's Who. Getting in is virtually impossible unless accompanied by a member, and the bill for two could easily top £100. In most other establishments you could expect to spend up to £50, depending of course on your liquor consumption. It is worth checking to see if there is any special low-price dinner-dance arrangement available before midnight. Since the recent licensing law amendments came into force, clubs have far more freedom in serving hours—but the law is still complicated so you'll have to check as you go.

For the latest "in" spots, consult *What's On, City Limits* or *Time Out,* but don't be surprised if you find it impossible to get in, for when a spot is "in" it's way in and crowded with the chinless and charmless —as well as the bright and the beautiful.

Barbarella's, 428 Fulham Road, SW6 (tel. 385 9434). One of the few discos where you can also eat in reasonable comfort, and hear each other talk. Suitable for all ages.

La Bussola, 42 St Martin's Lane, WC2 (tel. 240 1148). Convenient and elegant for a post-theater dinner-dance but prices require caution.

Dorchester Terrace Restaurant, Park Lane, W1 (tel. 629 8888). An exceedingly good choice for that "certain" evening, where you want to enjoy the food as well as the company.

Embassy Club, 7 Old Bond St., W1 (tel. 499 5974). Edward and Mrs Simpson dined here in the 1930's. Picking up after a period in the doldrums. Non-member admission £4.50 to £7. Membership £80.

Hippodrome, Hippodrome Corner, Leicester Sq., WC2 (tel. 437 4311). The very latest thing in nightspots. Reputed to have cost around £3 million for the original conversion this is a spectacular way of spending the evening. Entry fee £5 Mon., Tues., and Thurs., £7.50 Wed., Fri. and Sat. Closed Sun. Membership can be had for £50 for three months, £175 for a year. As this is strictly a jeunesse joint and style is vital if you want to get in, it is perhaps not a spot for the older, staider visitor—but if you can win through Checkpoint Charlie then the laser shows and general concept spawned by nightlife boss Peter Stringfellow may well make your trip. Live music Wed., other nights disco. 9 to 3 in the morning.

New Gaslight, 4 Duke of York St., SW1 (tel. 930 1648). Much advertised nightclub, working hard at living up to the Edwardian image. Striptease and cabaret from 9.

Raymond's Revuebar, Brewer St., W1 (tel. 734 1593). Two shows nightly of super-sexy striptease; the only one we can list as good value for money.

Samantha's, 3 New Burlington St., Mayfair (tel. 734 6249). An old disco with plenty of kooky atmosphere. Open Monday to Saturday, 8.30 to 3.30 in the morning; admission varies depending on the night, and on whether or not you are a member, from £4–5 for women, £4–7 for men (Gin and tonic £1.30). Annual membership £50 men, £15 women; strict dress code observed.

Savoy Hotel Restaurant, Strand, WC2 (tel. 836 4343). This granddaddy of all London's nightspots comes into its own for a special dinner out with dancing.

Stringfellow's, 16/19 St. Martin's Lane, Covent Garden (tel. 240 5534). One of London's brightest—the first born of Hippodrome's Peter Stringfellow. Open daily to 3 in the morning (closed on Sunday). Entrance for non-members £5–8. Membership (optional) £175. Operates strict dress code—smart and chichi.

Studio Valbonne, 62 Kingly St., W1 (tel. 439 7242). Stylish dining, dancing, disco, and cabaret. Monday to Saturday 9 to 3.30 in the morning (ladies free Tuesdays).

Tiddy Dols, 2 Hertford St., W1 (tel. 499 2357/8). British food, 18th-century setting, great wines, live entertainment 6–11, disco 11–2. Great evening for very reasonable cost.

Tingles, London Tara Hotel, Scarsdale Place, W8 (tel. 937 7211). Cocktail bar, steak and salad bar with the accent on American-style eating, and dancing to 1 A.M. Monday to Thursday, to 2 Friday and Saturday. Style is the name of the game here, with dress code scrupulously observed.

Xenon, 196 Piccadilly, W1 (tel. 734 9344/5). Highly publicized disco, which prides itself on a laser show, Hot Gossip-like dancers, and wild animals (in cages!).

Rock, Folk, Jazz and Bands

You'll find an exhaustive list of the week's gigs in *Time Out* and *City Limits,* the weekly listings magazines. These shows range from the great Wembley concerts, where the likes of David Bowie and the Stones appear, to hundreds of local pub and club scenes with up and coming groups. In between there are the discos and the halls.

The best big venue with regular concerts by recognizable names is the **Hammersmith Odeon,** which is the place in London where rock stars traditionally finish their British tours. The seemingly forever-changing fashions in rock music have seen a corresponding turnover in clubs, with yesterday's top-spot today's "nowhere." However, that famous name from the '60s, the **Marquee,** is still going strong—albeit in different premises from those heady days, in Wardour Street. Two more recent, though quite different, additions to the scene in the North London area are the **Electric Ballroom,** at the top end of Camden High Street, which is open Saturday and Sunday nights, and at the other end of the same street, the **Camden Palace,** something of a poseur's paradise, which you can enter five nights a week.

The pub-rock circuit, where the music usually comes with the price of your pint, is the source of some of the most promising up-and-coming musicians. Still notable here is the **King's Head** pub in Islington's Upper Street, where you will find live music in the bar itself every night, and in the adjoining theater some Sundays—everything from traditional folk music to jazz-rock-funk fusions. Down in Covent Garden there's the famous **Rock Garden,** which is right on the Piazza and features all kinds of fashionable rock and jazz.

However, the hottest jazz spot in London is **Ronnie Scott's,** in Soho. This is where the big boys come to blow—Dizzy, Monk, Jackson, they've all played here. But you should be warned that the entry fee is on the high side and the food poor. If you fancy old-time traditional jazz, head out to the **Robert Inn,** beyond Acton on the Great West Road, where every Friday night a six-piece jazz combo performs. It's a long trek but worth it—this is where Dixieland grew up in England, and years ago even saw the early rhythm and blues efforts of a group called the Rolling Stones. The **100 Club** in Oxford Street used to be Humphrey Lyttelton's old club. This is the last of the old-style jazz clubs in central London, and still has good jazz, reggae and rock every night.

An exciting development in 1985 was the opening of the **National Jazz Centre** in a converted warehouse (what else?) in Covent Garden's Floral Street. With live jazz—from Trad, through mainstream, to Modern—performed seven days a week in the 400-seater auditorium, also in the restaurant, not to mention rehearsal/practise rooms. For the use of aspiring musicians as well as established names, the Centre seems certain to prove a must for all aficionados of this sometimes neglected art form.

Cinema

Although the general state of the British film industry is never extremely healthy, and although the number of suburban cinemas is declining each year, and West End first-run cinemas are doing fair business. Unless you buy or book your seat in advance, always a wise move, be prepared to stand in line, for recent big hits at least. This is not always quite as deadly as it may sound, as the cinema queues are sometimes entertained by London's famous street buskers, who will sing, dance or perhaps even escape from chains for you, in return for a small "donation."

In most West End cinemas, seats are bookable in advance. Generally prices are around £3.50, though many of them have a discount policy on Mondays. In the suburbs—which *can* mean only a short bus ride from the West End—the neighborhood houses charge around £2.

The West End cinemas and their suburban brothers generally show popular entertainment films, the type of which is denoted, approximately, by the censors' rating. This appears in small print alongside the title of the film. Films with a *U* (for Universal) rating are considered acceptable for all audiences; those rated *PG* will require parental guidance; a rating of *15* means that the film has been passed for persons over 15; and lastly, replacing the infamous X-rating, comes an *18* which is meant only for the eyes and ears of those over 18.

In addition to the art houses such as the Screen on the Green in Islington, the Screen on the Hill (Belsize Park), the Gate (Notting Hill Gate) or the Everyman, Hampstead, there are two important cinema clubs, the National Film Theatre which is in the Festival Hall complex, and the Institute of Contemporary Arts on the Mall.

The NFT screens movies from its vast library, and specializes in series highlighting the films of famous directors or the work of a particular studio. It is possible for visitors to obtain temporary memberships.

One really imaginative chain of movie houses which is bucking the trend towards wholesale closure is the "Screen" group. The group has taken over interesting old cinemas in various parts of London—mostly out of the center—and after renovation runs them as front-rank art houses. Screen on the Green in Islington, Screen on the Hill almost into Hampstead, and the latest rescue operation of one of London's oldest movie houses, The Electric in Portobello Road near the celebrated antiques street market, are all doing a roaring trade in showing the movies that the normal big distributors won't touch. The Screens charge a 50p membership, available at the door. The Roxie Cinema-Club occupies the premises of the now defunct Essential Cinema in Wardour Street; a club in name only (i.e. there is no "fee," just a straight £3 entry), it concentrates on classics of the last 30 years or so.

There is a handful of sleazy all-night cinemas; otherwise, showings finish around 11 p.m. But there is a growing popularity for late night shows, starting about 11.30, on Friday and Saturday nights. Those lucky enough to visit the National Film Theatre can occasionally settle down for all-night screenings of horror, sci-fi or westerns.

Piccadilly Circus Rejuvenated

As we go to press, a new entertainment center is raising its sails above the London horizon. After decades of shilly-shallying, there have been developments in the plan to clean up London's major black spot—Piccadilly Circus. For years, the Circus has been a disgrace to a capital city—a haunt of the drug trade, lined with decrepit buildings and cheap souvenir shops, the whole sorry mess garishly lit by neon signs. But now a sizeable section of it has been redeveloped into a big modern entertainment center—The Trocadero.

With three floors of up-to-date design the complex contains an International Village with a provincial French street and an Italian piazza, replete with assorted shops and national restaurants to match; the Guinness World of Records, which brings to life facts from the best-selling *Guinness Book of Records,* using the latest display techniques; and a spacious atrium to tie the whole thing together.

The concept is one that will be familiar to New Yorkers, but is fresh to London. It is early days to estimate how the new complex will wear and how it will affect this central and all-important area. The signs are that it may go a long way to counteracting the sadly sleazy image that Piccadilly Circus has had for so long. One thing is already clear. There is emerging an entertainment district—running from Piccadilly Circus through Leicester Square (which is now a pedestrian precinct) and along Shaftesbury Avenue—where restaurants, movie houses and theaters will all share a unifying cohesion that has been lacking up to now. It is to be hoped that the hard-pressed administration of the area can find the resources to keep the area cleaner than they do at present.

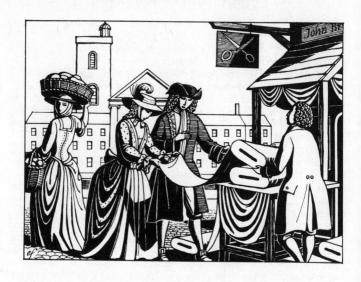

SHOPPING IN LONDON

The Sleek, Chic and Antique

by
PATRICIA HARRIS

Despite the ravages of inflation, the effect of soaring rents on prices, the get-rich-quick merchants, the crowds and the alarming increase in sheer shabbiness of so many of London's streets, shopping still ranks high among the delights of the British capital. For one thing, as you might expect in a great metropolis, many of the best shopping streets are in some of the smartest and most interesting areas of London. So, if the constraints of your budget won't allow you to do more than windowshop, you can combine this in itself frequently enjoyable process with an exploration of London. But if you do feel a little more flush, you'll find that the quality of traditional English goods has

114

declined not at all; cashmere scarves, sweaters and skirts, hand-made shoes, classic raincoats, silk shirts and, above all perhaps, the incomparable Savile Row suit still rule the roost in their respective fields. At the same time, London has consistently reaffirmed its position as a—if not *the*—leader in the fashion world, as the glittering shops in Mayfair and around Covent Garden make clear.

If high fashion is not your thing, however, how about antiques? London probably has more antique shops to the square mile than any other city in the world and in all price ranges. Or books? You'll find a number of strikingly excellent specialist and general bookshops. And then there are the department stores, covering the entire scale of quality and price, all the way from lofty Harrods to everyday Marks and Spencer.

One word of advice, however—do remember that London is a sprawling place and that its center alone is the same size as any number of respectably-sized cities. So try to confine your shopping activities to no more than one, or perhaps two, areas at a time. We would also recommend that you look at our remarks on V.A.T., the dreaded Value Added Tax, on p. 36 of the *Facts at Your Fingertips* section. You may be able to save yourself a pound or two.

Oxford Street

Oxford Street, the most famous shopping street in London, is unfortunately also one of the least appealing. Not only is it long and very crowded, it is also home to some of the most nondescript and drab shops in town, for the most part selling over-priced jeans and housed in decrepit Victorian buildings. However, to its credit, it does have a number of department stores, all of which are reasonably priced. The best, or at any rate the best-known, is *Selfridges,* a splendid pile of twenties Ben-Hur architecture, that dominates the whole of one block toward Marble Arch. It is London's equivalent of Macy's in New York.

Running from west to east, the other principal department stores are *C&A* at no. 505 (there's another smaller branch farther along and on the opposite side of the street at no. 200), for very reasonably-priced clothes for all the family, and some surprisingly bright fashions. At no. 458 there's a huge branch of *Marks and Spencer,* one of Britain's best-loved high street stores. It is inexpensive and the service is almost legendary for its friendliness and reliability. Grouped together, just before Oxford Circus, are *D. H. Evans* at no. 318, *John Lewis,* excellent for yard goods, and *British Home Stores* at no. 252—all of them reasonably priced, if perhaps also a little unexceptional.

At Oxford Circus itself, however, and occupying the whole of one corner of this great junction formed by the meeting of Oxford Street and Regent Street, is *Peter Robinson,* a department store of some style in comparison with its companions in Oxford Street.

From Oxford Circus, Oxford Street continues east to join Tottenham Court Road, but its proliferation of sad-looking boutiques and shifty street sellers makes this one of London's more discouraging areas.

Off Oxford Street

While Oxford Street itself may not offer much to the shopper other than the prospect of corns and exhaustion, many of the streets that lead off it count among London's prettiest and best shopping areas. They are worth exploring in some detail.

The first is St. Christopher's Place on the north side of Oxford Street and practically opposite Bond Street tube station. It's very tiny but well-signposted, so you shouldn't miss it. Opened in 1980, pedestrians-only St. Christopher's Place has convincingly established itself as one of the most attractive of London's chic shopping streets. Look in at *Under Two Flags,* at no. 4, which sells model soldiers of every type and period. *Rocks,* at no. 15, has jewelry galore—fashionable earrings, bracelets and necklaces of boldly cut glass and rhinestone. All that glitters is no necessarily gold here. *Mulberry & Co.* at no. 32 is almost equally chic and glamorous. *Cutler and Gross,* at no. 18, are London's most chic opticians and stock a wide range of fashionable frames. *Nicole Fahri,* at nos. 25/26 is known for her women's coats, suits, and dresses tailored in simple but sophisticated lines.

Just around the corner from St. Christopher's Place is *Ixiz,* at nos. 14/15 Stratford Place. It's a small store, packed full of shirts, trousers, sportswear, bags and notebooks, all in bold, simple designs and all from Japan.

South of Oxford Street this time, and just a little farther on from St. Christopher's Place, is South Molton Street. Walking down from Oxford Street, one of the first shops you'll come to is *Brown's,* five interconnected shops selling some of the smartest and most elegant clothes in town. The first, third and fifth shops are all branches of Brown's proper, the first selling clothes and accessories for women by some of the hottest designers around; the second specializing in shoes and handbags for women; the third specializing in menswear of considerable style. Sandwiched between these three, shops numbered two and four are *Giorgio Armani,* who sell Italian clothes for women. Farther down and on the opposite side of the street is another outpost of the Brown's empire, *Molton Brown.* Though they are essentially hairdressers, you can buy lovely tortoiseshell combs here, as well as very pretty hair slides and their own brand-name hair products.

Among the many other clothes shops in South Molton Street are *Joseph,* at no. 13, home for bold collections by British designers like Body Map and Street Clothes; *Next* at no. 15, the latest venture of fashion supremo Terence Conran, with an emphasis on economical chic; *Joseph Tricot,* at no.16, with knitwear for the whole year round (and owned by the same Joseph as that at nos 13 and 14); *Ebony,* at no. 45, currently *the* top man's shop in London—and the prices live up to the billing; and *Pacific,* on the corner at no. 34 Brook St., for denims in varied dyes made into multi-styled trousers, shirts and jackets. As a change from all this fashion, *Prestat* at no. 24 sell sensational handmade chocolates, while *Foto Inn* at no. 35 will develop and print photographs in only 60 minutes. Avery Row, the continuation of South Molton Street, boasts a branch of *The Cocktail Shop* at no. 5, where you'll find everything you could ever need to shake, stir and sip a cocktail, as well as some pretty remarkable recipes.Back in the world of high fashion, *Paul Smith* at no. 23 is one of the top names in town for elegant and distinctive men's clothes.

Bond Street (Old and New)

Returning to Oxford Street and continuing on a little, you'll come to New Bond Street, a street that has consistently maintained its reputation. It is a little less smart than, say, ten years ago, but it still has that certain glamorous quality. Aside from travel agents and airline offices, the bulk of shops that dot its length are ultra-sophisticated clothes shops, gift shops and jewelers. There are also a number of art galleries, some of great distinction. Needless to say, anyone subject to dizzy spells should not look at the price tags.

Starting from Oxford Street, you'll find *Smythsons* at no. 54, a home for the finest, featherweight leather pocket and address books. Something rather different is found at no. 76, the *Collection Venice Simplon Orient Express,* successfully recapturing the glamor of travel in the '20s and '30s; their sliver and glass tableware are exact replicas from the same period. No. 113 New Bond Street houses one of the great names in fashion design, *St. Laurent,* who has another alluring outlet at no. 73, this time for men only. *Fenwick* at no. 63 is a small but distinctive store with attractively cool clothes and accessories. Two attractive and unusual shops are *Louis Vitton* and *Ireland House* at nos. 149 and 150 respectively. At the former you'll find distinctive and elegant luggage—each piece is individually numbered and registered—and at the latter, Donegal trousers and Waterford crystal among many other delights from the Emerald Isle.

The White House, at no. 51, has gorgeous and very pretty linens and French couture. *Karl Lagerfeld,* at no. 173, is one of the world's great names in fashion. Here, in his London outlet ink-and-wash sketches of his lates collection hang on the walls to help you choose from his dazzling range.

Behind the rather nondescript facade of no. 34 New Bond Street, there lurks an organization that is known and respected the world over. This is the home of *Sotheby's,* largest and most successful of all the London art auctioneers. Their apparently rather pokey little building turns out, on closer inspection, to extend into and through a number of the adjoining buildings and is considerably larger than one would have thought. It can be fascinating to wander through the maze of rooms, big and small, viewing the objects coming up for sale, many of them surprisingly tatty, though some falling straight into the masterpiece category. Best of all, try to attend one, or at least part of one, of the auctions—but be sure you understand the prices before you bid!

A turn off the right towards Berkeley Square, down Bruton Street, will take you to *Holland and Holland,* at no. 33, one of those delightfully traditional English shops, with everything for the shooting gent; outdoor wear, a wide range of shotguns (they can advise on the necessary formalities), and many other shooting accessories.

Back in New Bond Street, *Ralph Lauren* at no. 143, *Hermes* at no. 156 and *Ted Lapidus* at no. 164 bring us back into the world of high fashion again. As with their more famous cousin in Paris, leather and silk are the Hermes trademark; their silk scarves in particular can be exquisite and make excellent gifts. Ted Lapidus, another of the great French names, has modern classics for both men and women, while Ralph Lauren specializes in equally stylish and glamorous clothes, again for both men and women.

Inexpensive gifts are not, however, high on the agenda at *Asprey,* no. 165. This is a world of luxurious glitter, deep soft carpets, glossy catalogs and chic gift wrapping. It's all very desirable and, somehow, very Bond Street. However, perhaps the ultimate Bond Street experience is to be had at *Cartier,* a little farther on at no. 175. This is one of the most exclusive jewelry shops in town. Old-fashioned class simply oozes out of the place.

Around about here, New Bond Street becomes Old Bond Street, but there is little difference in tone or atmosphere between the two halves of the street. At no. 3 you'll find *Ackermann,* who sell prints and paintings of all kinds. *Chanel* at no. 26, another of the great names, can supply you with their full range of skin products and perfumes, as well as their famous suits and gold chains, to complete the "Chanel look". *Charbonnel and Walker* at no. 28 sell fabulous French chocolates. They will make up special boxes of chocolates with the message of your choice inscribed on top. Finally, *Maud Frizon* at no. 31 have marvelously dainty shoes in beautiful colors created in conjunction with some of the top names in fashion.

Just past Charbonnel and Walker is the Royal Arcade, a sort of miniature version of the Burlington Arcade just round the corner. Among other shops you'll find the *Folio Society,* or rather their showroom. They produce special editions of famous books, with an emphasis on original bindings, and this is their principal outlet.

Back on Old Bond Street, you'll come across another of the great names in art at no. 43, *Agnews.* Their large and slightly unprepossessing galleries frequently contain stunning old masters. They also specialize in English paintings. The international stamp of style can be found again at *Gucci,* no. 27, famous the world over for leather goods marked with their red and green stripe.

The multitude of small and not-so-small streets running off Bond Street contain a number of shops, nearly all of them well worth investigating. In Brook Street, a busy road running across Bond Street at its northern end, you'll find *Halcyon Days* at no. 14. This could well be the place to pop into if you after a small and pretty gift. Their little enamel boxes are especially attractive and they are not outrageously expensive. Cork Street, which runs parallel to Bond Street between Clifford Street and Burlington Street, is home to three of the best modern galleries in London, the *Redfern* at no. 20, the *Waddington,* which has three addresses, nos. 3, 31 and 34, and the *Piccadilly* at no. 16. Visit any one and you could find yourself looking at the art of tomorrow. At no. 22 is *Knoedler,* specializing in contemporary art with a formidable list of artists on their books. Kitaj, Anthony Caro, Lichtenstein and David Hockney are among them, so walk in and look around—there's always something interesting to see. Also running parallel to Bond Street, though on the west side, Albemarle Street contains another of the most innovative and successful of London galleries, *Marlborough Fine Art,* dealers for Henry Moore and Francis Bacon among others. And in Maddox Street, running west off Bond Street, you'll find the *Francis Kyle Gallery* at no. 9.

Savile Row, the last of the Bond Street off-shoots, but certainly the most famous, has a name synonymous with the finest in British tailoring. Sadly, however, prices for a Savile Row suit are astronomic these days, but if you feel you can stand the shock of getting the bill, you'll find that the standards of tailoring are as high today as they have always been. Among the many tailors in Savile Row, *Gieves and Hawkes,* at no. 1; *Tommy Nutter,* at nos. 18/19, are distinctly less traditional stores than most of their counterparts here, yet true to form, still using only the very best cloths for both their custom-made and ready-to-wear collections (they are also the only Savile Row tailor to open on Saturdays). *Herbert Johnson,* at no. 13 Old Burlington Street, is one of the great names of British tailoring. They also sell hats, everything from to hats to berets.

The Burlington Arcade

A charming covered lane built in 1819, the Burlington Arcade, linking Piccadilly with Burlington Street and running up one side of the Royal Academy, is the perfect place to prowl on a wet day. The atmosphere here is terribly English, though in the nicest possible way and, not surprisingly, many of the shops sell mainly British goods, all of the highest quality.

At *James Drew,* no. 3, you'll find exclusive handmade silk shirts and dresses. *The Pen Shop* at no. 27 lives firmly up to its name, selling pens of all shapes and sizes. In this, the age of the ballpoint, a really good fountain pen can make a perfect present. *Sullivan Powell* at no. 34 was founded in 1880 and is one of a dwindling band of shops where you can still buy snuff. But they also sell a wide range of tobaccos, many of them rare and rather exotic. There's a branch of the *Irish Linen Company* at no. 35; while *N. Peal,* no. 37, has some of the softest and most appealing cashmere you'll ever hope to find. There are more traditional British shoes at *Church's,* nos. 58/59, smart and sturdy. *Lords* at nos. 66/70 are one of London's more exclusive hosiers. As you wander through the Arcade, you will also see miniature soldiers, china and glass—all kinds of items to pause over and enjoy.

Piccadilly

Piccadilly is not really much of a shopping street in comparison to Bond Street, yet it does have a number of delightfully English shops that are well worth visiting. Foremost among them is *Fortnum and Mason's* at no. 181, opposite the dignified Royal Academy. Fortnum's, as it is fondly known, ranks high among the untouchables of English life. It houses groceries on the ground floor, fashions and perfumery on the floors above. The pale-green decor and tail-coated assistants are reassuring symbols of permanence and English indomitability. Have tea or a light lunch here, too; not as grand as it once was, but still fair value for around £3.50 (tea) or £5 (lunch).

Other shops in Piccadilly worth investigating are *Hatchards* at no. 187/8, a superb bookshop (perhaps the best in London), and *Simpsons* at no. 203, home of elegant sports wear for both men and women, though they also do formal wear in the best tradition. For more traditional English country wear, in the best "gentry" tradition, try *Swaine, Adeney & Brigg* at 185, where Wellingtons (often surprisingly chic), shooting sticks and riding boots in the softest leather abound.

Jermyn Street and St. James's

Leading south from Piccadilly, beside Fortnum and Mason's, is Duke Street, a small road that slants downhill and plunges into the heart of St. James's, still an exclusive enclave of discreet clubs, art galleries and London's most traditional gentlemen's accessory shops. The major shopping street is Jermyn Street, which runs parallel to Piccadilly and is crossed at right angles by Duke Street.

Among the proliferation of splendidly elegant shops here, make for *Turnbull and Asser,* no. 71, where you'll find shirts, ties and handkerchiefs of distinction. *Floris,* a little farther down at no. 89, has marvelous and deceptively delicate soaps and perfumes, as well as gorgeously old-fashioned shaving brushes and bowls. In fact, the shop is a genuine survival—they still offer you your change on a velvet pad to enable it to be picked up by a gloved hand! For a more extravagant gift, pick up one of their lapis lazuli shaving brushes or an ivory toothbrush.

It will be easy to tell that you're getting close to *Paxton and Whitfield,* no. 93, you'll smell it long before you see it. The reason? An unusually potent collection of English and foreign cheeses, some the size of roulette wheels, that really have to be tasted to be believed. Try some Blue Cheshire or the Stilton, their specialty. *Astley's,* no. 109, has a superb collection of pipes, tobaccos and allied smoking impedimenta.

Though the art galleries of St. James's cater to a clientele that is, to put it mildly, well-heeled, there's nothing to stop anyone from walking into them and taking a look around. The main source of interest here is *Christies,* at no. 8 King Street, who, along with Sotheby's back in Bond Street, more or less run the auction game in London—and that means the world. St. James's Street, running up from St. James's Palace to Piccadilly, home of London's most discreet gentlemen's clubs, also houses London's most famous gentlemen's hatter, *James Lock,* at no. 6. You may not need one of their silk toppers, but what about a boater from £25 (or a cheaper version at £15)? And have a look in *Lobbs,* almost next door at no. 9. They've been making shoes for the gentry since the 1700s. Standards—and prices—remain unsurpassed.

Regent Street

Like Oxford Street, which it crosses, Regent Street is one of the great thoroughfares of London. It was built originally by John Nash for the Prince Regent (hence the name) and cuts a majestic swathe through Mayfair to the west and Soho to the east, as it runs down to and across Piccadilly Circus and thence to Pall Mall where it finally comes to an end. However, it offers considerably greater style and elegance for the shopper than Oxford Street, though it too has a tendency to overcrowding, but not to the tawdry bustle that so conspicuously bedevils Oxford Street.

The most splendid store in Regent Street is *Liberty's,* at no. 200. It is a labyrinthine building, full of nooks and crannies and surprising little corners. Its principal facade on Regent Street is a magnificent Hollywood-style classical structure that makes one suspect that the hand of Cecil B. DeMille has been at work, or that Charlton Heston might suddenly appear dressed as Moses from behind one of the columns. Around the side of the building, however, in Marlborough Street, the style changes quite unexpectedly to an equally magnificent —and inappropriate—Tudor idiom, all plasterwork and gnarled beams.

Liberty's are famous principally for their fabulous fabrics, which they design and print themselves, but they also have an Oriental department, full of gorgeous and mysterious saris and Arabian jewelry. The menswear section specializes in traditional clothes, with shirts made from their own prints. In the basement are selected and very attractive British crafts. All in all, the store is very hard to resist. You might easily pick up an original gift here—try the ties, for instance.

100 yards or so further down is *Hamley's,* London's premier toy shop and an institution. As well as their massive range of toys, there's an extensive sports department on the fourth floor. *Burberry's* at no. 161 does magnificent rain and trenchcoats, as well as a range of classic English sweaters, jackets, ties and so on. There is another, larger, branch in the Haymarket (no. 18) on the other side of Piccadilly Circus. *Gered,* at no. 158. is one of London's leading fine china shops. They specialize in Wedgwood and, not surprisingly, many of the most popular designs are the oldest, some dating back to the 18th century. *Aquascutum, at no. 100 is* another long-established and classic men's store, though the fashions here are definitely highly-priced.

Covent Garden

Covent Garden, for long the home of London's fruit and vegetable market, looked like proving all the theories about inner-city decay absolutely right a few years ago. The market, up until then the area's principal *raison d'être,* had moved to a new site south of the Thames, leaving the old central buildings, and dozens of warehouses in the peripheral streets, empty and derelict.

But suddenly the whole area sprang to life as a result of the decision to renovate the elegant mid-19th-century market building and its attendant fruit and flower markets. Today Covent Garden, with its shops and restaurants, publishers, public relations firms, the Opera House and, above all, the old market building itself, is the most attractive and bustling place in London, though the redevelopment of the area is by no means finished. If anything, the building sites and scaffolding and the potholes and the trucks tend to underline the vivacity and general bonhomie of the whole neighborhood and make it more appealing.

The heart of Covent Garden is the lovingly-restored market, a semi-open arcaded building on two levels, watched over by Inigo Jones's austere church of St. Paul's. Its light and airy interior is perfect for window shopping and walking around the stalls and many small shops. The front runners include *Pollock's Toy Theater* which has enchanting models and reproductions of toy theaters from the Regency, Victorian and Edwardian periods and a branch of *Culpepper,* which has good herbal soaps and lotions as well as attractive cosmetics and other delights in the cool, plant-filled interior. Also try *That's Entertainment,* specialists in rare and deleted records, especially of Hollywood and Broadway musicals, and the *Doll's House,* for dolls houses, of course, but of a very superior kind; they will for example design especially for you. They also have a marvelous range of miniature fixtures and fittings from Regency four-poster beds to microwave ovens. *Original and Rare Newspapers* at no. 46 have papers and periodicals dating back to the early 17th century. Some cost as much as £250, but you might pick one up for as little as £10. Finally, try the *Light Fantastic Gallery,* alive with holograms and lasers; their exhibitions change every three months and are well worth catching.

To the east of the market in Drury Lane, you'll find the *Drury Lane Tea and Coffee Company* at no. 57, with teas of a hundred different fragrancies and coffees from all over the world. In Wellington Street, round the corner from Drury Lane, is *Penhaligons,* no. 41, established in 1870 and hardly changed since. If you are looking for traditional English perfumes, soaps and aftershave, this is definitely *the* place to drop by. The delightful Victorian interior and the superb packaging of all their goods only adds to the pleasure.

Running north from the market is James Street. On the right is the new Opera House extension, while on the left are a series of attractive little shops. Try the *Poster Shop* at no. 28, home to a huge collection of posters from all over the world, or *Les Amis Gourmands* at no. 30, which does its best to live up to its name. It has a splendid selection of cheeses and croissants, cakes and ice creams among the many tempting delicacies.

A few yards up on the left is Floral Street, home to a number of quirky and intriguing spots. Try *Paul Smith* at no. 44, sister shop to that in South Molton Street, for excellent men's fashions. The *London Bicycle Shop* at no. 41 sells and hires bikes (of the pedalling variety) of all kinds, and has a wide variety of bicycle impedimenta—including bike radios. Also in Floral Street, is the *National Jazz Centre.* It promises to be a must for jazz freaks and will comprise auditoria for live performances, a shop and a restaurant. Both modern and trad jazz will be covered.

Backtracking to James Street, its continuation is Neal Street, a narrow and rather cramped street, but, like so many around here, full of interesting shops. *The Cocktail Shop* at no. 30 and *The Postcard Gallery* at no. 32 are two newcomers here. The former is great for anyone with a yen to sip an exotic concoction and only needs the means to do so; the latter for literally thousands of different postcards, though all with the accent on zaniness. Both are excellent for inexpensive, albeit hardly traditional gifts. Those in need of something a little more old-fashioned, should head for *The Copper Shop,* on the same side of the street at no. 48. Glowing, glistening copper pots and pans hang from the ceiling and crowd the shelves. Opposite is the *Bead Shop* with trays full of beads of every shape, size and color. *The Hat Shop,* at no. 58, has hats for every occasion—trilbys and panamas for men, cocktail hats and boaters for women. *The Kite Store* is at no. 69; it's alive with billowing colored kites, both traditional and zany.

Backtracking down Neal Street will bring you to Long Acre, whose mixture of wholly different shops and thronging people makes an invigorating change. On the corner of Neal Street and Long Acre you'll find *The General Store,* full of teapots with funny faces on them, cane and bamboo tables, jokey alarm clocks and a whole host of other pretty and silly—though in the nicest possible way—bits and pieces. Turn left down Long Acre for *The Glassblower,* at no. 65. As well as watching glassblowers at work, you can buy fine, original examples of modern glass by some of Britain's best-known names. To the right down Long Acre, *Bertram Rota,* at nos. 30/31, in a delightfully converted building, sells secondhand books, but these are nearly all first editions and a really magnificent collection, too. Over the road is *Flip* at no. 125, as different as can be. It's brash, modern, noisy and nearly always full; but it is also fairly inexpensive (check out especially the bargain basement).

Back on the other side of the street again there are two more bookshops, *Stanford's* at nos. 12/14, which has practically every travel book and map going—ours included, bless their hearts—and at no. 8, the *Arts Council Shop.* This is a great place for postcards and posters, as well as for catalogs of exhibitions from all over, and books on all the arts, including film, theater and ballet.

At the foot of Long Acre, turn left into Garrick Street and continue along past the dignified and sooty face of the prestigious Garrick Club. A step or two more will bring you to *Moss Brothers* (always called Moss Bros) who hire out dinner jackets (and complete morning suits for weddings and Ascot races) for the busy man on the move who does not have these clothes in his luggage. The same organization also hire out furs of the mink category, and couture evening dresses for ladies suddenly faced with a formal invitation while traveling. Moss Bros. is also a straightforward menswear shop with a very good range of middle-priced clothes. And in Bedford Street (the continuation of Garrick Street and just a little way beyond Moss Bros) is the *Button Box,* at no. 44, with more than 500 different types of buttons, from delightful little pearl buttons to brilliantly-colored wooden buttons. Backtracking a little, you'll come to New Row on the left where at no. 13 is *Naturally British,* a most enjoyable place, full of very British goods, handmade of wood or clay, with soft toys and some knitted sweaters and such, too. An attractive idea for that distinctive gift.

Three more shops just on the northern borders of Covent Garden are *Dobell's* at 21 Tower Street, a little lane of a street running into Cambridge Circus (connoisseurs of blues and jazz should definitely look in here where you'll find blues and jazz records, old, modern, obscure and famous, jamming the racks), *Foyles,* at nos. 119/125 Charing Cross Road, and *Zwemmer's,* also on Charing Cross Road, at no. 78. Zwemmer's is small, slightly musty and, for devotees, addictive. It is an art book shop. Foyles, on the other hand, is large (in two separate buildings, either side of a narrow lane), rambling and more nearly resembles a rabbit warren than any self-respecting store has a right to. Be warned, though, not only is it nearly impossible to find the department you want, let alone any specific book, but you can also face up to twenty minutes grappling with the lines at the old-fashioned tills that, for some arcane reason, have been retained. But the stock is incredible, with nearly every book in print somewhere in the store. In all, it's an essential part of London's book scene.

Knightsbridge

Knightsbridge is home to the most famous store in London, and one of the most famous in the world, *Harrods.* Its gaudy Edwardian bulk, all delicate red brickwork and gold detailing, dominates the stretch of the Brompton Road in which, serene and plush, it rules supreme.

Times change, though, and Harrods changes with them. The service is not quite so punctilious as it was before (indeed, there have been complaints that some of the gaucher members of the staff have hardly a nodding acquaintance with stock); the lush floors are far noisier than they once were and often uncomfortably crowded; but the refurbished food hall is still superb, the menswear department remains excellent and there are many treasures to be found all over the labyrinthine departments. The Queen still does her Christmas shopping here, and sheiks do theirs all the year round.

The problem is that success has bred success, and in pursuit of incredible profits the store has sacrificed some of the quiet dignity on which those profits were originally built. It is still an experience to shop here, with a pause for refreshment at one of the excellent coffee bars or restaurants, but it would be wise to do so at one of the comparatively quieter times, such as in the first couple of hours in the morning or during the evening opening time on Wednesdays.

A few blocks down (westwards) from Harrods is Beauchamp Place (pronounced *Beacham*). It is small and pretty and packed with dotty and attractive little shops. Try *The Map House* at no. 54 for antique prints and original maps dating back to the 15th century. Prices range from £8 (prints) and £25 (maps) to £600 and £3000 respectively. *Luxury Needlepoint,* with tapestries both old and new for firescreens, and wallpapers and prints from many periods, is at no. 36, while *Bruce Oldfield,* at no. 27, is an elegantly-designed pink-and-gray shop, housing his entire ready-to-wear collection. *Julip Model Horses,* with handmade model horses and riders, and assorted equine paraphernalia, is at no. 18. *Caroline Charles* has ball gowns galore, as well as more everyday wear and raw silks in brilliant colors. She's at no. 19.

Running off Beauchamp Place at right angles is Walton Street, a charming little road of pink, yellow and blue Victorian villas that is perfect for browsing. *Stephanie Hoppen* at no. 17 is an exclusive and very unusual book shop specializing in—believe it or not—antique cook books. The oldest volumes date back to 1492! But they also have plenty of more recent, and less expensive books on offer. Prices start from around £50. Try *Dragons* at no. 25. Downstairs you'll find children's painted furniture, lovely little toy boxes, clocks and pencil cases, all of which you can have painted to order, as well. Upstairs there is rather unusual French and English bric-à-brac.

Nina Campbell at no. 48 specializes in stationery, most of it Italian—marbled-paper boxes, fluffy cushions and Edwardian inspired lamps. Still on the subject of stationery, The *Walton Street Stationery Company,* no. 97, established in 1800, still provides superb cotton-fiber writing paper, as well as cards of all sorts and fabulous wrapping paper. The *Monogrammed Linen Shop,* at no 168, has a wide range of fine Italian bed linen, with matching towels, bathrobes, and nightshirts, plus tablecloths, mats and napkins—all of which they will have monogrammed for you. *L'Artisan Parfumier* at nos. 194/6, has terrific sprays positively reeking of whole baskets of flowers, scented candles and luxurious bath oils.

Back on Brompton Road, the *Reject Shop* at no. 245 sells seconds of all kinds at very reasonable rates. If you are in need of a last minute present and funds are running low, this might be the place to try.

The same cannot be said of a cluster of desirable shops at the opposite (eastern) end of the Brompton Road. *Fogal,* at no. 51, has a vast range of stockings and pantyhose in silks, nylon and cashmere. Over the road at no. 2, *The Scotch House* has excellent traditional woolen goods, superb scarves, gorgeous cashmere jerseys and super-smart skirts.

On the corner of Knightsbridge and Sloane Street is *Harvey Nichols,* considered by many to be London's most attractive department store, rivaled only by Liberty's. One major plus here is that, unlike most department stores, it is small and comparatively uncrowded. It also has some of the most elegant clothes in town, as well as an atmosphere of well-heeled plush.

Sloane Street

Harvey Nichols has introduced us to Sloane Street, a long straight street leading down to Sloane Square and the beginning of the King's Road. At the top end of Sloane Street there is a pleasant gathering of shops, some of them quite sleek. *Truslove and Hanson* at no. 205 is one of London's better bookshops. Across the road, take a look at *Joseph— Pour La Maison,* no. 16, for this is the latest outpost of Joseph's stylish London empire—there are 4 shops in South Molton Street—clothes, furniture, jewelry, books and gifts of all kinds vie with the collections of leading designers. *Taylors of London* at no. 166 specialize in hand-made floral-scented colognes, seductive bath oils and delicate pot-pourris. *Courtney* at no. 188 has silks and satins, lingerie, robes and other delightful nightwear. *Bendick's* at no. 195 have chocolates, chocolates and more chocolates—try their bittermints.

The other shopping section of Sloane Street is right at the bottom, quite a long walk and about two bus stops away, but the walk is a pleasant one, as the lefthand side of the street is filled with a long, long leafy garden. At the bottom end, just before Sloane Square is *Partridges,* no. 132, a very superior food shop; try their baked meats if you are having a picnic, very English and quite delicious. At no. 144 is *The General Trading Company,* full of garden and household goods, exactly the sort of place for that offbeat present. It is rather like New York's Hammacher Schlemmer.

Chelsea

At its southern end, Sloane Street runs into Sloane Square, a surprisingly attractive little square that marks the meeting point of ponderous and stately Belgravia, away to the east, with Chelsea, away to the west. For long one of the prettiest areas in London, Chelsea has always enjoyed a rather raffish reputation. This quality was well to the fore during the heyday of the swinging sixties, when Chelsea reigned supreme as the beating heart of all that was modern and daring in London (an atmosphere well captured in the film *Blowup*). Those days are long passed now, but Chelsea still retains a vigor and spontaneity that can be hard to resist.

Nowhere is this more evident than in the King's Road, an endlessly long road that runs from Sloane Square all the way to Putney. However, the part that is most Chelsea-like occupies only the first quarter of its total length. To see it at its most amusing and enjoyable, full of outrageous fashions and wonderfully bizarre characters, walk down it on a sunny Sunday afternoon when the whole place buzzes and hums with movement and color.

As if to belie its true nature, the King's Road starts off very soberly with *Peter Jones,* a decidedly respectable department store (one of the John Lewis chain), which fills out the corner of the King's Road and Sloane Square. They stock a fine range of attractive fabrics, china and glass, all at reasonable rates. The next stretch of the King's Road houses an assortment of boutiques and clothes shops of a type that can be found more or less anywhere in London. Some are smart and modern, some a little more conservative, none is especially exciting. But as the King's Road unwinds take the chance to pop down some of the little side streets, which are among the most delightful and unexpected in London. These side-trips apart, more interesting shops begin to crop up. At no. 135 is *Antiquarius,* an antique market packed with little stalls. Though well past its better days, when it was the center of trendy antique dealing, it is still worth a visit. At 181/183 is an antique market, the *Chenil Galleries,* with around 150 stalls and a bewildering range of goods, many small and not too pricey. Back at no. 141 is *Edina and Lena* for designer knitwear and hand-made jumpers made from old patterns. The *Designer's Guild* at no. 271 and 277 is an Aladdin's Cave of fabrics and wallpapers, lamps and chairs in Tricia Guild's exclusive designs. At no. 207 is *Givan's Linen Store,* home to high-quality linens with a charmingly old-world atmosphere.

A turning to the right past the Town Hall and a row of pretty antique shops reveals Old Church Street, one of the most desirable addresses in London. At no. 49, Manolo Blahnik at *Zapata* will sell you women's shoes in a Louis Quinze setting at prices that would make even Louis blink. Back in the King's Road again, *Johnson's* at no. 406 is a brand-new spot making a name with its classic rock-and-roll styles.

World's End is an area that sits in the middle of the King's Road and does its best to live up to its name. But if you continue on through its dreary council buildings and drab shopping complexes, you'll come to perhaps the prettiest stretch of the whole King's Road. It is only 300 or 400 hundred yards long, but a pub or two, a lovely 19th-century arcade and a refreshing mixture of shops, some grand, some rather sheepish and rundown, contrive to give this little patch an irresistible flavor. Watch out especially for *Christopher Wray's Lighting Emporium* at no. 600. It's alive with delightful and amusing lights from the 1880s through to the 1920s. Just beyond at no. 86 New King's Road, as it then becomes, is *Lunn Antiques,* a treasure trove of old lace; delicate, intricate and charming. Continuing down, you come to the Fulham Pottery at no. 210, founded in 1671.

Fulham Road

Almost as long as its more famous neighbor, the King's Road, though certainly not so exciting, the Fulham Road does have in one relatively short span of its great length a collection of shops as tempting as any in London.

Starting where the Brompton Road—on which Harrods sits—comes to an end, the Fulham Road runs away southwest, roughly parallel to the King's Road. *Conran* at no. 77 has gifts of all sorts downstairs; upstairs, you'll find the best of modern furniture as well as elegant bathroom and kitchen fittings. At *Night Owls,* no. 78, everything you could want to buy in the way of ladies' bedroom wear will tempt you. A sidetrip here down Sydney Street is in order now, to *The Chelsea Design Company* at no. 65; sailor suits in silk, velvet-and-cotton stripes for women and children are the attraction.

Continuing on . . . *Whittards* at no. 111 is one of London's superior delicatessens. They've been in the business now for over 100 years or more and stock delicacies of all kinds. But their specialty is tea and coffee. They have over 50 different teas from all over the world and almost as many coffees. *Divertimenti* at no. 139 has delightful cooking pots and pans, glassware and pottery, as well as rugs, mats, cushions and bed covers—altogether a good place for that unusual gift. The *Pan Book Shop* is at no. 158. It's a reasonable shop of its kind with a good selection of books, mostly paperbacks, but what really singles it out are the great opening hours: from 10 a.m. to 10.30 p.m. Monday to Saturday and 2.30 to 6 p.m. on Sundays and Bank Holidays. *Souleiado,* at no. 171, have printed scarves, shawls and bedcovers in traditional, sunbaked Provençal patterns.

Butler and Wilson, no. 189, are the most imaginative and fashionable designers of costume jewelry in town. Their new designs are based on old Baroque pearls. There is also lots of diamenté. No. 341 is home to *L'Herbier de Provence,* really the most spectacular and splendid shop on the whole Fulham Road and quite the most beautifully-scented place in the metropolis, if you have a nose for herbs and spices. As the name suggests, the shop specializes in herbs grown in the south of France. They are stacked in baskets and sacks around the floor and include leaves and flowers for health-giving *tisanes,* special teas, bathroom oils and essences.

Kensington

Though primarily a residential district of considerable charm and chic, Kensington nonetheless has a certain amount to offer the shopper. Sadly, the principal shopping street, Kensington High Street, is little more than a scaled-down version of Oxford Street. Only *Hyper Hyper* at nos. 26-40, easy to recognize with the hectic caryatids and neon abounding on the outside, is worth more than a glance; the large interior houses 70 stalls manned by young British designers offering startling fashions at low prices.

The real charm of the area is to be found in Kensington Church Street, a long and winding road that snakes uphill from the High Street to Notting Hill Gate. Aside from a few good clothes shops, Kensington Church Street is notable principally for the endless array of antique shops that line both sides and the small turnings that run off it. You'll find jewelry, clothes, paintings, glass, ceramics, furniture, Japanese prints, dolls—just about everything you can think of. It is the perfect place for window shopping. At the beginning of the street, drop in on *Crabtree and Evelyn* at no. 6, yet another preserve of delicious smells, for their fabulous soaps with sophisticated packaging. *Distinctive Trimmings* at 17d is great for braids, trimmings, cords and assorted fabrics in all shapes and sizes. *Roxy* is at no. 25, a must for those after the best of modern British designers. *Monsoon,* a few doors down, offer glittering, Oriental inspired clothes.

A small turning, Holland Street, just beside Monsoon reveals one of the delightfully quiet little streets that make London such a joy to explore, it has many attractive 18th-century houses and a very pleasant pub on a corner. Watch out for *Academy Books* (there's one on either side of the road) who specialize in books on Art Deco and Art Nouveau subjects, though they have all the latest titles as well. Turn left down

Kensington Church Walk, a little country lane with some pretty, tiny shops, and so back to the High Street.

Hampstead

Hampstead, away to the north of London, is always worth a shopping trip. There is none of the overcrowding and jostling here that seems so inevitable in the center, and even if you buy nothing at all, it is a delight to wander in the attractive, hilly streets. The major shopping route is Rosslyn Hill, though, confusingly, it changes its name twice as it unfolds, becoming in turn the High Street and then Heath Street.

Starting up Rosslyn Hill, you'll find *Benetton* at no. 40, with gorgeous rainbow-colored knitwear for men and women, with jackets, trousers and skirts to match. No. 60 is home to the *Kilim and Nomadic Rug Gallery,* which specializes in high quality modern Turkish rugs, they change their stock every three months, so there's always something new on offer. As you come into the High Street, watch out for *H. Knowles-Brown* at no. 27, excellent for antique jewellery and watches and clocks, as well as more modern work, much of it produced right here.

Just before Heath Street begins, turn right into Flask Walk where, among the pastel cottages you will find *Culpepper,* specialists in herbs and cosmetics, *Lodder's Coffee and Tea Warehouse,* a treasurehouse of coffee and tea, *The Flask Bookshop* which, apart from the rest of its stock, has the widest range of P.G. Wodehouse in London and *Fawks and Stanley Smith Antiquarian Books,* where you can browse away an hour among the fascinating shelves.

Continuing into Heath Street, watch out for *Fouquets* at no. 6—the London home of a famous French name—offering fruit compotes, unique oils and vinegars, preserves and honey. Further up is *Chic* at no. 74/82, where you'll find tempting lingerie, exotic shoes and the best of British designers. *Elena,* over the road at no. 87, sells delicious handmade chocolates.

Markets

Fun as it is to wander around the formal shops of London, there is nothing like a street market for stimulating the acquisitive juices. The difference between this kind of shopping and the more sedate kind is that you would be wise to get to the markets as early as you can, both to watch how they gather impetus during the day, and to find those worms that are most tasty for early birds. You should also remember that you can make mistakes in purchasing as long as you don't spend too much on them. You will have to be very certain of your own taste and knowledge to spend more than, say, £20. But, above all, it isn't the bargains that really count with street markets, it's the unbeatable atmosphere. Here are the major markets, with a few helpful facts about them.

Bermondsey (New Caledonian), one of London's most extensive. Hundreds of booths and stalls, with a wealth of junk from the attics of England. A special stamping-ground for dealers. Take the 15 or 25 bus to Aldgate, then the 42 over Tower Bridge to Bermondsey Square. But get there early and remember, you may have to walk a lot. The market can start as early as 4 in the morning and runs till about midday *on Fridays only.*

Camden Lock (Dingwalls Market), (Tube or buses 24 or 29 to Camden Town). Antiques and crafts market. Open Saturday and Sunday, 10–5:30, though individual craft shops are open weekdays around the picturesque lock.

Camden Passage, Islington (Tube or buses 19, 38, to "The Angel"). Openair antique market, Saturdays. Fascinating antique shops in Camden Passage and Pierrepont Arcade, particularly for silverware. Stick to Association of British Antique Dealers members here. Shops open daily, 10:30–5:30; market Wednesday and Saturday. Also a good spot for a Sunday morning wander.

Leadenhall Market, EC3. A Victorian covered arcade with food and plants; lashings of atmosphere. Monday to Friday, 9–5. Tube to Bank.

Leather Lane, Holborn EC1. A blend of traditional fruit, vegetable and crockery stalls with new-fangled wares like spare Hi-Fi parts. Monday to Friday, 11–3 p.m.

Petticoat Lane, in Middlesex St., E1. Open on Sunday mornings (9–2) only, for pets, clothes, fabrics and curios of all descriptions. (Watch your wallets!)

Portobello Market, Portobello Road, W11. (Take 52 bus or tube to Ladbroke Grove or Notting Hill Gate.) Best day is Saturday, from 9 a.m. to 6 p.m. (though it is open during the week—not Thursday afternoon) for all kinds of curios, silverware, antiques, etc. Several dealers with shops in other parts of London have booths here. No bargains and sometimes can be a trap for tourists, but is bursting at the seams with local color.

Smithfield, EC1. London's main meat market and one of the biggest in the world. Best days are Mondays and Thursdays. Tube to Farringdon or Barbican.

EXPLORING CENTRAL
LONDON

"The Flower of Cities All"

by
RICHARD MOORE

London has changed dramatically over the last few years. The great open spaces are still green and filled with flowers; there are still wild-fowl in St. James's Park and boats on the Serpentine. But behind them, the skyline has assumed a new profile, with familiar shapes set in a new perspective of towering office blocks, of which the latest, the NatWest building, soars to 600 feet, dominating nearby St.Paul's.

The enforcement of smokeless zones across the middle of London has had two effects. The deadly autumn fogs have been abolished, and a sweeter atmosphere has inspired a wholesale cleaning of the city's older, more remarkable buildings. But even though those choking fogs have gone and the mists no longer wreathe the street lamps on winter evenings, London is still essentially a place where the quality of the light, diamondhard or softly opalescent, governs the city's mood. It is a mood which the visitor can share with complete enjoyment. For London is a city which loves to be explored; it only reveals its real self to those who are prepared to wander into its hidden courts.

The biggest city in Europe, London sprawls over more than 600 square miles. Through its center curls the River Thames bending and twisting from beyond Richmond and greener fields, past the Houses of Parliament and the Tower, to slide alongside the docks, now largely derelict (though there are imaginative redevelopment plans afoot), on towards Greenwich and Woolwich—the latter with its majestic new Flood Barrier a prime attraction—and ultimately out to the sea. Sometimes London is criticized for not making more of its river; a strong and beautiful attraction, it is the most spectacular throw-away in the country and the farther one moves away from it, the less interesting London becomes. Yet you can enjoy its drama, real and potential, anywhere from London Bridge itself up to Chelsea, by walking alongside it or by taking one of the cruises upriver to Windsor and downriver to Greenwich.

All of which is true—romantic, but true. There are, however, other truths about London that must be faced. It is fast becoming a city of cleaned buildings and dirty streets. Garbage collection is hugely expensive and London has been no more successful in solving its financial problems than has New York, though they are not quite so acute. But it is not just the uncleaned streets that will greet the visitor. Once there were many little shops in the West End, established in the same place for decades, sometimes for centuries. Soaring rents and property taxes have forced them to close and where they once were are now dozens of cheapjack stores, selling the same tawdry trinkets from the Far East that can be found all round the world. The area around Piccadilly Circus has been seriously affected by these get-rich-quick merchants.

Another unhappy truth that will hit the visitor especially hard is the rocketing costs of hotels and restaurants. London has been among the most expensive cities in Europe for some years now and, sadly, the services that are offered are frequently not the equal of the costs.

We point out these facts not in any mean carping spirit, but because the visitor to London usually has a very clear picture of what he expects to find. Nowadays he will have to look harder to find it. Beneath the rampant commercialism, the untidy streets, the occasional petty crime, the London of the posters is still there, the London of *Upstairs, Downstairs,* the London engraved on the world's imagination by a thousand years of history, art and literature, the city which provided the backdrop for the pageantry of the wedding of the Prince and Princess of Wales. It will just require a little more patience to find it.

Thirteen Million Can't Be Wrong

There is one point that should be made about visiting London, before we launch into the details of our *Exploring* section. Currently about 13½ million visitors arrive in Britain every year and nearly all of them inevitably want to see London. Now, London is a working city. Its residents have to get to and from their jobs every day; they have to eat lunch and generally do all the things that you would do yourself back home. More than 13 million visitors make it a little bit more difficult for them to do those things; and the situation is exacerbated by the fact that the influx is concentrated in the summer months when the buses and the Underground are at their least attractive—and least efficient.

Londoners are among the most hospitable people anywhere, but the vast number of travelers that surrounds them for so many months in the year does create a new situation to which they have to adapt. The message is, therefore, try to travel during the out-of-peak periods when sightseeing (it's cheaper anyway), and remember that if you ask a Londoner the way somewhere he may have been asked the same question already a dozen times. Our bet is that he will still answer in a friendly, helpful way. The only trouble is that, the odds being what they are, you'll probably find you are asking another one of your 13½ million fellow visitors!

Piccadilly Circus

All explorations have to start somewhere, so we have chosen Piccadilly Circus as the point to begin ours. That is about its only useful function, for Piccadilly Circus these days is noisy and sordid. In some ways, it is a symbol of the state of British life in general, once a proud hub of empire, but now haunted by junkies and the sellers of cheap souvenirs. However, most major cities have such a center, and much as it would like to be, London is no exception. But it is safe enough in the daytime, we just suggest that you avoid it like the plague late evening and in the small hours of the morning. Luckily there are signs of improvement. There have been plans for the rehabilitation of the Circus for 40 years, and at last change seems to be coming. The Trocadero complex was opened in 1984 with its restaurants and exhibitions, and it heralds a new era.

The Circus is always crowded. At the times of big hoop-de-doos, New Year's Eve or the evenings of Cup Finals, it throbs with noisy, drunken crowds. The Angel of Christian Charity, designed in 1893 and mistakenly called Eros (the God of Love), is poised for flight at one side of the Circus looking strangely diminutive for such a famous figure. On days of big celebration the water in his fountain is shut off and he is boarded up, to prevent him being used as a miniature Matterhorn. The statue actually commemorates a Victorian philanthropist, Lord Shaftesbury, who is remembered, too, by nearby Shaftesbury Avenue. The bow and arrow of Eros is a play on Shaftesbury's name.

On the corner of Piccadilly in 1612, there was a shop owned by Robert Baker, a tailor, selling pickadells or lace collars. These collars, some say (though there are several other theories), gave their name to the now famous thoroughfare.

Select whatever area of Central London you want to explore, go to Piccadilly Circus, face in the appropriate direction and start. To the north runs Regent Street, curving up one side of Mayfair. To the south is Lower Regent Street, leading towards Whitehall, the parks and the palaces. To the east are Shaftesbury Avenue and Coventry Street, for theaters and Soho; to the west is Piccadilly itself, heading off for Hyde Park, Knightsbridge and, eventually, Land's End. Piccadilly Circus is also one of the embarkation points for the London Transport round-tour bus, which is a very good way of getting to know the center of London quickly. Once you have acquired a two-hour orientation that way, you can return to the parts that interested you and explore them in greater detail.

St. James's

Looking south from Piccadilly Circus, down the wide stretch of Lower Regent Street, you will see the towers and spires of Whitehall. The area bounded on the north by Piccadilly, on the east by Lower Regent Street, on the south by The Mall and on the west by St. James's Street, is known as St. James's. It is one of the very few areas of London whose plan has barely changed from the time it was laid out in the late 17th century.

At the bottom of Lower Regent Street, you will find Pall Mall leading off to your right. Pall Mall has a dignity and elegance brought about by the presence of many important clubs. These are not open to the public, but it's always possible you'll meet someone who is a member and invites you to lunch! The exclusive Reform Club, at No. 104, is a favorite with many famous writers and was where Jules Verne's Phineas Fogg made the wager that he could go round the world in 80 days. The even more prestigious Athenaeum, with its frieze copied from the Parthenon, embellishes a corner of Waterloo Place. At the foot of this attractive, elongated, tree-lined square stands the Duke of York's Column, a 124-foot memorial to the second son of George III, actually an efficient administrator, but one who now lives in the children's jingle which remembers that he had a terrible time leading ten thousand men up and down a hill.

There are dozens of statues around London, but hardly anywhere has such a concentration as does Waterloo Place. Apart from the Duke of York up on his column, there's Florence Nightingale, the heroine of the Crimea, with her famous lamp; two great explorers, Sir John Franklin, who died trying to find the Northwest Passage, and Captain Scott, who died in the depths of the South Polar icecap; three monarchs, Edward VII, Victoria and George VI (the last two a few yards off to each side); Sir John Burgoyne, son of the General Burgoyne who surrendered at Saratoga; Sir Colin Campbell, who rose from being the son of a Glasgow carpenter, to become the leader of the relief of Lucknow during the Indian Mutiny; and finally, Lord Curzon, the "very superior person" who lived close by at no. 1, Carlton House Terrace.

Pall Mall ends by St. James's Palace. Of recent years this lovely brick palace has taken a back seat in the affairs of the nation. About its only claim to fame as an integral part of the government of Britain now is that all foreign ambassadors are still officially accredited "to the Court of St. James's."

The palace was called after St. James because, early in the 11th century, not long after the Normans had conquered the country, there was a leper hospital on the site for unfortunate women suffering from that mystically dread disease. Henry VIII built the beginnings of the present structure in the 1530s. Although it remained a royal residence, the focal point of government for the next century and a half was the sprawling colossus of Whitehall Palace. St. James's regained favor when Whitehall burned down in 1698; but Victoria (trying to escape the wicked aura of her uncles, no doubt) moved to Buckingham Palace in 1837 and thus put paid finally to St. James's central function. It is possible to see a small part of the palace (through the entrance to the Ambassadors' Court), and, of course, there is always the superb Tudor gateway, facing the foot of St. James's Street, which usually has a splendidly uniformed Guard on duty and makes an excellent subject for the photographer in search of atmosphere.

The internal interest in the palace for visitors will be the Chapel Royal, said to have been designed by Holbein, though it was heavily redecorated in the mid-1800s. The ceiling still has the initials H and A, intertwined, standing for Henry VIII and his second wife, Anne

Boleyn, the mother of Elizabeth I and the first of Henry's wives to lose her head.

Nearby is the Queen's Chapel, on the left across Marlborough Road, which joins Pall Mall with the Mall. This chapel is one of the forgotten glories of London, small but exquisite. The lovely structure is one of the very few pieces of architecture that can be definitely attributed to Inigo Jones. It was built between 1623 and 1627, among the first purely classical buildings in the country. It is possible to visit both these chapels for Sunday services. To find out when they are held, consult the Sunday papers.

At 66 St. James's Street, on the left going up from the palace, is one of London's most striking new buildings. Like a grouping of bronze rockets about to take off, it provides a challenging contrast to virtually every other building in the street, creating an exhilarating feeling of sheer bravado.

St. James's is an essentially masculine area; Jermyn Street cuts across, parallel to Piccadilly, and contains splendid shops, mostly for men's clothing and accessories, although there is a sprinkling of antique shops and art galleries. This is the mecca for lovers of hand-made shoes, shirts and other symbols of a vanishing way of life. Lobb's, on St. James's Street, is a world-famous bespoke shoe-maker. James Lock, on the same street, has been making hats for over 200 years. The window of this classic shop is always a slightly dusty delight. The district is historically interesting in a general way and exudes a slightly pompous elegance which is ideal for the discriminating shopper.

Tucked away in the center of this area is St. James's Square, the very first of the breed. The square is lined by attractive buildings, mostly from the 18th century, which are worth spending a moment looking at. For those interested in books the narrow facade of No. 14, in one corner, will be specially fascinating, for behind it lurk nearly a million books belonging to the London Library, one of the best private lending libraries in the world. The equestrian statue in the middle of the square is of William III (William of Orange).

St. James's Park and Buckingham Palace

If you return to St. James's Palace, go down Marlborough Road, past the Queen's Chapel and the art nouveau memorial to Queen Alexandra, Edward VII's deaf and understanding wife, you will reach the Mall and St. James's Park. The park consists of 93 acres, developed at different times by a series of monarchs (one must not forget that this is the heart of what used to be the private purlieus of the crown, the royal back-garden). Henry VIII drained the marshes that were here, so that he could have a handy hunting preserve. Charles I took his last walk across the park en route to his execution.

Charles II began to convert it to its present shape. He employed Le Nôtre, a famous French landscape gardener who had worked for the Sun King, and had him redesign the area. So successful was Le Nôtre, that it became *the* fashionable playground for many decades. Pepys often mentions walking there. "Found the King in the Park. There walked. Gallantly great."

In 1829 the great architect John Nash worked the park over once more, making the lake and generally giving it the look it has now. Although it is a lovely spot to walk in during the day, with its exotic birds and superbly kept flowerbeds, it is especially attractive at night when the illuminated fountains play and the floodlit Abbey and Houses of Parliament beyond the trees look like a floating fairyland. St. James's Park is the apotheosis of the strange ability Englishmen have to translate what are essentially private gardens into public domains.

The Mall itself is decorated with gilded crowns and banners whenever there is a State visit or any other excuse for a grand procession. It is the site of several great houses occupied by various members of the Royal Family. The most important of these is Clarence House, where the Queen Mother lives. At the eastern end of The Mall is Carlton House Terrace, a fine row of Georgian houses with colonnades, in the basement of which are the Institute of Contemporary Arts galleries, often occupied with shows that are at extreme odds with the dignified terrace rising above. Across the Mall, almost at Admiralty Arch, is the great ivy-covered bulk of the block-house that was Churchill's wartime headquarters.

At the other, western, end of the Mall from Admiralty Arch stands Buckingham Palace—historically important, though visually dull. It won't be dull trying to cross the street to see it, however; the authorities refuse to put traffic signals or marked crosswalks in front of the Palace as they don't want to "spoil the beauty of the place"—so lots of luck en route! The Palace was first built in the 18th century for the Duke of Buckingham who sold it to George III for £21,000. Initially it stood on three sides of a courtyard, the east-facing end open to St. James's Park. The heavy facade of the east front, which the tourist sees through the iron fence, was added later (the present one in 1913) and is much less pleasing than the west front, which the public cannot see. The interior and the gardens are never open to the public (except for the lucky few who are invited to Garden Parties or attend formal investitures at which the Queen confers knighthoods and lesser awards).

On the site where Buckingham Palace stands there once stretched a mulberry garden—planted at the time when James I wanted to encourage the making of silk in England.

The Queen's Gallery (adjoining the Palace on its south side) is one of the best small galleries in Europe, and regular exhibitions drawn from the vast and spectacular royal collections are on display. The royal standard flying above the east front indicates that the Queen is in residence. The Changing of the Guard is one of London's most popular tourist attractions. So much so, that the number of tourist coaches that can park in the immediate vicinity has had to be limited. Since a guardsman had an unfortunate altercation with an importunate tourist a few years ago, the sentries have been moved inside the Palace railings.

The large monument in front of the Palace is the Queen Victoria Memorial, an epic recapitulation of Victorian ideals, with Motherhood, Truth, Justice, Peace and Progress all represented. The best thing that can be said for this mammoth celebration of everything but Virginity and The Right To Vote, is that it makes a wonderful grandstand from which to view processions and the Changing of the Guard. From the Palace (on the right as you face it) an avenue, Constitution Hill, leads alongside Green Park, to Hyde Park Corner.

From the other side of this triumphal circle, Birdcage Walk leads along the south side of St. James's Park towards Westminster. The first buildings on the right are the Wellington Barracks. This was the site of a tragedy in the Second World War. The Royal Military Chapel was destroyed during a service on June 18, 1944, by a flying bomb and 121 people were killed. By one of the freaks of bomb-blast that wartime London got to know well, when the dust and rubble settled it was found that the candles on the altar were still burning. The Chapel was rebuilt in the early 1960s in a naturally rather somber style, incorporating what was left of the old building. The public is welcome to Sunday services.

A comfortable stroll down Birdcage Walk will bring you eventually into Parliament Square. Halfway along you might want to make a small detour and take the little turning which leads into Queen Anne's Gate, lined with really lovely early 18th-century houses (many of them now occupied by government offices). Tucked away here is a rather stiff and formal statue of Queen Anne herself.

The Houses of Parliament

Seen across Parliament Square, the Houses of Parliament seem at first an incoherent complex of elaborate spires, towers and crenellations. But their medieval look is quite spurious. Visitors are often surprised to discover that they were built between 1840 and 1850, the exception being the genuinely ancient core of the complex, Westminster Hall, which was first built in 1097. The designer of the New Palace of Westminster, Sir Charles Barry, the country's leading architect in the period following the death of John Nash, selected the richly decorated Perpendicular style, probably in order to harmonize with Henry VII's chapel opposite. Seen from across the river, it is clear that the Houses of Parliament are planned with classical simplicity, the towers and roofs just giving the impression of confusion from some viewing angles.

Parliament Square itself was designed by Sir Charles Barry to give the very best views of his great building, and to act as a sort of garden connecting the Houses of Parliament with the Abbey. The statues in Parliament Square are an interesting round-up from many times and nations. Field-Marshal Smuts appears as a rather clumsy statue by Sir Jacob Epstein; Palmerston, Disraeli, Peel are among the eminent British statesmen who are there; Abraham Lincoln is represented by a copy of the Chicago statue, the work of Saint-Gaudens; Richard Coeur de Lion and Oliver Cromwell exist in unlikely proximity—in life they would have undoubtedly hated each other's guts; but by far the most impressive of this frozen throng of great men is the figure of Sir Winston Churchill sculpted by Ivor Roberts-Jones (1973), a presence of such dynamic power that it still dominates the Houses of Parliament with as much force as did that brilliant leader in life.

Westminster was the first major settlement outside the City of London; Roman remains have been found and Edward the Confessor built a palace here between 1050 and 1065 in order to be close to the abbey which he refounded. William Rufus in 1099 completed the vast Westminster Hall, and his medieval successors made many further additions. The present Houses of Parliament, therefore, occupy the site of a palace and so still rank as such (hence the term, the "Palace of Westminster," in references to Parliamentary news). English kings lived here up to the time of Henry VIII, but from the mass of buildings only a few survived. Westminster Hall stands in the center, facing across Parliament Square; it has a fine hammerbeam oak roof, put there by Richard II in 1399, and to its east, the crypt of St. Stephen's Chapel (14th-century), still used occasionally for weddings and christenings by Members of Parliament and their families. Across Old Palace Yard is the moated 14th-century Jewel Tower.

The Houses of Parliament and Westminster Hall are no longer open to the public on Saturdays. In fact, Westminster Hall is closed to the public at all times, unless you are fortunate enough to know, or to meet socially, a tame M.P., and can persuade him to take you around. Tea on the terrace with a Member is a memorable experience. Watching the House of Commons or the House of Lords at work, from the Strangers' Gallery, is probably the best free show in London. (See *Facts At Your Fingertips,* page 52, for details.)

The palace covers eight acres, has two miles of corridors and more than 1,000 rooms. The large, square, 336-foot-high Victoria Tower is supposed to be the tallest square tower in existence, while the 320-foot clock tower is the universal symbol of London, "Big Ben." (Actually, this is the name of the 13½-ton bell on which the hours are struck, named after Sir Benjamin Hall, First Commissioner of Works when it was hung.) It has now been discovered that the clock tower is leaning slightly, its top being some nine inches off the perpendicular; however, there are no worries at present about its future. The interior of the palace is a treasurehouse of Victorian design, recently cleaned and restored with great care and craftsmanship.

When Parliament is sitting, a flag flies from the Victoria Tower by day and a light shines by night.

Westminster Abbey

Across Parliament Square stands Westminster Abbey. The first authenticated church on this site was a Benedictine abbey, established in 970 and dedicated to St. Peter. In fact the official name of the Abbey is still the Collegiate Church of St. Peter. West Minster means "western monastery," indicating its geographical position in relation to the City of London. It is a key part of British history, for here most of the kings and queens since the Conquest have been crowned and here many of them lie.

The finest architectural aspects of the Abbey, and the most impressive views, can be obtained by wandering round the outside, down some of the narrow streets, even into the atmospheric cloisters. You will notice very quickly that the Abbey is by no means all of a piece. It has

Westminster Abbey

1. West Entrance and Bookshop
2. Tomb of Unknown Warrior and Memorial for Sir Winston Churchill
3. Chapel of St. George
4. Organ Loft
5. Sanctuary
6. High Altar
7. Poets' Corner
8. Chapel of St. Faith
9. Chapel of St. Benedict
10. Chapel of St. Edmund
11. Chapel of St. Nicholas
12. Tomb of Mary, Queen of Scots
13. Tomb of Henry II
14. Royal Air Force Chapel
15. Tomb of Elizabeth I
16. Chapel of St. Paul
17. Chapel of St. Edward the Confessor—Henry V's Chantry
18. Chapel of St. John the Baptist
19. Coronation Chair
20. Chapel of Abbot Islip
21. Chapel of St. John the Evangelist
22. Chapel of St. Micheal
23. Chapel of St. Andrew
24. North Entrance
25. Belfry Tower
26. Jerusalem Chamber (closed to the public)
27. Jericho Parlour (closed to the public)
28. Stairs to Library
29. Chamber of the Pyx
30. Norman Undercroft and Museum

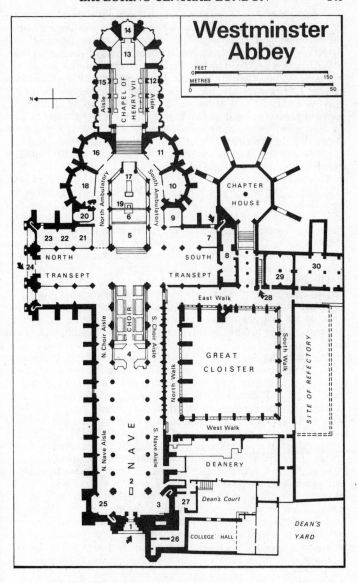

Westminster Abbey

FEET
0 | 150

METRES
0 | 50

N

CHAPEL OF HENRY VII

14
13
15 | 12
Aisle | Aisle

16 | 11
18 | North Ambulatory | South Ambulatory | 10
17
20 | 19 | 9
6
5

CHAPTER HOUSE

23 | 22 | 21
7
NORTH | **SOUTH**
8
TRANSEPT | **TRANSEPT**
24
29 | 30
28

East Walk

CHOIR
N. Choir Aisle | S. Choir Aisle
4

GREAT CLOISTER

North Walk | South Walk

SITE OF REFECTORY

N A V E
N. Nave Aisle | S. Nave Aisle

West Walk

DEANERY

2
25 | 3 | 27 | Dean's Court
1

DEAN'S YARD

26 | COLLEGE HALL

been restored and reshaped down the centuries with insistent regularity. The last major building work to be carried out was the erection of the two great west towers, which were not finally completed until 1745 by Nicholas Hawksmoor, a very stylish architect of the period, who, nevertheless, was able to instill a certain amount of Gothic feeling into his work, so that they are moderately in keeping with the rest of the Abbey. These towers have been the subject of controversy since the day they were finished, and, if you wander round the outside of this huge, sprawling mass, you will see that they do indeed seem light and delicate in contrast with the almost brutal strength of the rest. It is no coincidence that the favorite public image of the Abbey is of the west front, with these gentle soaring towers, not of the dark, somber, intricate power of the medieval building behind.

The Abbey, by the way, is an anomaly. It is not the seat of a bishop (the seat of the Bishop of London is St. Paul's Cathedral) but is run by a Dean and Chapter, who are responsible to the monarch alone—always excepting the Higher Power, of course. The technical term for the Abbey's status is "royal peculiar," a delightful distinction which it shares with St. George's Chapel at Windsor. In pre-Reformation days there was an abbot in charge of the resident monks, and the office was one of enormous power, political and religious.

The great English essayist, Joseph Addison said, "When I am in a serious humor, I very often walk by myself in Westminster Abbey." It is a place for serious wandering. Well-informed guides are easily available, so we will just concentrate on a few of the more outstanding elements that go to make up this treasure house of religion, history and art.

The first thing that will strike the visitor is the fantastic proliferation of monuments, tombs, statues and tablets. At one or two points the place takes on the aspect of a stonemason's store. A great many of these relics are of little interest to the ardent genealogist and none whatever to anybody who cares about art; they mostly serve to make it more difficult to appreciate the splendor of the interior. To add insult to artistic injury, many of the memorials are not graves. H. L. Mencken was annoyed to realize that "when you examine it, you find that two-thirds of the graves haven't even got a dead man in them."

It would be wrong to forget that the Abbey is a place of worship, wrong but quite forgivable. The vast crowds of visitors who fill it on almost every day of the year do give the feeling of an art gallery, a museum, rather than an ancient house of the mysteries of religion. It's a feeling that may well be accentuated when you find that you have to pay to get into parts of the building. Try, if you can spare the time, to attend a service there as well. It will help to put the experience in perspective.

Just inside the great west door is a memorial to Sir Winston Churchill, who is buried at Bladon, near his beloved Blenheim. Straight ahead is a tomb of the Unknown Warrior, a nameless soldier of the First World War, buried in earth brought with him from France. It is one of the very few floor-level tombs in the Abbey over which the countless thousands do not walk. By the tomb hangs a Congressional Medal, an echo of the Victoria Cross awarded by Britain to the Unknown Soldier in Washington.

As you wander up the aisle to the right you will see, among many others, memorials to such diverse men as Baden-Powell, founder of the Scout Movement, Major John Andre, the Wesleys and William Congreve. Further on you will come to the Poets' Corner, and perhaps wonder if stone and brass can outlive the works of the pen. Here are immortalized writers, and some composers, from Chaucer to the present day; a few of them are actually buried here, too. T. S. Eliot, Henry James and Longfellow are remembered beside Tennyson, Milton and Noel Coward, the latest addition. This small corner is more interesting than the forest of Victorian marble elsewhere.

Behind the high altar lie two of the most interesting parts of the Abbey, the Chapel of Edward the Confessor and Henry VII's Chapel. This is an area in which are the royal tombs. It is a roll call of the romantic past, with many of the striking effigies bringing the mighty dead to life. Edward the Confessor himself, lying in his own church in the spot to which he was transferred in 1268; Queen Elizabeth I and her sister "Bloody" Mary; Mary, Queen of Scots, magnificently entombed by her son James I; Henry V, minus the solid silver head that was stolen at the Reformation (it was replaced by a polyester resin one in 1971); Queen Anne, who had to wear layers of leather petticoats at her coronation, to keep out the Abbey's bitter damp; Richard II, one of the very first portraits of an Englishman extant, lies beside his wife, Anne of Bohemia; Edward III, his life of conquest and tumult quietened to a figure of patriarchal peace. They are all here or hereabouts. The cleaning and repainting of most of the Abbey's memorials has restored a vividity to them which gives a marvellous idea of their original splendor.

The focal feature of Edward's Chapel, apart from his own massive tomb, is the Coronation Chair. This hastily made, and extremely uncomfortable, seat was knocked together in about the year 1300 at the orders of Edward I. The chair encloses the Stone of Scone (pronounced *skoon*), or Stone of Destiny, which has long been a source of friction between England and Scotland. The kings of Scotland were crowned on it and it was used for the coronation of Macbeth's stepson at Scone in 1057. It was carried away from Scotland by Edward I in 1296 but has, over the centuries, become a symbol of Scottish independence. It has been removed from the Abbey only three times—once to Westminster Hall for the installation of Oliver Cromwell as Lord Protector; once for safety from German bombers in 1940; and finally, by Scottish nationalists in 1950, who took it far north. (It was returned six months later.)

Henry VII's Chapel is one of the miracles of western architecture, and should be savored. Dating from 1503, it is the last riot of medieval work before the rebirth of classicism and, one has to admit, is very un-English in its exuberant richness. It would be as well to have a pair of binoculars along, because much of the delightful detail, such as the small saints high up, cannot be seen easily. The tomb of Henry VII and his wife, Elizabeth of York, is a masterpiece of the Renaissance, being the work of Torrigiano, an Italian artist who is famous, apart from his superb creations, for having broken Michelangelo's nose (for which he was banished from Florence).

The Chapter House and Cloisters

Before leaving the Abbey, you must be sure to visit the Cloisters and the other parts that lie on the south side. These are the areas most connected with the life of the Abbey when it was still a monastic foundation. The octagonal Chapter House was the center of the Abbey's religious life, but it has also been called the "cradle of all free parliaments," for the King's Council, and later Parliament, met here from 1257 until the reign of Henry VIII. It is one of the great interiors in Europe, not only for its feeling of space, but also for its daring technical assurance, and for the beauty of the single column, like a frozen fountain, sustaining the roof.

In the Norman Undercroft, just off the Cloisters, is an excellent small museum. Among the treasures it contains are some effigies that used to be carried in funeral processions. These are mainly of monarchs, clothed in their robes and, since the faces were mostly taken from death masks, they give an impressive idea of how they actually looked. The figure of Nelson (not a funeral one, but made long ago to attract visitors) is one of the most striking pieces of portraiture extant, as a likeness it has Madame Tussaud's beaten hollow; you would swear it is alive.

After the time you have spent absorbing impressions in the Abbey itself, a quiet session in the Cloisters is refreshing before emerging into the bustle of London. Here, in the old days, the Abbot washed the feet of thirteen old men as part of the Maundy Thursday celebrations; here, too, the monks walked and discussed affairs of state and of their souls; here, perhaps more easily than elsewhere in Westminster, you may recapture the lost sounds of the past. We recommend that you poke around as much as you legally can, as there are so many nooks and crannies and lovely views to find.

St. Margaret's

Nestling near the Abbey is the church of St. Margaret where Sir Walter Raleigh lies buried. Beheaded in nearby Old Palace Yard, when he saw the blade above him, he remarked: "This is a sharp medicine, but it is a physician for all diseases." His wife then kept his head in a velvet bag to show to visitors with the macabre words "Have you met Sir Walter?" The east window, made in Flanders in 1509, was a gift from Ferdinand and Isabella of Spain. The church has an intimate atmosphere and is the scene of many smart weddings; Pepys, Milton and Sir Winston Churchill were all married here. In a niche on the facade of the church is a lead bust of Charles I, looking with a reflective air at Cromwell across the square.

Also buried here is William Caxton, the father of English printing. He had two presses nearby and is commemorated, too, in the name of the Caxton Hall, not far off, where many notable marriages were once performed in the registry office.

Millbank and the Tate Gallery

After leaving the Abbey, turn once more towards the Houses of Parliament and continue to the right, parallel with the river. This will lead you past the Victoria Tower Gardens, where stand the statue of Mrs. Emmeline Pankhurst—who suffered prison and hunger-strike for the cause of women's suffrage—and the noble group, *Burghers of Calais,* by Rodin, now placed on a low plinth in accordance with the sculptor's wishes.

Off to the right, (turn up Dean Stanley Street), is the renovated church of St. John, Smith Square. It represents a perfect solution to the mammoth problem of redundant churches which is increasingly afflicting Britain as it slowly swings away from a total involvement with the Established Church. The church was burnt out during the Second World War and rebuilt in the mid-'60s. It is now used as a concert hall, and a more delightful ambience for hearing music, particularly baroque music, could hardly be imagined. The BBC have frequent lunchtime concerts there. The streets in this area, especially Lord North Street, which leads out of Smith Square, are largely inhabited by Members of Parliament who want to be near their work. Lord North Street is a delightful example of the domestic architecture of Georgian London, the kind of houses where Handel and Johnson would have been at home.

Further along Millbank (passing Lambeth Bridge and looking across the river towards Lambeth Palace, the London home of the Archbishop of Canterbury) you will find the modern bulk of the Vicker's Building, a strangely light and sweeping construction, much favored by film makers as a background. Just beyond is the Tate Gallery, a must for all lovers of modern art as well as those who want to find out more about British art in general.

The Tate, like so many great galleries, reveals more gems the more one explores. The works of William Blake and Turner, two English artists poles apart and yet bringing contemporary visionary skills to their craft, hang here in profusion. Elizabethan and Edwardian portraits show the Briton down the years. Degas, Giacometti, Rodin, Gainsborough, Hogarth, Henry Moore, Bacon, Dali, Warhol, Lichtenstein, Hockney—the cream of European and American creativity is here.

In 1979 the Tate opened its long-awaited extension, over 22,000 square feet of exhibition space, with backstage facilities that were much needed. The new galleries are frankly functional, there was no attempt to create visually satisfying architecture, everything was subordinated to the need for uncluttered space and a controlled environment, both in terms of light and of temperature. The result is rather like a well-equipped factory. The one thing that the new extension has immediately provided is the wall space to show much more of the Gallery's huge collection than ever before. There is a strong feeling that the space is also revealing more of the controversial purchases that the Tate has indulged in over the last few years, giving the public the chance to see them to better advantage—or to their detriment, depending entirely on one's own reactions.

Quite apart from the excellence of the works on view, the Tate has a dynamic marketing policy, with reproductions, books and other Tate-oriented items. There is also a very good restaurant (lunch only) and an adequate, though cramped, coffee shop.

Past the Tate you will come to the end of Vauxhall Bridge, and find an abstract sculpture by Henry Moore, *Locking Pieces.*

Westminster Cathedral

Another side trip to be made from Parliament Square is to Westminster Cathedral, the Roman Catholic equivalent of the Abbey. To do this, walk along Victoria Street, which runs straight ahead from the west front of the Abbey. Victoria Street used to be a delightful thoroughfare of Edwardian shops and apartment blocks, but it is now entering the modern world with a vengeance. Slowly the whole length of the street is being demolished to make way for the latest in current architecture, most of it unimaginative and a very poor advertisement for British taste.

On the right is an undistinguished block that houses the headquarters of New Scotland Yard, the *new* New Scotland Yard, so to speak. Further along, the Army and Navy Stores has painfully risen from the wreckage of its former self. And, further along again, in a gap between two new buildings, you will see the Cathedral.

This view of the Cathedral is one of the happier decisions of modern London, a city where all too few imaginative combinations of old and new have been attempted. The usual pattern has been to tear down old buildings (some of them fine examples of their era) and replace them with pitifully conceived new ones. London has been at the mercy of unimaginative architects in the service of commercial convenience. The situation is changing. It has been discovered that to convert and modernize attractive old structures is preferable to demolition and rebuilding—it is amazing how the simplest concept that has been obvious to the majority of people for years, can appear like a vision on the road to Damascus to others! In far too many cases the change of heart is too late.

But the treatment of the Cathedral is a shining exception to the depressing rule. It used to be that the building was completely hidden and only the tip of its campanile could be seen, but now it stands at the back of a small piazza, framed by the new blocks and cleaned of its years of grime. This is the premier Catholic church of England, built between 1895 and 1903, and still unfinished inside. The tower is 284 feet high and the top can be reached by a lift. Unfortunately, the view is rather circumscribed by the new buildings round about.

This Cathedral is not a museum, a depository for the past, it is pre-eminently a place of worship, a function not always to the fore in other British cathedrals. Designed in a Byzantine idiom, as foreign a style in the heart of London as can be imagined, it yet exists triumphantly as a House of God. A fully choral service there, especially on an occasion such as Christmas Eve, with the choir singing from its place behind the high altar, will prove a memorable experience.

Unfinished as it is, the interior is a strangely attractive mixture of brick, marble and mosaic. The marbles come from all over the world, Greece, Italy, Ireland and Norway, among other countries. Scattered around inside are carvings by Eric Gill, an English sculptor fashionable when the original impetus of the building was strong. It will be many a long year before the Cathedral is complete since today's feelings run more to using money to help the poor rather than in ecclesiastical building schemes, but meanwhile, as a church in the making, it is a fascinating study.

A very short distance beyond the Cathedral is Victoria Station, a convenient center for tubes and buses.

Whitehall

Yet another walk that can be taken from Parliament Square will lead up Whitehall, passing the end of Westminster Bridge. Once, this whole area from the river to about where Trafalgar Square now is, was an extensive and fascinating palace, which has simply disappeared, most of the buildings being destroyed by a devastating fire in 1695. It was a series of courts, lawns, walks and buildings wonderful in conception, but never fully completed. According to a historian it was: "A glorious city of rose-tinted Tudor brick, green lawns, and shining marble statues." Today Whitehall is a rather dull, wide, curving street.

Without realizing it, perhaps, you will be walking through the heart of Britain's bureaucracy, pumping its diktats through arteries of red tape. The big government buildings that line the first part of the street are slightly brutal, but impressive. To the right is New Scotland Yard, its rather quaint brick exterior familiar from a thousand detective and police films set in London. The headquarters of the Metropolitan police was moved in 1967 to a vast modern block off Victoria Street. Since the police moved, the building has been used as extra offices for Members of Parliament, who were sadly squashed in the cramped conditions of Westminster.

Leading off to the left (west) from Whitehall is King Charles Street. If you follow it nearly to the end (just before Horse Guards Road) you will come to Clive Steps and the entrance to Winston Churchill's

Westminster Cathedral

1. High Altar and Baldachino (Sanctuary)
2. Chapel of the Blessed Sacrament
3. Lady Chapel
4. Chapel of the Sacred Heart and St Michael
5. Chapel of St Thomas of Canterbury (Vaughan Chantry)
6. North Porch (Visitors' Entrance)
7. Chapel of St Joseph
8. Chapel of St Paul
9. Chapel of St George and the English Martyrs
10. Chapel of St Andrew and the Scottish Saints
11. Chapel of the Holy Souls
12. Chapel of St Patrick and the Irish Saints
13. The Campanile or St Edward's Tower
14. Chapel of St Gregory and St Augustine
15. North West Porch
16. Main Entrance
17. Baptistery

A. Archbishop's Throne
B. Choir Organ
C. Stairs to upper galleries
D. Pulpit

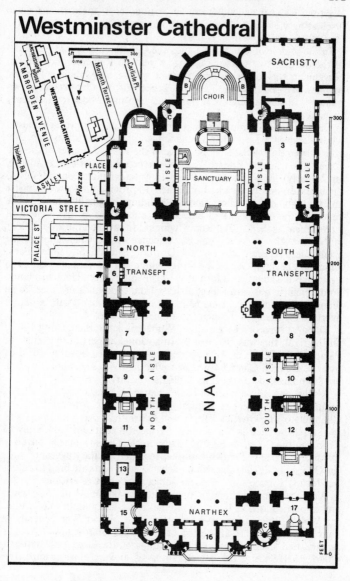

Westminster Cathedral

Wartime Cabinet rooms. Restored at huge cost, these rooms make fascinating viewing for visitors both old and young, and give a vivid idea of life during World War II.

In the middle of Whitehall stands the Cenotaph, a simple memorial to the dead of two wars; here, once a year on Remembrance Day in November, the sovereign lays the first tribute of symbolic Flanders' poppies. At this time the nation is supposed to be blanketed in two minutes' silence, though it is now a custom more honored in theory than in practice.

On the left is Downing Street, a pleasant row of 18th-century houses, where Boswell lodged when he made his famous visit to London. No. 10 has been the official London home of the Prime Minister of the day since 1732, when Sir Robert Walpole was presented with the residence. In the early 1960s both Nos. 10 and 11 were extended considerably to the rear, leaving the facades untouched, to provide the Prime Minister and the Cabinet more room than the buildings originally afforded. The center of the complex, and indeed the hub of the British system of government, is the Cabinet Room, which is situated on the ground floor of No. 10. No. 11 is the official residence of the Chancellor of the Exchequer. You can walk through Downing Street to St. James's Park, which lies beyond. One of the things which strikes so many visitors to London is the complete informality of Downing Street. Here, in a house no different in outward aspect at least from thousands of others to be found in London, the Prime Minister lives and works, with no more overt guard than a policeman positioned in front.

The next item of interest along Whitehall is the Banqueting House on the right; this was designed by Inigo Jones as part of the extensive Palace of Whitehall in 1625, to replace one burned down in 1619. In front of the hall, Charles I was beheaded in 1649. The whole building has been cleaned to reveal its Palladian beauty.

Almost opposite is William Kent's Horse Guards, a not very tall, but beautifully proportioned, building with a clock tower. Here, the Changing of the Queen's Life Guard takes place every morning, and in the Horse Guards Parade beyond the forecourt, the ceremony of Trooping the Colour is held annually on the Queen's official birthday in June. It is one of London's most spectacular military pageants, with the Queen taking the salute on horseback; good seats are hard to obtain but luckily it makes an excellent subject for color television.

We have mentioned one or two statues so far, and will do so when any of particular note occur. Whitehall has a fairly motley collection. Sir Walter Raleigh, an assortment of First World War generals, a couple of Dukes and, at the top of Whitehall, almost into Trafalgar Square, one of London's loveliest memorials, the equestrian statue of Charles I. He sits astride his elegant steed looking down towards the spot where he was executed. This statue is by Le Sueur, made in 1633, secretly preserved during the Commonwealth by a brazier who refused to melt it down, and brought back into the light of day when Charles II regained his father's throne. In a delicate show of achieved vengeance, it stands on the very spot where some of those who signed the king's death warrant were themselves executed. There is a plaque in the pavement behind which marks the center of London, from which all distances are measured.

Trafalgar Square

Trafalgar Square may rival Piccadilly Circus as the tourist's center of London and does so in an infinitely more dignified way. Laid out in 1829, it was finished in 1841. In the center is another celebrated London landmark, Nelson's Column, erected in the 1840s to celebrate the victory of Nelson at the Battle of Trafalgar in 1805. The statue of Nelson on the top of his pillar is 17 feet high, and the overall height of the column 185 feet. Four massive lions by the popular Victorian artist, Sir Edwin Landseer, guard the base of the monument, which is decorated with four huge bronze panels, cast from French guns captured in the battles of St. Vincent, Aboukir Bay, Copenhagen and Trafalgar—and which depict scenes from the same battles. The fountains are fairly modern, the old ones having been sent as presents to the Canadian Government; one is happily ensconced in Regina, Saskatchewan.

There are pigeons everywhere, and also many photographers, equipped with birdseed to entice the semi-tame birds to settle on snap-happy tourists. Trafalgar Square is a focal point for rallies, marches and political meetings; on evenings of high jinks and celebrations, crowds throng the square, and even on cold winter nights—like Bonfire Night or New Year's Eve, though the latter can be dangerous. In 1982 two people were killed and 502 injured during the celebrations, since when stricter crowd control has had to be exercised. At Christmastime a huge tree, the gift of the people of Norway, is set up in the Square and forms a focus for carol singers and other seasonal entertainment. It is the delightful way that the Norwegians have chosen to remember the help given them by the British during the Second World War.

The north side of the square is formed by the long, low National Gallery, housing the national collection of art and containing some of the world's greatest paintings. An extension, opened in 1975, allows for more of the priceless collection to be put on show. An excellent guide to the collections has been published which should prove a very useful *vade mecum* when faced with the seemingly endless rooms of masterpieces. Even if you can only spend a short time here, try to do so, the collection of Rembrandt's works alone would justify a quick visit. The collection is very well hung and lit, especially in the newer rooms.

Outside the Gallery, on the grass verges, stand two small statues. At one end is the luckless James II in Roman dress, sculpted by his contemporary Grinling Gibbons; at the other is George Washington, a replica of the famous statue by Houdon at Richmond, Virginia, presented to Britain by the Commonwealth of Virginia in 1921.

Across from the end of the National Gallery is St. Martin-in-the-Fields, built in the 1720s to the design of James Gibbs. It is a church not only beautiful in its architecture, but actively carrying on a Christian tradition of caring for the poor and destitute (though itself needing funds for essential repairs and refurbishment). It has also made a great reputation for itself round the world as a "radio church."

Opposite St. Martin's is the National Portrait Gallery, tucked in behind the National Gallery itself. This is an unusual gallery, specializing in British portraiture down the centuries. Of late it has expanded into photographic records and caricature as well, in an effort to bring together in one place the faces of the known and the unknown in British life. The display techniques are excellent and the special exhibitions that are regularly organized here are well worth visiting.

Just above St. Martin's is a Post Office with a philatelic counter selling all the latest British commemorative issues.

Running up from the Post Office is St. Martin's Lane, a fairly narrow street full of theaters, restaurants and bookshops. The first theater on the right is the Coliseum, now home of the English National Opera Company, where opera in English is performed during most of the year and visiting ballet companies fill the weeks when the Opera is on tour. Off the Lane, to right and left, are small "courts" or alleys, full of bookshops. Mozart stayed in Cecil Court, on the left, in 1764. Goodwin's Court, on the right, has a row of delightful old bow-fronted shops, now converted into offices. At a junction of seven streets lies the Arts Council shop, just inside Long Acre. It has a wonderful collection of postcards, posters, books and pamphlets—all concerning the arts in Britain.

Soho and Leicester Square

A swing to westwards now will take you through Soho, back to Piccadilly Circus. Soho is conveniently regarded as being bounded by Shaftesbury Avenue, Charing Cross Road, Oxford Street and Regent Street, making a small, nearly square area, its geometry emphasized by the way in which the streets run east to west or north to south, crossing each other neatly, a very unusual system for London where the streets are normally like a tangle of spaghetti. It is associated with food, foreigners and sin, the latter much overrated.

The development of Soho as a place of dubious reputation came late. The food aspect arrived only early in the present century, the sin label even later. Originally, the district was developed (residentially) after the Great Fire of London in 1666, when many people wanted new homes. The parish of St. Anne was formed out of St. Martin's in 1686, and splendid streets and squares of great houses rose. Earlier it had been a hunting spot, which is where the name derives from, *So! Ho!* being a call of the field. Historically and architecturally, it should be one of London's glories, but it isn't. Most of the original houses have been demolished over the centuries, many going when Shaftesbury Avenue was laid out.

But the atmosphere is intriguing. There is a high density of continental residents, which means a variety of food shops, delicatessens and, naturally, one or two of London's best foreign restaurants. There is, too, a continental feeling, with cosmopolitan newspaper shops, a freedom about the pubs and a general air of happy drifting. At night comes the neon, and the slouching figures in doorways tout for strip shows. There are many such dives and clubs, most of them squalid and unattractive. Soho has for long been a haunt of the underworld and is reported to have more porno movie houses than there are legitimate cinemas in the whole of the West End—though latterly there has been something of a moral backlash directed at some of the worst excesses.

Curiously, the east-west streets are more interesting than the north-south ones. The latter, though boasting a few clubs and restaurants, are dull, full of offices and the headquarters of film companies. The lateral streets, however, are lined with shops and restaurants and you will still find hidden 18th-century gems.

Just off the Regent Street side of the area is Golden Square, architecturally dull, but with perhaps one house indicating its 18th-century grace. Nearby is Carnaby Street, which became a synonym in the '60s for swinging youth. It is now a depressing, dirty mess, without a shred of Beatle magic left. Some of the side streets, however, are worth exploring for such shops as the Craftsmen Potters Assoc. on Marshall Street.

The other main square is Soho Square, near the Oxford Street side—again fairly dull, though it has an early-1700s statue of Charles II and a small rustic tool shed in the middle (about 1870). Elsewhere, the main part of the church of St. Anne, on Wardour Street, was destroyed by bombing in 1940, but the tower remains. There are some interesting pubs and colorful street markets, selling some of the best fruit, meat and vegetables in London.

Shaftesbury Avenue cuts through the southern part of Soho; this is the main street for theaters. Between this street and Coventry Street, Soho still runs but here a small Chinatown changes the atmosphere from Mediterranean to Oriental.

Below Shaftesbury Avenue lies Leicester Square, another center of entertainment, this time cinemas. At the end of the last century it was famous for its music-halls, now either demolished or turned over to the movies. The square has been paved and converted into a pedestrian-only zone, except for one side where the confused traffic can filter past. But, however smart the new paving is and however pretty the new flower tubs, it is impossible to avoid the fact that it is more than just a little bit insalubrious these days, with hotdog stands, cheap bars and a general air of sleazy honky-tonk. Shakespeare stands on his plinth in the middle of it all, chin on hand, clearly wishing he were somewhere else. In one corner of the square stands the new statue of one of London's favorite sons—even if he did spend the majority of his life elsewhere—Sir Charles Chaplin, Charlie to his friends. It's one of the few fun statues in London, placed in position in 1981 and sculpted by John Doubleday.

Quite close to Chaplin's statue is a booth for cut-price theater tickets. A vital place for theater lovers, especially those on tight budgets.

Piccadilly

Taking Piccadilly Circus as the starting point once again, the next walk should be along Piccadilly itself. Piccadilly is a rather strange amalgam of sophisticated shopping and tree-bordered avenue, half and half. The first stretch, from Piccadilly Circus to the Ritz, is the home of several famous shops, making the northern edge of the St. James's area.

The first building to notice, on the left, is St. James's Church. This is one of Wren's churches and betrays its origin in every elegant line. It was built between 1676 and 1684 but damaged in the blitz of the winter 1940–41. There is much lovely craftsmanship in the interior, including a limewood reredos by Grinling Gibbons, the sculptor of the statue of James II in Trafalgar Square. He also carved the organ case and font. The new spire (made of plastic!) was added as late as 1968. The area around the church has been designed as a garden where the passer-by can rest in the middle of a busy day. St. James's also houses a brass rubbing center, where the visitor can take his own brass rubbings from specially made copies, thus preserving the original tombs from erosion by elbow-grease.

The next few blocks on both sides contain many well-known stores and the headquarters of such airlines as Air France. Among the shops are Simpson's, excellent for men's wear; Hatchards, one of the best bookshops anywhere; Fortnum and Mason's stocking fine food. Fortnum's have a small restaurant, down the side and on a corner, which is a comfortable spot for mid-sightseeing lunches or pre-theater dinners. Also on the south side of Piccadilly, and about here, is the Piccadilly Arcade, not so large or well-known as its big brother, the Burlington Arcade, opposite, but still worth investigating.

The north side of Piccadilly, in this reach, has three major points of interest. There is a small courtyard which is the entrance to Albany. This is an extremely exclusive set of apartments, built in the early 1770s and extended in 1803. Over the years many famous people have lived there from Byron and Gladstone to Edward Heath. Just beyond Albany stands the massive bulk of Burlington House, the home of the Royal Academy of Arts and six other learned societies (Antiquaries, Geological, Royal Society etc.). There is a statue of Sir Joshua Reynolds in the forecourt; he was the first President of the Academy. Burlington House now houses some of the most prestigious loan exhibitions, as well as the famous—or infamous, depending upon your artistic point of view— Summer Exhibitions. These are massive affairs, open to all comers. The Academy selection committees have broadened their horizons immeasurably of recent years, but the modernity on view is, for the most part, heavily imitative. There are some fine works in the permanent collection, but the prize, now on regular public view, is a tondo (a bas-relief disc) by Michelangelo, called the *Madonna Taddei*.

Running up beside Burlington House is the Burlington Arcade, a long, covered lane of delightful wee shops. This is the place to wander through on a wet day, or to search for that slightly extravagant present to take home with you. Most of the shops stock British-crafted goods.

A slight detour is in order here. If you turn right when you leave the top of the Burlington Arcade, you will find the Museum of Mankind, the popular name for the British Museum's Department of Ethnography (and a popular name doesn't come amiss!), housed at the back of Burlington House. The Museum contains a good part of the British Museum's collection of Aztec, Mayan, African and other ethnic artifacts. They are very imaginatively displayed and worth visiting. There are exhibitions, from time to time, of a particular ethnographic theme.

Back on Piccadilly, shops, airline offices (including that of Aeroflot with a cooly conceived statue by Elizabeth Frink outside) fill the next few blocks until the Ritz Hotel looms on the left. From here, all the way to Hyde Park Corner the south side of Piccadilly is taken up by Green Park, around 53 acres of quietness that has a very French feel about it, reinforced by avenues and decorative wrought-iron gates. The Piccadilly railings are festooned with art for sale at weekends; it gives a colorful, slightly raffish air to the normally staid street.

At the end of Piccadilly you will reach Hyde Park Corner, a huge, busy junction of several major roads. The center of the traffic whirl is occupied by a well-laid-out island of surprising tranquility, containing a couple of rather good statues—including a fine *David* by Derwent Wood on a memorial to the Machine Gun Corps—and the Constitution Arch, a triumphal arch which was originally intended to act as a sort of monumental back gate to Buckingham Palace. It used to have a huge statue of Wellington on the top of it, a pair for Nelson on his column, but in 1912 the present Victory in her chariot took his place. It also houses London's smallest—and most unlikely—Police Station.

This is Wellington country, for just across from the Arch, beside the entrance to Hyde Park, stands Apsley House, the Wellington Musuem. It was originally built in the 1770's, but Wellington did a great deal to it after the British Government had bought it for him in 1816. It is full of memorabilia of the Iron Duke, some of it attractive, but much consisting of heavy ornate pieces more impressive than beautiful.

Mayfair

Broadly speaking, the confines of Mayfair are drawn by Regent Street, Oxford Street, Park Lane and Piccadilly. The main interest of this area lies in its fine shops, beautiful residential houses and squares. As it represents all that is gracious in London living and shopping, there is an air of wealthy leisure, even on the busiest days. In the 17th century, Mayfair was a quiet country spot, popular as a residential area away from the bustle of Westminster and the City.

The western limit of Mayfair is Park Lane, which faces Hyde Park, and which once was synonymous with high living and beautiful houses. Most have now been demolished to be replaced by hotels. Here are the Inter-Continental (next to Apsley House), the Inn on the Park, the Hilton, the Dorchester, Londonderry House and Grosvenor House. These tall buildings have created an entirely new problem for the royal family, whose garden, secluded behind its high brick wall and groves of trees, is now not quite as private as it used to be. At the north end of Park Lane is Marble Arch, another traffic whirlpool, where you will find, on the park side, Speakers' Corner, a space specially reserved for anyone with anything to say that they *must* say publicly. Great entertainment for a Sunday afternoon.

Marble Arch itself is not particularly impressive; it used to stand in the forecourt of Buckingham Palace, until brought to this spot in 1850, near the place where once stood the public gallows known as Tyburn Tree.

In Mayfair three blocks east of Park Lane, is Grosvenor Square and the American Embassy. The large, graceful square, laid out in 1725, has in its center Sir W. Reid Dick's memorial statue to President Franklin D. Roosevelt, erected in 1948. The British had an especially soft spot for Roosevelt and they demonstrated it by the way they raised the money to pay for this statue; the open subscription list was limited to entries of only five shillings, and the whole amount was gathered in next to no time. Eero Saarinen designed the embassy, which takes up the entire west side of the square, often called "Little America" by Londoners. When the building first went up, there were some wry comments about the huge eagle poised over the facade as if waiting to pounce. But it has long since become the big brother of the London pigeons. John Adams, first American ambassador to Britain and second president of the United States, lived in the house at the corner of Brook and Duke Streets here.

Another spot of considerable charm within this area is Shepherd Market (lying between Piccadilly and Curzon Street; turn off Piccadilly at White Horse Street), a network of narrow streets with some attractive houses and fascinating shops. There are no sheep here, but a couple of rousing pubs and the vestiges of what was once London's leading red-light district (recently the area has been making strong claims to regain this title). There is also Berkeley Square, where the nightingale sang, with some good hotels and distinguished night spots. Berkeley Square, still beautiful with its fine trees and gardens, was once one of London's most distinguished residential centers. Robert Walpole, his son Horace, Charles James Fox, and Clive of India lived here; as much as two million pounds has been asked for one of the houses.

Going still further east, towards Piccadilly Circus, you will come to Bond Street. Divided into two sections, New and Old, Bond Street is the home of more luxury shops. Many of the internationally-known names like Asprey's are here, as well as some of the foremost art dealers, and the great auction house of Sotheby's. The Time and Life building stands at the corner of New Bond Street and Bruton Street. This was one of the major buildings of the 1950s, and has some panels carved by Henry Moore in the facade, as well as one of his statues. The Bond Street area forms an interesting counterpart to St. James's, on the other side of Piccadilly; both, in their own way, wonderful areas for spending happy hours window shopping, though Bond Street has a definite edge where international shops are concerned. In case you wonder just why a street that is apparently continuous should be divided into "Old" and "New," the answer is quite simple. Old Bond Street was created around 1690 and New Bond Street some twenty years later. Somehow a slightly snobbish air of superiority clings to the elder brother.

The next major thoroughfare to the east is Regent Street. If you walk there along Burlington Gardens, you will pass the Museum of Mankind, already mentioned. There are several interesting commercial art galleries in the surrounding streets.

Regent Street is impressively wide and curving, running from Piccadilly Circus to Oxford Circus. It was originally conceived by John Nash as a triumphal way connecting the palace of the Prince Regent with Regent's Park. The Prince Regent, who became George IV, was a man of considerable taste and imagination, (as the Pavilion in Brighton witnesses), but little staying power. The original scheme went through many changes and not much of it survives today. The present street, sweeping away almost all of Nash's work, was built in the early years of this century in an empty grandiose fashion. It is now the haunt of those airlines that are not located on Piccadilly and some excellent stores, especially Liberty's, with its mixture of styles and feeling of the elegant '20s inside. The Regent Street frontage is surmounted by impressive carvings and a 115-ft. frieze celebrating trade with exotic places. Round the corner in Great Marlborough Street, the mock Tudor façade masks a rich interior, partly built from the carved timbers of two old fighting ships, the *Hindustan* and the *Impregnable,* which were broken up in 1921. There is a large oil painting of them in the bridge on the second floor, immediately behind the animated clock.

Oxford Street

The north limit of Mayfair is Oxford Street, a long straight shopping thoroughfare containing many department stores and shops of all kinds. It begins on the east at Tottenham Court Road, and continues to Marble Arch.

There are very few visitors to London these days who do not do the obligatory stint of Oxford Street shopping, especially at Marks and Spencer's or Selfridges. Unless you manage to begin your expedition there early in the day it is likely to prove a very exhausting experience indeed. And not merely exhausting, but frustrating, too. Apart from the main points along the street—such as John Lewis, with its great stock of yard goods, or H.M.V. simply bursting with discs and tapes—a great deal of the merchandise on offer is the same endless cheap jeans at high prices and many of the shops, cheek-by-jowl with the reputable stores, are get-rich-quick enterprises to beware of.

Turn up at the westerly corner of Selfridges and you come shortly to Baker Street, a place of pilgrimage for admirers of the greatest detective of all, though you'll look in vain for the house where Sherlock Holmes "lived." The Abbey National Building Society, at Holmes' address, however, still deals with many letters every year addressed to the sleuth from all over the world. In Manchester Square, off the bottom of Baker Street to the east, was the town house of the Marquis of Hertford, now the home of the Wallace Collection. Attractively redecorated, it contains some of the most delicate and beautiful things in any London museum. Among the joys of the collection are Limoges enamels, paintings by Fragonard, Boucher and Watteau, and much French furniture. While much more extensive, the Wallace Collection is the London counterpart of the Frick, having similar treasures and being a gallery to which no additions are made.

Turn back down to Wigmore Street and walk east to Harley Street which is mainly devoted to medicine; most of Britain's greatest specialists have their consulting rooms there. High on a wall in Cavendish Square, just behind John Lewis department store, is the *Madonna and Child,* one of the most moving sculptures by Jacob Epstein.

North of Soho Square and Oxford Street is the Post Office Tower (now known as British Telecom Tower), at 619 feet London's tallest building. This is a landmark that can be seen from all over London, and can act as a useful pointer if you manage to lose yourself. For a top-to-bottom view of it stand at the junction of Great Portland and Clipstone Streets.

Hyde Park and Kensington Gardens

After wandering for so long among buildings, it would be relaxing to spend some time among trees, although it must be said that one is never very far from trees in London. Not only are many streets lined with them, but all the squares are islands of greenery. The cleaning-up of London's terrible pollution has helped greatly to give the multitude of trees a new lease of life. Except for the ugly gaps left by the death of so many elms from Dutch elm disease, London's parks have never looked so healthy.

London has developed, over the centuries, an awareness of the importance of having wide, green spaces in the center of the city. They are frequently called "London's lungs." St. James's Park, Green Park and Buckingham Palace Gardens make a large open swathe in the middle of central London; this is continued westwards by Hyde Park and Kensington Gardens, which together make many hundreds of acres of space to play in, walk babies and dogs, lie in the sun, boat, swim, make love and generally romp about. London takes advantage of this opportunity and Hyde Park is a focal point for relaxation. You can walk steadily for two or three hours among trees and flowers, all the way from Kensington Palace to the Houses of Parliament (or vice versa), with only a couple of ventures into the real world of London traffic, and be all the time in the very heart of the metropolis.

The main gate to Hyde Park is Decimus Burton's screen at the south end of Park Lane, just by Apsley House. To the left is Rotten Row,

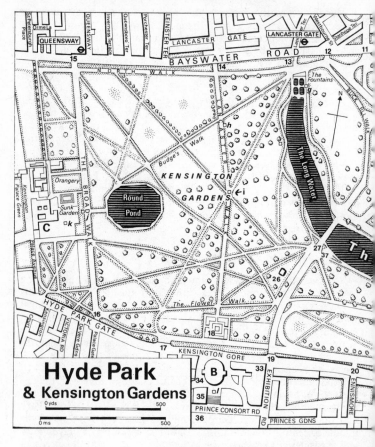

Hyde Park
& Kensington Gardens

0 yds ————— 500

0 ms ————— 500

Hyde Park

& Kensington

Gardens

A Apsley House
(Wellington
Museum)

B Albert Hall

C Kensington Palace

1. Hyde Park Corner Decimus Burton
   Screen. Main Entrance
2. Stanhope Gate
3. Grosvenor Gate
4. Underground Car Park
5. Speakers' Corner
6. Marble Arch
7. Cumberland Gate
8. Stanhope Gate
9. Albion Gate
10. Clarendon Gate
11. Victoria Gate
12. Westbourne Gate

13. Marlborough Gate
14. Lancaster Gate
15. Black Lion Gate
16. Palace Gate
17. Queen's Gate
18. Albert Memorial
19. Alexandra Gate
20. Prince of Wales Gate
21. Edinburgh Gate
22. Albert Gate
23. Bird Sanctuary
24. Police Station
25. Ring Tea House

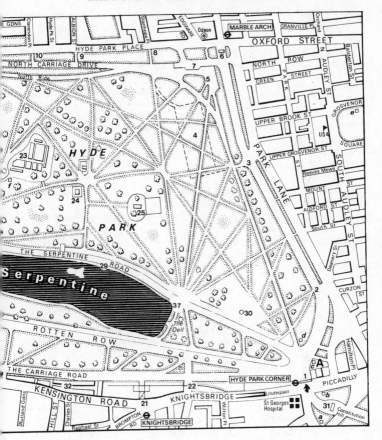

26. Serpentine Gallery (The Temple)
27. Rennie's Bridge
28. The Lido Bathing Station
29. Boats for hire
30. Band Stand
31. Wellington Arch
32. Knightsbridge Barracks
33. Royal Geographical Society
34. Royal College of Art
35. Imperial College
36. Royal College of Music
37. Cafeterias

Statues etc.

a. Artillery Memorial
b. Wellington
c. Byron
d. Achilles
e. Roosevelt
f. Rima: Hudson Memorial
g. Edward Jenner
h. Speke Memorial
i. Physical Energy
j. Queen Victoria
k. William III
l. Prince Albert

a sand track for horse riders who use it daily. The paths either side of the Row have always been a popular strolling place, particularly on Sundays after church, in the days when Londoners still went to church. Today you will find the park much less fashionable than of old—mostly because elegant lounging is out of fashion. But there are still riders on the Row, and you can join them by hiring a horse from one of the livery stables scattered in the areas adjacent to the park.

A little way into the park, by Hyde Park Corner, is the statue of Achilles, standing twenty feet high on a mound which raises him even higher. It was yet another tribute to Wellington, this time paid for by subscriptions from the women of Britain. The assembled ladies must have been rather shaken when, in 1822, this colossal nude, cast from the metal of guns captured in some of the Duke's famous victories, was finally unveiled.

Running across both parks, Hyde Park and Kensington Gardens, is a crescent of water called the Serpentine in Hyde Park and Long Water in Kensington Gardens. The poet Shelley liked sailing paper boats on the Serpentine. He once made himself one from a banknote which, luckily, was blown back to him. Less luckily, his first wife, Harriet Westbrook, drowned herself here. Peter Pan, the hero of J. M. Barrie's play annually revived at Christmas, lived on an island in the Serpentine, and on the bank of Long Water is the famous statue of him. Barrie lived at 100 Bayswater Road, just north of where the statue stands.

Strolling along the edge of the Serpentine is one of the most delightful of all rural pleasures that London can offer. At any season of the year the lake has its own atmosphere; in the summer it is almost a seaside scene, the grass thronged with deck chairs and couples strewn thick as leaves, the water busy with boats and swimmers; in winter it is a scene of gentle melancholy, the trees bare medieval traceries against the grey sky, the water feathered by swooping gulls, the wandering couples fewer, but still as self-absorbed.

Past the bathing place you will arrive at the bridge that carries the main, bisecting road. It is a lovely construction, built in 1826 by George Rennie and looks like a stage setting come to life among the trees, especially at night. It is also one of the best points to view the skyline of Westminster to the southeast. At the southern end of the bridge is a restaurant and bar. It makes a very useful point to rest for a spell and watch the life of the park. There is another snack bar at the eastern end of the Serpentine. You should be warned, though, that the standards of food are not very high.

Once across the main road—and it isn't always that easy to cross it—you are in Kensington Gardens. It was once part of the private purlieus of Kensington Palace and had been enthusiastically landscaped by Queen Caroline, wife of George II, who created most of the present features. The long avenue that runs right across the bottom of Hyde Park, Rotten Row, now used exclusively for horse riding, is so called from the fact that it was the route taken by the king's carriage when going to Kensington Palace from Westminster—the English name is a corruption of *route du roi*. It must have looked very attractive with hundreds of lamps hung in the trees to light the king's way.

Just inside Kensington Gardens, on the left, stands the 175-foot-high Albert Memorial. This monument to Victoria's reverence for her dead husband was for many years considered as the most grotesquely ugly landmark in the whole country. Tastes change, and there is a growing affection for this exuberantly eclectic "memorial of our Blameless Prince." The designer was Sir Gilbert Scott, who, quite seriously, intended to build a "kind of ciborium . . . to protect the statue of the Prince." So there Albert sits, under his canopy, like a fragment of the true cross, or one of St. Vitus's toebones in a Gothic shrine. In a way the whole memorial is a symbol of the South Kensington complex that lies across the road, from the Albert Hall down to the Victoria and Albert Museum (*see* the section on South Kensington), for the plinth of the memorial is decorated with carefully accurate portrait-figures of poets, composers, architects and sculptors, drawn from all ages and lands. The corners have four marble groups symbolising Agriculture, Manufacture, Commerce and Engineering—the Victorians loved to convert abstract concepts into stone—another four groups take up the outside corners, this time dividing the world in a thoroughly Kiplingesque way, Asia, Europe, Africa and America.

From just above the Memorial, a Flower Walk angles westwards. This is a superbly kept area of flower beds, with many changes of plants during the year. It makes an ideal spot for a gentle walk on a spring or autumn day.

In the avenues and paths that lie to the north of the Flower Walk you will find several statues. We have already mentioned the delicate little one of Peter Pan by the Long Water. The most impressive is called *Physical Energy*. It is actually a version of the main figure in the Cecil Rhodes Memorial, near Cape Town, and stands in Kensington Gardens as an explosion of power at the point where several paths cross. It is one of the very few massive statues in London that reflects an idea rather than commemorates a military or civic bigwig.

Kensington Palace stands at the western edge of the Gardens. The palace was the residence of the reigning sovereign until 1760, when George II died. It has been altered by two great architects, Wren and William Kent. Queen Victoria was born here and also Queen Mary. Present residents include Princess Margaret and the Prince and Princess of Wales. Victoria was told of her accession to the throne here, and there is a statue of her by her own daughter, Princess Louise, outside facing the Round Pond, where children of all ages sail toy boats.

This is no pompous palace, it has none of the grand architectural features which characterize the major palaces of the world; this is the next best thing to a bourgeois palace there is; in English terms a slightly bigger version of the normal country house. The state apartments are open to the public and contain some excellent paintings as well as many mementos of Queen Victoria. Queen Mary, who was born here, as we have said, was a royal collector. One of her major interests was in collecting pieces which had once been in the royal possession or which had connections with the crown. The palace now houses a collection of court dress too, some 60 costumes dating from the 18th century to the 1970s are displayed in these evocative surroundings. The exhibition can be seen at the same time as the State Apartments.

Kensington

Even in these democratic days, one occasionally hears someone say that the *only* area where one could *possibly* live in London is "north of the river and south of the park." The park is Hyde Park, the area, the Royal Borough of Kensington (amalgamated with raffish Chelsea). Though the district has many contrasting facets, this really sums up the basic tone: it is a grand residential area. Unfortunately, many of the rather pompous houses have been broken up into flats, but the feeling of stuccoed wealth, the pillared porches and tree-filled squares remain.

It was King William III who, socially speaking, really put Kensington on the map. "The Smoak of the Coal Fires of London much incommoded his Majesty," wrote a contemporary, "who was always troubled with asthma and could not bear lying in town." The king found the Thames mists that frequently veiled Whitehall particularly trying. So, in 1689, he bought Nottingham House, as it was then called, rurally sited in the village of Kensington, and there he was able to lie comfortably in state. Renamed Kensington Palace, and enlarged from time to time, it still acts as the spiritual heart of the neighborhood.

With the arrival of royalty the village "flourished almost beyond belief," according to a chronicler writing in 1705. Court personages hastened to follow the royal example, and Kensington Square (just behind Barker's department store) was built to accommodate them. In the reign of Anne, the demand for lodging became so pressing that at one time an ambassador, a bishop and a physician occupied apartments in the same house in the square. With the court and society came the wits and the men of letters.

Immediately behind the palace runs Kensington Palace Gardens (called Palace Green at the south end), a wide avenue of large houses set in their own grounds and mostly the work of the leading architects of the 1850s and '60s. Thackeray, the novelist and author of *Vanity Fair,* died at No. 2, in a house he had built. This is one of the few private roads in London, with a uniformed guard at either end, and its secluded nature makes it ideal for foreign embassies. There are several here. At the northern end the Czechs have built an interesting one, and closeby the Russians preserve their anonymity.

Just past the towering, modern Royal Garden Hotel runs Kensington Church Street. With St. Mary Abbots Church on the corner (which, although it looks properly medieval was, in fact, built in the 1870s by the same architect who designed the Albert Memorial) this is territory for the antique enthusiast. All the way up this winding road are antique shops, specializing in everything from Japanese armor to Victorian commemorative china. Tucked away behind the Church is Kensington Church Walk (go down Holland Street, take the second on the left), which is a microcosm of the area, containing tiny shops full of dolls and prints, pottery and pictures. Holland Street, itself, is pretty, with an excellent pub and a tiny little flowered cul de sac almost opposite. A little farther on is the brick bulk of the municipal offices, modern and massive.

If you walk along Kensington High Street, now a busy and flourishing, if slightly tacky, shopping area, you will come to the Commonwealth Institute, with a huge, tentlike copper roof, standing back from the street in its own spacious grounds. Although the Commonwealth concept is shrinking at a rate of knots, this Institute is very much alive, with excellent, attractively displayed exhibits, frequent concerts and film shows and a general air of international goodwill.

Behind the Institute lies the park of Holland House. The house itself was mostly destroyed by incendiary bombs during the Second World War, but the grounds have been preserved, with their peacocks and roses. The house was first built in Tudor times and was the lively center for artists and wits during the residence of the third Baron Holland between 1773 and 1840. The brilliant circle was largely attracted there by his wife, a dynamic hostess and, like many of the breed, an impossible woman. Among the notables who frequented the house were Talleyrand, Humboldt, Gladstone, Macaulay (who described the circle in his essay on Lord Holland) and Metternich. The Garden Ballroom— one of the few parts of the house remaining—now houses an attractive restaurant, especially good for summer dining.

A little further along the High Street, on the other side, is Edwardes Square. It was developed around 1802 by a Frenchman named Changier—in perfect taste, though entirely English in atmosphere and architecture. The story goes that Changier was really one of Napoleon's agents and as such built the square to house the Corsican's civil servants after England had been successfuly invaded!

A little way past the Commonwealth Institute, on the same side of the High Street, is a turning, Melbury Road, that leads to Holland Park Road. Here, at No. 12, lived Lord Leighton, the Victorian painter *par excellence.* You can still recapture some of the exotic richness of the artistic life of the last half of the 19th century in the interior decorations here, especially in the Arab Hall, lavishly lined with Persian tiles and woodwork.

On the other, eastern, side of the Commonwealth Institute is Linley Sambourne House, at 18 Stafford Terrace, a little masterpiece of Victoriana. Managed by the Victorian Society, this fascinating survival was sold intact to the City of London by the Countess of Rosse, mother of Lord Snowdon, the granddaughter of Mr. Sambourne, who built and furnished the place in the 1870s. For anyone interested in the Victorian era, it's a must. (Note that groups are catered for by appointment only.)

South Kensington

Although it is not generally recognised by visitors as such, partly because it covers such a large area, the district that runs southwards from Kensington Gardens to the Cromwell Road is a huge cultural complex, probably the most extensive and comprehensive in the world. It was planned as such by the Victorians, and it is no accident that Albert the Good sits pensively under his canopy, looking down on such a magnificent tribute to his own considerable achievements.

It is perhaps best to begin from the Brompton Road, having, with unlikely self-discipline, passed Harrods. On the right is the Brompton Oratory, a very Italianate Roman Catholic church, inside and out. It was built in that mid-Victorian period when the English Catholics, who had suffered eclipse and worse for centuries, were emerging into the light of tolerance. A clue to the quality of the meaning of that renaissance is given by the gentle statue of Cardinal Newman outside, for he was the standard bearer of the vast upsurge in Catholic activity.

The next building is the Victoria and Albert Museum, cliff-like and surmounted by cupolas and a structure like a cross between a crown and a wedding-cake. This is the heart of the whole area. It would seem strange that there can be two museums such as the British Museum and the V&A in the same city, but they really do serve two fairly distinct purposes. In some realms they overlap a little, as with drawings and water-colours, but the main function of the V&A is to act as a "Museum of Ornamental Art," with the object of "the application of fine art to objects of utility and the improvement of public taste in design." It is essentially a teaching museum, heavily committed to design from every age and country. As such it has an unrivalled collection in many spheres, and one can spend hours wandering through its endless rooms, surrounded on all sides by the most lovely things from France, Italy, the East and, of course, Britain itself. Arm yourself with a plan when you go in, if you don't you may feel utterly bewildered.

The collection is so vast, and so rich, that it is difficult to pick out some of the most exciting elements. The paintings of Constable rank very high on any list; the jewel rooms, especially the massive baroque jewels; the delicate miniatures, with some of the loveliest painted in Elizabeth I's reign; the medieval church art, with its elaborate workmanship and occasional glimpses into a world haunted by the fear of death and damnation; a profusion of Renaissance art, especially a series of magnificent Raphael cartoons; costumes from many periods, excellently exhibited in the Costume Hall; musical instruments bewildering in their complexity and craftsmanship, and frequently played in fascinating recitals; Chinese, Islamic, Indian art . . . the list is endless. A newly-opened wing, the Henry Cole, round the corner in Exhibition Road, gives a chance for even more of the collection to be displayed. In the main building there is a functional cafeteria.

Next to the V&A come the three museums devoted to science, the Natural History Museum, the Geological Museum and the Science Museum itself. These are extremely informative especially for young people, who find the working models and the detailed explanatory displays absorbing. If you go there with children of school age be fully prepared to spend the rest of the day!

Across the road from the front entrance to the V&A is a brand new building which is rather unexpected in this heartland of Victorian London—the Ismaili Center. With strong Moslem elements, this hybrid structure is a place of meeting and worship for London's large Ismaili community and was opened by Margaret Thatcher in 1985.

Exhibition Road, the wide road which runs up beside the V&A, will take you back to Kensington Gardens through the heart of this cultural complex. On the left is the Imperial College of Science, now part of London University. On the right is a large Mormon Chapel, with a thin spike covered in gold leaf.

To the left runs Prince Consort Road, and, above it, the Royal Albert Hall, scene of the summer series of Promenade Concerts which will celebrate their 92nd birthday in 1986. These concerts, sponsored by the BBC, are one of the most comprehensive festivals of music in the world, eight weeks of international music-making with a concert every day. The vast, circular interior of the Hall used to have an abominable echo, it was said that the visitor got two concerts for the price of one. But science is a wonderful thing; after much experimentation, the dome was turned into a parking lot for flying saucers and now even Wagner, let alone Mahler, can be enjoyed at their normally excessive (but not doubly excessive) length. The huge amphitheater, resplendent in wine-red and gold, is a truly Victorian temple to Art and Science.

Chelsea

Begin your exploration in Sloane Square, where the Royal Court Theatre stands. In the area surrounding the Square are the quiet, rich residential streets of Belgravia and, on Sloane Street, the Cadogan Hotel, where Oscar Wilde was arrested and taken to prison. Westward from the Square runs the King's Road—packed with boutiques, bistros and antique shops. This is the road to visit on Saturdays from about noon onwards, when the pavement is crowded with a jean-clad army, strengthened by punk platoons, bristling with pink and green hair. It long ago lost the attractive look it had when it superseded Carnaby Street, but it can still offer intriguing shopping, especially for clothes. Streets leading south from the King's Road bring you to the Chelsea Embankment; those to the north lead to Kensington.

The most interesting part of the King's Road is not the section from Sloane Square to the Town Hall, but the stretch beyond that. Here there are good small restaurants, lots of excellent antique shops and places to browse in for ages. The walk could well be a long one, for the road continues all the way to Putney Bridge (becoming New King's Road en route).

For the visitor the joys of Chelsea lie in the area south of the King's Road, and the main of these joys is the Chelsea Hospital. The easiest way to reach it is to turn left down Cheltenham Terrace, just past the Duke of York's Barracks, continue down Franklin's Row and there the Hospital is, straight ahead. It was built around 1690 by Sir Christopher Wren as a refuge for old and disabled soldiers. It had the seal of approval of Charles II, though the happy legend that it owed its origin to his mistress, Nell Gwynn, is sadly not true. There is a fine statue of the Merry Monarch by our old friend Grinling Gibbons in the grounds. The statue is decked with oak leaves on the 29th of May each year, Oak Apple Day, in commemoration of the time when Charles hid in an oak tree to escape the troops of Oliver Cromwell.

The Hospital is a peaceful place, and one can understand why it is that old soldiers never die but only fade away; it would be a fine spot to fade in. The building itself is worth visiting, it is open to the public in the mornings and afternoons, and the manicured grounds are ideal for strolling about. In the spring each year, the Chelsea Flower Show is held here. Garden-lovers (who rival dog-lovers in Britain for their ubiquity) troop to the Show to see the latest improvements in gardening and to carry away samples and ideas.

The comparatively new National Army Museum is just past the Hospital, on Royal Hospital Road. This museum celebrates the exploits and achievements of the Army from 1485 to 1914. It is an excellently conceived display, and for anyone who finds the progress of the art of warfare interesting it will prove a rich mine. The sad thing about it is that the outside of the building is monumentally ugly. A couple of blocks further on is the Chelsea Physic Garden, started in 1676 and fascinating to anyone interested in plants and their uses in medicine and cooking. It was from here that the first cotton seeds were sent to Georgia in 1732.

One of the most intriguing parts of Chelsea, especially for the visitor who is attracted to houses with histories, is the long riverside walk from just past the Chelsea Hospital, westwards beyond Battersea Bridge. This street of houses overlooking the river is called Cheyne Walk and has been the haunt of many poets, painters and other assorted notables. Here you will see many of the blue plaques put up all over London to commemorate famous residents. Starting at No. 4 with George Eliot, one continues with Dante Gabriel Rossetti who lived at No. 16 for twenty years, and kept a small zoo in a garden; Scott of the Antarctic lived in Oakley Street, just round the corner; Carlyle, the Victorian pundit, lived in Cheyne Row at No. 24, which is open to the public Wednesday to Sunday; Henry James died in Carlyle Mansions in the First World War; and suddenly one faces one of the area's most famous inhabitants, Sir Thomas More, the Man for All Seasons.

His statue, seated and looking out across the river, is modern, set up in 1969, but it has a strongly Tudor look to it, square, gilded and hierarchic. It portrays More the saint, rather than More the richly, humorous, warm human being. Across the base is carved an enlarged facsimile of More's own signature. The statue stands outside All Saints' Church, which was badly damaged in the blitz, but rebuilt and contains many interesting memorials that survived nearly untouched. This area is full of associations with More and his family, for he lived in Crosby Hall, which was moved from its original site in Bishopsgate and re-erected on the Chelsea Embankment in 1910 on the area that used to be More's orchard. His first wife is buried in All Saints, part of which he designed.

One of the most attractive sights here is the Albert Bridge, an 1873 suspension bridge which, when it is lit up at night, looks like the work of a talented spider with an eye on posterity.

Cheyne Walk continues westwards. It was along here than J. M. W. Turner and Whistler lived (Nos. 118 and 96 respectively). The misty light on the river formed the subject of many of Whistler's best paintings. Turner, who lived here under the name of Booth, was also captivated by the quality of the light, and painted Battersea Bridge, which lay outside his windows.

Regent's Park and the Zoo

We have had one change of pace, walking in Hyde Park, and it is now time to take in another of London's "lungs," Regent's Park.

The park, as its name implies, was laid out for the Prince Regent by John Nash, the work beginning in 1812. The idea was to provide a northern terminus for the stately triumphal way, Regent Street, that was to run from the Prince Regent's house in St. James's to a country villa. The southern edge of the park is still fringed with the lovely Nash terraces that were part of the overall design. They are worth looking at on your way into the park. Walk up Regent Street from Oxford Circus, then into Portland Place at the point where the BBC and All Souls, Langham Place stand. All Souls was created by Nash to act as an exclamation point to the view up Regent Street. It has an attractive, round portico and a high pointy spire, which were much more effective before the competition of surrounding modern blocks dwarfed them.

Portland Place was the work of the Adam brothers, but is now rather a mishmash of styles, including the home of the Institute of British Architects, half-way up on the right hand side. It used to be much reviled, but is now revealed as a 1930s period piece of considerable merit.

The top of Portland Place is Park Crescent, a sweep of Nash buildings, that leads well into the park itself. The damage done by bombing during the Second World War has been repaired and some of the terraces (especially those to the left by Ulster Place on Marylebone Road) have been gutted and rebuilt behind, with the façades carefully preserved.

Enter the park by the gate at the top of Park Square East, just across the road from the Royal College of Physicians building, a strangely effective structure designed by Denys Lasun (who also conceived the new National Theatre). It could easily be taken for a temple of some dark cult.

Once into the park and London drops away like a discarded life; peace (broken only by the distant roar of traffic and lions) will invade you and you will be able to stroll, looking at flowers, to your heart's content. The flowerbeds between this gate and Chester Road which crosses the park are all formal ones. Like those in other London parks, they are regularly restocked as the seasons pass, and you will be able to see some quite stunning displays of, for example, fuschias if you are there at the right time of year. The park also contains a semi-permanent display of large pieces of sculpture by British artists. The main avenue is called the Broad Walk and, geographically, it is a long, leafy continuation of Portland Place.

When you reach Chester Road, turn left and walk towards the Inner Circle. This road is lined with cherry trees which are magnificent for a few weeks in spring. Arriving at the Inner Circle you will be opposite the wrought-iron gates to Queen Mary's Gardens. If you only have time to visit one London park, it is here that you should go. The gardens are not all that large, but within their spherical boundary they contain an incredible variety. Their chief glory comes in May to July when the endless beds of roses are at their peak. The scent and the shadings of color are enough to send the most casual visitor into a Persian dream. Evergreens, heathers, azaleas and much more beside keep the interest going the year round. On an island in a little lake is a Japanese garden, where all sorts of small plants are delicately tended.

The delights of this part of the park are not ended there. Hidden behind a high hedge is the Open Air Theater, where Shakespeare is performed in the middle months of summer. It is a magical setting for the plays, especially those like *A Midsummer Night's Dream* which have an openair theme. The seating is now of a more permanent kind than it used to be, when deck-chairs would lull one into a false sense of security. As the sun sets and the stage lights take over, the sense of being transported to a place of magic is strong. But the evenings can be chill, so go prepared.

There are several ways to reach the Zoo, but the easiest is to return to Chester Road and then turn left on to the continuation of the Broad Walk. It is quite a distance up to the Zoo, after all there are around 470 acres in the park, all told.

The Gardens of the Zoological Society of London are, for good reason, just known as the Zoo. They have been going for over 150 years, absorbing, en route, such collections as that of the royal menagerie, which used to be housed in the Tower of London. The Zoo itself is one of the busiest mazes in the world, and one can wander round in circles for hours, happily taking in the incredible variety of animals living there. Focal points are: firstly the Mappin Terraces which were orginally built some 70 years ago, and were an early experiment in trying to create fairly natural, cageless conditions for such animals as goats, pigs and bears; the Children's Zoo, where children can play with the smaller animals; the Snowdon Aviary, designed by Lord Snowdon in 1965 (this lies across the Canal); the exciting Lion Terraces; the Elephant and Rhino Pavilion (an oddly delicate name for such a massive castle); the Small Bird House and the Tropical House with its darting hummingbirds. One fascinating and unique exhibit is the Moonlight World, on the lower floor of the Charles Clore Pavilion. Here night-time conditions are simulated so that nocturnal animals are busily leading their

The Zoo

1. Main Gate
2. Giant Pandas
3. The Michael Sobell Pavilions for Apes and Monkeys
4. Aquarium Entrance
5. Sheep and Goats
6. Bears
7. Wild Pigs
8. Pelicans
9. Reptile House
10. Stork and Ostrich House
11. Southern Aviary
12. Sealions
13. Wild Dogs
14. Elephant and Rhino Pavilion
15. Seals
16. Penguins
17. Children's Zoo and Farm
18. Lions
19. New Lion Terraces
20. Tigers
21. Water Birds
22. Pheasantry
23. Bird House & Tropical House for Humming Birds
24. Pea Fowl
25. Wolf Wood
26. South Gate & Party Gate
27. Birds of Prey Aviaries
28. Three Island Pond
29. Camel Riding
30. Gibbons
31. Aviary
32. Parrot House
33. British Crows Aviary
34. Flamingos
35. Members' Lawn
36. Eastern Aviary
37. Children's Playground
38. Zoo Shop
39. Society's Meeting Rooms
40. Society's Offices, Enquiries & Lost Property
41. Insect House
42. Otters
43. Great Apes Breeding Colony
44. The Charles Clore Pavilion for Mammals and Moonlight World
45. Waterbus landing stage
46. Beavers
47. Camels & Llamas
48. Giraffes and Zebras
49. Horses and Cattle
50. Deer
51. Antelopes
52. Zoo Study Centres & XYZ Club
53. Snowdon Aviary
54. Pheasantry
55. Owls
56. Cranes & Geese
57. Owls
58. North Gate
59. First Aid and Lost Children
60. Clock Tower

R. Refreshments
☆ Lavatories (female)
★ Lavatories (male)

Regent's Park

1. Clarence Gate
2. Sussex Place
3. Hanover Terrace
4. Hanover Gate
5. Grove House (Nuffield Institute)
6. Winfield House
7. North Gate
8. Regent's Park College
9. Gloucester Gate
10. Cumberland Terrace
11. Chester Terrace
12. Chester Gate
13. York Gate
14. Bedford College
15. The Home
16. Open-Air Theatre
17. University of London Institute
18. Royal College of Physicians
19. Royal College of Obstetricians & Gynaecologists

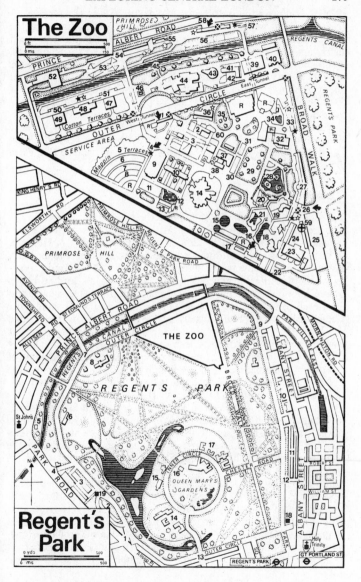

night lives during the outside world's daytime, with the process reversed at night, when the lighting in the cages grows bright and the animals progress to their daytime activities. A visit to the Zoo could last hours and, for an especially interested child, even a whole day. Although it is one of London's major tourist attractions, the Zoo is actually the private gardens of the Royal Zoological Society, which it finds increasingly difficult to finance. The entrance fees for a family plus refreshments are high—though the last year or so has actually seen a reduction in entrance charges in the face of mounting criticism.

Having walked to the Zoo, it might be fun to take a waterbus to Little Venice, near Warwick Crescent. The Regent's Canal (Grand Union Canal) borders the whole northern side of the park, adding that extra dimension of water to all the other attractions.

Bloomsbury

Before the redivision of London into the Greater London Council's new areas, Holborn was a borough. It is now joined with others into the much bigger area called Camden. An important part of Holborn, to the north of Holborn underground station, is called Bloomsbury, associated with students, the university and the self-centered literary set of the twenties (of which Virginia Woolf was the leading light). Bloomsbury consists mainly of a series of beautiful, linked squares and fine streets of 18th-century origin. Not the least remarkable thing is the fact that Bloomsbury Square itself, lined with huge trees, was excavated to a great depth a few years ago and now hides a vast underground car park. Not all recent work has been so well disguised, and much ugly rebuilding has been done during the past 50 years or so. But some of the charm remains. Here can be found the London University, the British Museum and the Courtauld Institute Galleries (the latter destined to move eventually to Somerset House in the Strand).

It is a district of neat squares. Macaulay reports that foreign princes were taken to see it as one of the wonders of England, a veritable "little town." In Bloomsbury Square, Herbert Spencer wrote his *First Principles,* and Sir Hans Sloane started the collection that was to be the nucleus of the British Museum. Steele, the writer, entertained his friends in one of the prim houses—using the bailiffs as waiters. In his youth Disraeli was a resident. And other Bloomsbury squares—Russell, Bedford, Woburn—have had almost equally distinguished pasts.

A suggested itinerary for a walk around Bloomsbury: starting from Holborn underground station, cut north through Red Lion Square (not so pretty, but Dante Gabriel Rossetti lived there) into Theobalds Road, a wide, noisy, boring thoroughfare. Walk east, past Great James Street (a narrow street built in 1722 and a fine example of domestic Georgian architecture—many of the original glazing bars and fanlights remain) until you reach the pleasant greenness of Gray's Inn. Opposite, turn north on John Street, which also contains some good 18th-century houses. In John Street's continuation, Doughty Street, is Dickens' House, where the writer lived from 1837 to 1839. It contains a good library museum and plenty to interest the Dickens' buff.

At the end of Doughty Street, turn left along Guilford Street past Coram's Fields, a children's playground on the site of the Foundling Hospital which was started by Captain Coram, a friend of Handel's. The composer gave proceeds from early performances of *Messiah* to help support the work of the orphanage. Turn left into Lamb's Conduit Street, in which is a pub called The Lamb, interestingly decorated and very crowded indeed in summer. Opposite the pub is a small commercial art gallery, The Workshop, where you can buy cartoons and other drawings and prints very reasonably.

From Lamb's Conduit Street, turn right into Great Ormond Street, with its famous Hospital for Sick Children, through Queen Square (surrounded by hospitals), and through a little walk (beside another charming small pub, The Queen's Larder) westward into Southampton Row. Turn right until you reach Russell Square, very large and full of trees, lawns and fountains. In Montague Place, in the west side of the square, is the back entrance to the British Museum.

The British Museum

There are two ways of approaching the British Museum, either through the wide forecourt on Great Russell Street, where the huge columns of the portico rear up, dwarfing the mere mortals scurrying around below, or through the more matey back-door on Montague Place (just off Russell Square) through which one can insinuate oneself without feeling overawed, though getting through to the front of the Museum from here isn't easy. As we suggested for the V&A, arm yourself with a free ground plan, the place is a maze. The main shop of the Museum, where you can buy posters, postcards, transparencies and so on, is just inside the Great Russell Street entrance.

For the culture vulture, serious or not, the British Museum is a must. Not only is it one of the world's really great museums, but it is also one of the great libraries, and on both scores has been enriched by the natural acquisitiveness of the British over two hundred years. The Library, now known as the British Library, has been hived off from the Museum to become a separate body. While the average visitor is unlikely to be using the Library for study purposes, the displays of manuscripts, bindings and rare printed and illuminated books is always fascinating. The Library benefitted from a gesture made by George II, in 1757, when he gave the Royal Library to the Trustees. Along with the priceless volumes went the right to have a copy of every book published in Britain . . . free. The Reference Division alone has around ten million books, and they still flood in.

A description of a few highlights will introduce the Museum's wealth. First and foremost come the Elgin Marbles, brought from Greece by the seventh Earl of Elgin at the beginning of the 19th century, and now wanted back by the Government of Greece. As the Parthenon itself is in a very bad way, worn by the grossly polluted atmosphere of Athens, these portions of the original carvings, superbly displayed, give a better idea of the detailed artistry of the original sculptors than can be got in Athens. The display techniques now employed at the British Museum have banished for ever the old junk shop feeling that the place used to have. Some of the display cases would do credit to a Fifth Avenue store. One of the sections that has been totally rethought is the Egyptian Collection, always a major part of the Museum, but previously poorly displayed. In the new layout many of the huge figures have taken on a different aspect. The Rosetta Stone, which helped archeologists to interpret Egyptian script, stands in an important place at the beginning of the exhibition.

In 1985 seven new basement galleries were opened, displaying sculpture which had been in storage since 1939 when it was put away to protect it from the bombing. The riches—mostly Greek and Roman—in this collection are astonishing.

Upstairs, one of the most intriguing displays is that of the Mildenhall treasure, a cache of Roman silver found in a field in Suffolk in 1942. On this floor, too, are delightful displays of Greek and Roman art, the grisly remains of Ancient Egyptians and the delicate jewelry found on the site of Ur of the Chaldees by Sir Leonard Woolley.

It is not the slightest use thinking that you could cover the British Museum in one short visit, so don't try to. See what you can, and savor what you see in the hope that you can return again.

North of Russell Square are Woburn Square (where the Courtauld Galleries are), Gordon Square and Tavistock Square, pretty, green places with some attractive town houses. Running along the western side of Gordon Square is University College London, founded by the Utilitarian philosopher, Jeremy Bentham, whose embalmed body is still on the premises and has been known to attend student functions. The college was the first in England to admit Jews, Catholics and women.

Holborn

Two major highways link central London with the City; the Strand and Holborn. Strand here means "beach," as it was originally a riverside road along the Thames. Holborn derives from Hole Bourne, or "stream in the hollow," as it lies along the route of the little Fleet River (it runs underground now). Between these two arteries lie the great Inns of Court, and round them the first urban development outside the cities of London and Westminster took place; so while much ugly rebuilding has been done, there are still quiet streets of genuine historical charm.

Begin at Holborn Underground station, at the north end of Kingsway (a wide, dull street linking Holborn with the Strand) and walk eastwards. At first, the street is unexciting; shops, big office blocks, a pompous insurance company building. Soon, on the right, comes Chancery Lane. A detour along this narrow street leads you to several interesting and unusual places. On the left is the Public Record Office, whose archives include Britain's national records since the Norman Conquest—and the Domesday Book. On the right are old arched gateways that take you from the roar of the traffic into the cloistered 18th-century hush of Lincoln's Inn, part of London's legal quarter.

The slightly odd name "Inns of Court" is originally a medieval term. There are four of them, Gray's Inn, the Inner and Middle Temples and Lincoln's Inn—all of them here or hereabout. The Inns provide the manpower for the English legal system, those, that is, who actually plead at the Bar (hence the name "barristers"). The Inns are their college, union headquarters, club and licensing authority all rolled into one. Students who wish to become lawyers have to "keep term," which means that they must eat a regulation number of dinners in hall, while studying.

Lincoln's Inn is very old. Law was associated with the site as far back as 1292, and proper records begin with the year 1424. The buildings reflect both the age of the institution and that slightly other-worldly serenity which is such a feature of scholarship—and the Inns of Court are very much places of learning. Although parts of Lincoln's Inn suffered during the blitz, the rebuilding was skillfully done and the scars are now forgotten. A lot of the buildings are Tudor, the Gatehouse being built in 1518. The Chapel was rebuilt under James I between 1619 and 1623, but has a fair bit of Victorian addition. New Square is a lovely late-17th-century creation, not originally part of the Inn, but absorbed at a later date. The Hall and Library are Victorian (started in 1843) and their romantic version of the Tudor style blends in well with the real MacCoy. Many famous names have been on the

Inn rolls, among them Sir Thomas More, John Donne the poet, William Penn, the politicians Pitt, Canning, Disraeli and Gladstone, the writers Macaulay and Galsworthy and even the actor David Garrick.

A slight back-track westwards will lead into Lincoln's Inn Fields, a wide, almost park-like square, which is very busy during the week but relapses into rural tranquility at weekends.

There are some fine buildings around the square. The south side is taken up mostly by the interesting quarters of the Royal College of Surgeons, with a magnificent 1806 portico. Nos. 59–60 (on the west side) are Lindsey House and may have been the work of Inigo Jones in about 1640. Nos. 13–14 house Sir John Soane's Museum. Soane's portrait, a superb painting by Lawrence, is in the dining room of the house and it can be seen, even from this fashionable likeness, that the man was both intelligent and odd. He was a great architect, though almost unknown now, and a collector of genius. In many ways this house is a fantasy world, containing some of the most lovely paintings in Britain as well as priceless Egyptian relics, especially the sarcophagus of Seti I, which Soane bought for £2,000 after the British Museum had turned it down. For a glimpse at what the English eccentric-cum-genius can do with money, the Soane Museum is not to be missed.

Back in Holborn now, just past the entrance to Chancery Lane is Staple Inn, a romantic-looking, half-timbered block. It is not original (having been blown up by a V-bomb in 1944), but has been rebuilt so that it does in fact look exactly as it did in Elizabeth I's London; the original dated from 1586. Inside are two pleasant courtyards, on one of which Dr. Johnson lived for a while. Here, too, in the street are the Holborn Bars, two small obelisks that mark the western limits of the City of London (the originals were placed here in 1130).

Farther along is Holborn Circus, in the center of which is an equestrian statue of Prince Albert, politely raising his hat as if to salute a lady on the top of a passing bus. On the left is Hatton Garden, occupied by diamond merchants. A little way along Hatton Garden, on the right, is The Mitre, a small historical pub hidden away down a narrow alley (well signposted outside). Just off Holborn Circus, too, is Ely Place, where the Bishops of Ely had their London house from the late 1200s to 1772. The Place is still a private road with its own security guard (the police can only enter on invitation). Ely Place appears in Dickens and contains Ely Chapel (St. Etheldreda's), a noted example of 13th-century Gothic, which has a vaulted crypt standing on Roman foundations.

But let us continue along Holborn Viaduct. On the right is Wren's church of St. Andrew, whose tower interior dates from 1446. Wren did not alter it. It was here that David Copperfield married Dora Spenlow.

The street now becomes a viaduct, constructed in 1867 to take the road across the Fleet valley. It is an impressive construction with elaborate bridges. At the end of the viaduct is the 12th-century church of St. Sepulchre (where Captain John Smith, "sometime Governor of Virginia and Admirall of New England," whose life was saved by Pocahontas, lies buried), which had its bells rung when there was an execution at Newgate. Newgate Prison stood opposite, on the site now occupied by the Central Criminal Court (the "Old Bailey"), topped by the symbolic statue of justice. There are five courts, open to the public and usually crowded, especially when a sensational case is in progress. The more sensational trials are usually held in either No. 1 or No. 2 Court.

To the left of this corner (turn up Giltspur Street) is St. Bartholomew's Hospital, built by James Gibbs in 1730, though founded in 1123. In a niche above the main gateway of the hospital is a statue of Henry VIII done in 1702. The hospital was yet another of the king's thefts.

Just past the hospital (Smithfield Meat Market on the left), is the church of St. Bartholomew the Great, well worth visiting. Apart from the chapel in the White Tower, it is the oldest church in London, being part of the priory founded in 1123 in fulfillment of a vow made in Rome by Rahere, a courtier of Henry I. The church is approached through a charming gateway with an Elizabethan, timbered façade, revealed when a bomb explosion in 1915 shattered its covering. The interior is beautiful; the heavy roundness of Norman architecture is fully evident. The Normans were unique in that they built their churches with the same art and the same skill as they built their castles, not surprising when one remembers that Norman bishops were often in the forefront of battles, swinging their murderous "morningstar," a spiked ball on a chain since their religious profession forbade them to use edged weapons. The church is often used for concerts as are many old buildings in the city, and to hear Bach and Handel superbly performed in these surroundings is a memorable experience.

At the junction by the Old Bailey, Holborn becomes Newgate Street, leading to St. Paul's Cathedral and Cheapside.

The Strand and Covent Garden

The other major highway linking the West End with the City is the Strand, which runs from Trafalgar Square eastward to Temple Bar—main gate to the City of London—where it becomes Fleet Street, finally ascending to St. Paul's under the name of Ludgate Hill.

Between Trafalgar Square and St. Mary-le-Strand—a 1714 church designed by James Gibbs and islanded by traffic—the Strand is little more than an ordinary shopping street with three theaters, the Adelphi, the Vaudeville and the Savoy. There is one interesting feature, just behind St.-Martin-in-the-Fields, however. This is the massively restored West Strand Improvements, designed by Nash, with round towers at the corners. In the middle of the Strand frontage is an ultra-modern glass cliff, the new premises of Coutts Bank, and a startling contrast with the 1830 decorous façade that stretches on either side.

Off to the north, however, up Southampton Street, is Covent Garden, once the central fruit, flower and vegetable market—now moved to a new site south of the Thames. Since then the area has been—and still is being—extensively redeveloped. The born-again Covent Garden is an exciting mixture of shops, restaurants, a few building sites and potholes and some genuinely attractive buildings. The centerpiece is the old 19th-century market building itself which has been restored and converted into an elegant and delightful shopping center of considerable charm. It houses some of the capital's newest and trendiest shops which are not as expensive as they look. Opposite the market is Inigo Jones' rather forbidding church of St Paul's (main entrance from Bedford Street). The network of streets nearby contains the Royal Opera House and Drury Lane.

In and around the central market complex there is a regular program of street entertainers of all kinds who play everything from classical music to jazz, act out the most complicated plays or just simple mimes. They have turned the old colonnades into a lively place, easily rivaling the streets of Paris for fun and interest. The market buildings also house pubs, restaurants and wine bars, which are ideal for recovering from any lingering tourist traumas. Among the many attractions is the Cabaret Mechanical Theatre, full of fascinating automata which work at the push of a button and can give hours of fun. At 9–10 Floral Street is the National Jazz Centre, with 7-days-a-week live jazz in a 400-seat auditorium.

Just as no visit to Moscow is really complete without a visit to the Bolshoi, so no visitor to London should fail to see a performance at Covent Garden. This version of the opera house was built in 1857–58, after two earlier theaters on the site had burned to the ground, one in 1808 and the other in 1856. (By the way, the name Covent Garden is a corruption of Convent Garden—the monks of Westminster Abbey once had gardens there.) Not only are the acoustics of the theater excellent, but the Victorian gilt and plush seems to create an atmosphere in which ballet and opera can flourish. A scheme to increase the backstage and rehearsal facilities is in hand and phase one has now been completed; the second phase is planned for later in the decade, depending on whether cash for the astronomical cost can be raised.

The Theatre Royal, Drury Lane, is one of the largest in London and the fourth one to be built on the same site. The first was granted letters patent by Charles II in 1663. The third theater had been built for Richard Brinsley Sheridan in 1791–94 and was burned down in 1809 (since massive quantities of candles were used at performances, regular fires were not surprising). Sheridan was spotted by a passerby sitting in the window of a nearby tavern while the theater burned to the ground. When asked how he could possibly sit there so calmly, he replied, "Where else should a man drink but by his own fireside?" The present theater was built in 1809–12, but the auditorium was reshaped in 1922. It is now the home of lavish musicals, usually from Broadway, and the occasional West End comedy.

To the south of the Strand lies the Adelphi area, so called because it was originally built by the Adam brothers, though not very much of their 18th-century architecture remains. Along the side of the Thames here is an attractive garden, excellently maintained and providing a pleasant spot to listen to a brass band or sit in the summer sun.

While Lancaster Place leads off the Strand to the right to Waterloo Bridge, on the left is the Aldwych, a crescent containing more theaters. The massive building on the right-hand side (Bush House) is the home of the BBC World Service. Beyond is St. Clement Danes, a Wren church with a Gibbs tower and a statue of one of its regular worshippers, Dr. Johnson, outside the choir. The original "oranges and lemons, say the bells of St. Clement's" church, it is now dedicated to the R.A.F. To the south is Somerset House, whose spectacular façade, built in 1776, is best seen from the river. The huge house used to contain the office of the Registrar-General of Births, Deaths and Marriages (now moved to St. Catherine's House, 10 Kingsway, WC2); however, once the necessary 3 million pounds or so has been raised, it is planned to move the Courtauld Institute of Art to this new setting. Next door, under King's College, are the so-called Roman Baths.

The Strand becomes Fleet Street at Temple Bar, where traditionally, the Lord Mayor of London must challenge the reigning monarch when she (or he) enters the City. Sir Christopher Wren designed the old gate that stood here, but it was removed in 1878.

Just before Temple Bar (now marked by a rather uninteresting memorial with statues of Queen Victoria and Edward VII—though it is unlikely that any statue of Victoria could ever be called interesting) are the Royal Courts of Justice or Law Courts, amazingly Gothic in the Victorian style. It is possible to listen to cases in the courts, but, as they are mainly civil actions, they quickly become tedious to the inexpert. To get a better idea of how British justice deals with the man in the street, drop in at a Magistrates' Court, the main central one being in Bow Street, or, even better, visit the Old Bailey.

On the other side of the road is The Temple, approached by many unlikely-looking alleys. This is another part of the legal quarter, beautiful, with linked courtyards and a quiet atmosphere. The name derives from the Knights Templar, a powerful medieval order created during the Crusades. It was dissolved in 1312, and in 1346 the ground belonging to the Knights Templar was leased to law students; it has been, ever since, the home of lawyers. The Temple Church dates from the 12th century and was badly damaged during the Second World War but has now been restored. The Middle Temple Hall provides one of those rare glimpses of Elizabethan times, remaining just as it was when built. Explore this area one afternoon, using Wren's gatehouse in Middle Temple Lane (off Fleet Street) to enter.

Fleet Street is, of course, the main artery of the Press; on and around this famous street have been, at one time or another, the offices of most of the major newspapers. You will see the restrained Daily Telegraph, the shiny black Daily Express and many others; though the granddaddy of them all, The Times, has moved to Gray's Inn Road.

Just north of Fleet Street (turn down Bolt Court) is Gough Square, where, at No. 17, Dr. Johnson compiled his dictionary. At Ludgate Circus, Ludgate Hill rises to St. Paul's Cathedral. To the right is Blackfriars Bridge, and next to that the little Mermaid Theatre, at Puddle Dock, rebuilt as part of a development scheme.

St Paul's Cathedral

1. Great West Door
2. North West Door
3. All Souls' Chapel
4. St Dunstan's Chapel
5. Monument to Lord Leighton
6. Monument to General Gordon
7. Duke of Wellington
8. Lord Mayor's Vestry
9. Sir Joshua Reynolds by Flaxman
10. Chapel in the N. Transept
11. Dr Johnson by John Bacon
12. Minor Canons' Vestry
13. Chapel of Modern Martyrs
14. High Altar and Baldachino

15. The American Memorial Chapel
16. The Lady Chapel
17. The Donne Effigy
18. John Howard
19. Entrance to the Crypt and the O.B.E. Chapel
20. Dean's Vestry
21. Admiral Earl Howe
22. Admiral Collingwood
23. J. M. W. Turner
24. Nelson
25. Sir John Moore
26. Font
27. General Abercromby
28. Sir William Jones
29. Staircase to Whispering Gallery, Dome, and Golden Gallery

30. St Paul's Watch Memorial Stone
31. Chapel of St Michael and St George
32. Geometric Staircase and Dean's Door
33. South West Door

A Bishop's Throne
B Lord Mayor's Stall
C Sanctuary Screens and Gates by Tijou
D Lectern
E Pulpit
F *Light of the World* Holman Hunt

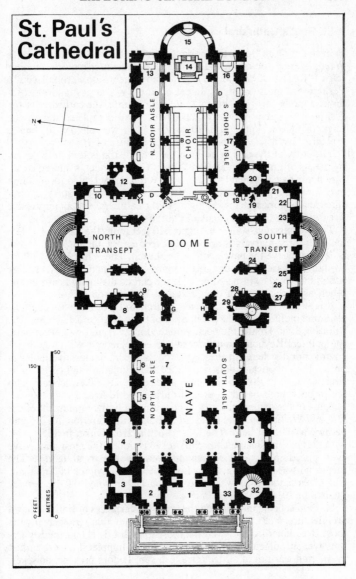

St. Paul's
Cathedral

St. Paul's Cathedral

In the crypt of this great monument is the tomb of Sir Christopher Wren, bearing the epitaph: *Lector, si monumentum requiris, circumspice* ("Reader, if you would see his monument, look around you"). Perhaps the most potent comment on London's largest and most famous church, this boast refers to a living church, the cathedral of the Bishop of London. It was begun in 1675 and completed during the reign of Queen Anne, in 1710, when Wren was almost 80, and it replaced an earlier one, burnt in the Great Fire of 1666.

The story of the design of the present cathedral is told in the crypt by means of graphic panels and Wren's Great Model, a superb structure made by craftsmen to a design by Wren not accepted for building but showing a great dome. The crypt also contains a display of treasures and historical items belonging to the cathedral and an impressive Treasury with over 200 items of church plate.

The Renaissance-style building is 520 feet long (the nave is 125 feet long), and the marvelous dome is 112 feet across; the top of the cross is 365 feet above the pavement of the church. The Whispering Gallery around the base of the dome is a source of fascination; it is 112 feet across but words whispered on one side can be distinctly heard on the other, as in the dome of the Capital in Washington DC.

It is an enormous and impressive church and crowded with memorials, some indifferent, some good, most of them large and elaborate. Dr. Johnson, John Donne the poet, who died in 1631 and was Dean here, the painters Reynolds and Turner and even George Washington are commemorated here. In the crypt, too, is a commemorative tablet to one of the American pilots who "died that England might live." The Jesus Chapel, in the Apse, is dedicated to the 28,000 Americans who fell in operations based in Britain during World War II.

Some of the memorials are gigantic, especially the monument of the Duke of Wellington, who defeated Napoleon at Waterloo in 1815 and became a national hero. The funeral of the Iron Duke, in 1852, was, with that of Sir Winston Churchill in 1965, among the most impressive ever staged in London for anyone outside the royal family. The memorial was erected in 1875. Lord Nelson, the victor of Trafalgar, was given a statue, as was Lord Kitchener, drowned off the Orkney Islands in 1916.

St. Paul's, being modeled on the great masterpieces of Italian church architecture, lacks the atmosphere and intimacy that strangely invests most British cathedrals, even the most splendid. It is enormously impressive, but somehow chilly, as if it would be happier if it were bathed in the rich warmth of a Mediterranean sun. It does provide, however, a splendid setting for pageantry, as shown most recently by the wedding of the Prince and Princess of Wales, which was seen all over the world.

The great cathedral was cleaned completely in 1965–66 and now looks even more spectacular from this approach, though as one gets nearer, a new (and highly controversial) office block masks part of the façade. Illuminated at night, the cathedral is at its most splendid. One of the best ways to see all that the great cathedral has to offer is to take the conducted tour that lasts around two hours.

There is a delightful ecclesiastical story attributed to the great Regency wit and a Canon of the cathedral, Sydney Smith, who, when he heard that there was a proposal to surround St. Paul's with a wooden pavement, said, "Let the Dean and Canons lay their heads together and the thing will be done." The area around St. Paul's has long been the subject of debate. The devastation of the 1666 fire gave the chance for a spectacular redevelopment, which was not acted upon. The equally catastrophic havoc caused by the Blitz gave yet another chance for careful planning and rebuilding, and the schemes that were hatched, perhaps too quickly, in the aftermath of war have produced sadly shoddy work, by and large.

To the left of the cathedral is Paternoster Square, a modern pedestrian complex of plazas with shops, restaurants and pubs. It has been designed to afford unexpected views of Wren's cathedral, which stands moored like a vast ship among the smooth surfaces of concrete and glass. Just behind the cathedral is the new Choir School.

The scheme for St. Paul's precinct was devised by William Holford, with the intention of framing the cathedral from various angles, with paved courts, flights of steps and lawns. Some voices urged for wide open spaces around the cathedral, and a stroll round the new developments quickly indicates that this might have been preferable to some of the crowding modern buildings that have been erected.

While you are here, it is well worth having a look at the Barbican, an area just to the north of St. Paul's, which after 1940 was reduced to 35 acres of complete devastation. Tower blocks march two abreast down London Wall (a street so called because it follows the route of the Old Roman Wall, remains of which are incorporated into the new scheme) and are connected by pedways, above traffic level. Sadly, much of the development is showing signs of wear—the materials used are not always well-chosen. Bang in the middle of the area is the Barbican Center, home of the London Symphony Orchestra and the Royal Shakespeare Company's London base. (We discuss the Center in more detail in our *Entertainment* chapter.) Lying between St. Paul's and the Center is the exciting Museum of London, tracing the history of the metropolis from the earliest times, by means of relics, dioramas, costumes, all superbly displayed. A must, especially for those who like their history brought vividly to life.

Opinions are very sharply divided about this huge development—especially among some of the 6,000 residents who have found that it is not the easiest place in the world to live in—but it is worth visiting, particularly if you are interested in modern city planning. Getting in and out of the area is extremely confusing, and if you are intending to go to a performance at the Center by public transport, give yourself lots of time.

The City

Known as "The Square Mile," the City of London is an irregularly defined crescent stretching from Temple Bar to the Tower of London. Its heartbeat is at the giant crossroads, a meeting of seven streets, where stand the Bank of England, the Royal Exchange and the Mansion House, official residence of the Lord Mayor. On-the-spot information about the City is obtainable from the information bureau across the road from St. Paul's in St. Paul's Churchyard.

From behind St. Paul's, the most immediate approach is a walk along Cheapside, past the church of St. Mary-le-Bow to the big seven-way intersection. Tradition has it that to be a true Cockney you must be born within the sound of Bow Bells—which these days severely limits the number of genuine Cockneys available.

Memories of Saxon times haunt the streets near Cheapside; indeed, the very name Cheapside is of Saxon origin; *ceap* meaning barter. The earliest Saxon (if not Roman) relic in the City is claimed to be the famous London Stone. The Stone was formerly embedded in the wall of St. Swithin's Church, in Cannon Street, but the church, damaged by bombing, was demolished in 1958. The stone is let into a wall of the Bank of China, near its old site. All round Cheapside and east of St. Paul's Cathedral, street names (Bread Street, Ironmonger Lane, Wood Street) indicate that busy trades flourished there in medieval times. In Pudding Lane, the Great Fire of London is said to have broken out.

Buried in the entrails of Bucklersbury House are the remains of the Temple of Mithras. If you visited the Museum of London, you will be keenly aware of the Roman past of the city, and here is one of the major evidences of that past. If you walk along Queen Victoria Street, you will find the temple in the side of Bucklersbury House—not that there is very much of it, but what there is serves to remind one of the antiquity of life on this same spot.

Off Cheapside to the left, down King Street, is the Guildhall, the center of the City Corporation and the City guilds. Only the porch and one 15th-century window survive; otherwise, it is a mass of replacements. It was destroyed by the Great Fire of 1666 and again by German bombs in 1940. This restored, but still very impressive, building is the scene of the election of the Lord Mayor each year and of other City officers, and it is here that the City stages banquets to honor visiting Heads of State and other bigwigs. Behind the Mansion House is the church of St. Stephen Walbrook, considered to be one of Wren's finest works.

The Bank of England, another citadel of Britain's financial power, faces the Royal Exchange. An important aspect of the Bank, the long windowless wall broken by Corinthian columns, is the work of Sir John Soane, whose museum activities we remarked earlier. One of the small odd facts about the Bank is the type of civil servant who has worked there, many of them eccentric and following strange hobbies out of hours. It is ironic, for example, that Kenneth Grahame, author of *Wind in the Willows,* should have been an executive there.

The Monument and a Roman Site

Farther east, near London Bridge, stands a towering 200-foot Monument, built as a memorial to the Great Fire of 1666. It was built between 1671 and 1677, designed by Wren, and so almost literally emerged like a phoenix from the scarcely cold ashes. The fire had begun nearby in Pudding Lane and ended near Pie Corner five days later. A culinary conflagration, one might say. The great column is surmounted by a huge ball of flame, and its flanks are covered with bas relief sculptures and large tablets in Latin and English.

Only a few steps from here is the River, with London Bridge, and just beside it the former site of Billingsgate Fish Market. There has been settlement on this site for well over two thousand years. It was a Roman wharf and acted in a similar capacity for every subsequent wave of inhabitants of the area. Before rebuilding began, London's archeologists had a year to excavate the area, an opportunity which has provided the most extensive examination of a site vital to the understanding of the whole history of London from the Roman and Saxon periods onwards. The extensive finds will take about fifty years to study, and are now housed in the Museum of London's stores. They are not open to public viewing.

The Tower of London

The long-planned system of roads and subways designed to improve traffic and pedestrian circulation in the Tower area has been completed. Visitors arriving at Tower Hill underground station can walk to the Tower without crossing any roads along a system of steps, terraces and ramps. The subway system also extends to St. Katharine by the Tower and to the Royal Mint.

The Tower celebrated its 900th birthday in 1978, taking that date from the year that William the Conqueror began to build on the site. But in reality the foundations he laid were solidly placed on fortifications that were even then a thousand years old. The Tower is the root of London's history, with the constructions of the centuries from the Normans onwards well preserved. Seen at night when floodlit it becomes a setting more evocative than any stage designer could create.

The White Tower, in the center, is the oldest part of the fortress, having been built for William the Conqueror. Wren, who had a hand in so many of London's buildings, made some alterations to the exterior, but inside, the Norman origins are still self-evident. The Bloody Tower is the most infamous, for here most of the important prisoners in bygone days were confined and tortured. One particularly nasty cell was called Little Ease. The unfortunate inmate couldn't stand, sit, or lie down. It's said that at the Tower on the rack, in 1546 a woman called Anne Askew was tortured so greatly to the delight and interest of the Lord Chancellor, who attended the proceedings, that he himself pressed on the levers and almost tore the woman's body apart. Some years ago a well was found in the lower part of the tower—filled nearly to the top with human bones!

The White Tower is surrounded by nineteen others, each individually named, the whole complex resting across the ancient wall of the City of London. A Roman fortress, mythically ascribed to Julius Caesar, certainly occupied the site, and later a Saxon castle stood there. Since

The Tower

1. Entrance
2. Middle Tower
3. Byward Tower
4. Bell Tower
5. St. Thomas's Tower
6. Traitors' Gate
7. Bloody Tower
8. Wakefield Tower
9. St. John's Chapel
10. Armories
11. Tower Green
12. Site of the Scaffold
13. Chapel Royal of St. Peter ad Vincula
14. Beauchamp Tower
15. Yeoman Gaoler's House
16. Princess Elizabeth's Walk
17. Queen's House (not open to public)
18. Raleigh's Walk
19. Entrance to Jewel House
20. Crown Jewels
21. Heralds' Museum
22. Devereux Tower
23. Flint Tower
24. Bowyer Tower
25. Brick Tower
26. Martin Tower
27. Constable Tower
28. Broad Arrow Tower
29. Salt Tower
30. Lanthorn Tower
31. New Armories
32. Hospital Block
33. Royal Fusiliers' Museum
34. Wardrobe Tower (on site of Roman Bastion)
35. Wall of the Inmost Ward and Coldharbour Gate
36. Legge's Mount
37. Brass Mount
38. Develin Tower
39. Well Tower
40. Cradle Tower
41. Site of Lion Tower & Drawbridge

R. Refreshment
☆ Lavatories (female)
★ Lavatories (male)

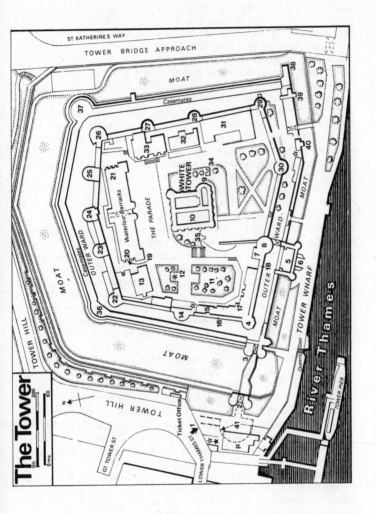

it was built (William the Conqueror wanted to frighten the Londoners), the Tower has never been seriously attacked and served more as a state prison than a fortress. Innumerable famous people have been immured here and many lost their heads on the block.

A good three hours is needed to do the Tower full justice (there are a cafe and restaurant here). Things to see are St. John's Chapel—the oldest church in London—the various rooms of armor, with a collection begun by Henry VIII, and the site of the scaffold on Tower Green. You may see the Tower's tame ravens hopping about on the Green. There have always been ravens here, and legend says the Tower will crumble if they should ever leave. Since their wings are clipped, that's unlikely. The raven has great significance in history and myth. Odin had two of them as his eyes and ears, and throughout the early days of northern Europe the raven was known as "corpse goose" and, as a haunter of battle grounds, "osprey of the spear-storm."

The Beauchamp Tower has had a most distinguished list of prisoners —from Sir John Oldcastle (possibly the model for Shakespeare's Falstaff), who was executed on Tottenham Court Road in 1418 for his religious beliefs, to Robert Dudley, a favorite of Queen Elizabeth I. Inscriptions on the walls of the tower total nearly a hundred. The list does not, of course, comprise all the victims, most of whom were buried in the Chapel of St. Peter ad Vincula, or in the burial ground close by (now part of the Green). The great English historian, Macaulay, said of the Tower that "in truth there is no sadder spot on earth."

Of the famous people who were beheaded in the Tower at least four should be mentioned: the philosopher, creator of Utopia, saint, and statesman, Sir Thomas More (1535); two wives of Henry VIII, Anne Boleyn (1536) and Catherine Howard (1542); and that versatile courtier and hot-headed lover of Queen Elizabeth, the Earl of Essex (1601). When the axe fell for the last time in 1747, it was upon a rebel's head—that of Lord Lovat, a Scotsman. The axe, execution block and instruments of torture can still be seen in the White Tower.

Elizabeth I (while still Princess) knew something about the Tower from personal experience. Queen Mary imprisoned her in the Bell Tower. She arrived by water at Traitors' Gate. It was raining, but she sat on the steps and refused to budge. Looking at the grim place, you'll scarcely blame her.

Perhaps the most famous part is the Bloody Tower—the name seems to sum up the history of the place. Some inmates, however, must have found it tolerably comfortable, as jails go. Sir Walter Raleigh spent thirteen years there—for seven of them his wife was permitted to be with him, and his son, Carew, was actually born there. He had visitors and wrote his *History of the World*.

Of course, you'll want to see the Crown Jewels, and you'll be impressed by the elaborate precautions taken to ensure their safety and by the striking way in which they are displayed. Formerly they were kept in the Martin Tower, and while they were there a Colonel Thomas Blood made a determined effort in 1671 to steal them, actually getting as far as Traitors' Gate before he was stopped. Instead of being punished, he received a royal pension. Understandable perhaps, when rumor said that Charles II, being short of ready cash, had connived with Blood over the attempted theft. Since most of these jewels were scattered during Cromwell's Commonwealth, the ones you see today are largely post-Restoration (after Charles II). Since 1967, the jewels have been kept in the Jewel House, a depository below the Wakefield Tower. Be prepared for a long wait, since there is always a long line during the height of the tourist season.

There are two recent additions to the attractions of the Tower. One is the Heralds' Museum, opened by the College of Arms Trust in the Waterloo Building. The exhibits are changed annually, but they always include various aspects of heraldry, with documents, painted shields, coronets and crests together with much of the panoply that makes this such an intriguing subject to so many people. The other new attraction is the walk along the battlements, which at the moment extends from the Wakefield Tower as far as the Martin Tower, and which will eventually stretch all the way to the Flint Tower, giving a completely new dimension to viewing the whole complex.

The Tower is a peaceful enough place today, and it is pleasant to sit in the gardens near the ancient cannon and watch the Thames roll by. Remember, however, that the Tower is still a military fortress. You'll see the troops of crack regiments as well as the Yeoman Warders in their picturesque Tudor-style uniforms.

Tower Bridge, nearby, is frequently mistaken for London Bridge, upstream. But, for all its air of antiquity, Tower Bridge is comparatively new, having become operational at late as 1894. The Bridge is open to the public, with wonderful views from the walkways and the massive operating mechanism laid bare.

Near the Tower is All Hallows church, important to American visitors as it was the site of both William Penn's baptism in 1644 and the marriage of John Quincy Adams, sixth president of the U.S.A. in 1797. Also close to the Tower is the quay where you can catch a boat either up or down the river to see some of the other historical buildings at Greenwich or Hampton Court.

St. Katharine's Dock

As we mentioned at the beginning of this section on the Tower, you can also reach St. Katharine's Dock by using the system of subways from Tower Hill tube station. This is an intriguing area, strongly reminiscent of the small harbors that fringe the coast of Cornwall. Once a busy dock, with cargos arriving from all over the world, it fell, with most of this part of the Port of London, into disrepair and decay. But little by little it has found a vivid new life.

Part of the dock is now a marina for small craft, with boats from the Historic Ship Collection of the Maritime Trust, including Captain Scott's Polar ship *R.R.S. Discovery*. One of the old warehouses, the Ivory House, which got its name, very simply, from the kind of cargo that was stored there, has been converted into a magnificent set of apartments, imaginatively using the resources of the old building. There is a series of shops and bars here and, across the dock, the Dickens Inn, a completely reborn building—even its site has been moved—which hosts evenings of rather rowdy Dickensian entertainment.

The River Thames

London has rather turned its back on the Thames since the 19th century. From the beginning the river was *the* major highway, and in the days of the Tudors and Stuarts it was thronged with boatmen plying from shore to shore and carrying passengers down to Greenwich or up to Hampton Court, shooting the turbulent water under the narrow arches of the bridges in much the same way as men try their skill on the white water of rapids in their canoes today. With the vast increase in road transport since those far-off days, the river has become littlemore than an ornament, running almost unheeded through the very heart of London.

There was a time, unbelievable as it may seem today, around the middle of the 18th century when the apprentices of London complained that they were given salmon to eat too often. The Thames was that good a fishing river in those days. But the increase in the sewage from the increasing population and the effluent from factories turned the stream into a really appalling state by the mid-1950s, when it stank of rotten eggs and ships painted with lead-based white paint turned black.

But the river is making a slow comeback. The terrible pollution of the last century is almost at an end. By the 1950s all fish life was gone from the river, with the exception of the occasional eel which must have been poison-proof. New anti-pollution controls in the early '60s reversed the apparently irreversible state of affairs and now the river teems with the most unlikely life. Smelt, shrimps, bass, seahorses, even salmon have returned. In all 91 species had been recorded by the late '70s and one expert estimated that in the stretch of river from Richmond to Tilbury tens of millions of fish were living it up. Not that you would guess it from looking at the water. It is a murky, swift-flowing river, but those who have the courage of their convictions insist that the murk is due to silt, not pollution.

There are two walks in central London which follow the river, one along either bank. The one on the north side (which you can easily follow on our maps) can be started at the western end of Cheyne Walk in Chelsea, past Battersea Bridge and the decorative Albert Bridge, along the Chelsea Embankment, past Chelsea Bridge, along Grosvenor Road to Vauxhall Bridge, along Millbank (where the Tate Gallery stands) to Albert Bridge, the Victoria Gardens and the Houses of Parliament. We have mentioned most of that walk in previous sections. You will only lose touch with the river at one or two points, and the views that unfold themselves are really delightful, as are the glimpses of the unusual aspects of London life, such as the house-boats moored off Cheyne Walk.

From Westminster the walk becomes a trifle more formal and ornate. First the Victoria Embankment is lined on the left hand side by massive government blocks, like New Scotland Yard. Across the river you can see the dignified bulk of County Hall, the upwardsweep of the Shell Building and the glass front of the Festival Hall. The road passes under the skeletal Hungerford Bridge that carries trains from Charing Cross to the south. Now the character of the Embankment changes. On the left, after the Embankment Tube station (which used to be called Charing Cross, much to the mystification of visitors, since it wasn't actually at Charing Cross) there are the well-kept Embankment Gardens; neat flower-beds, a bandstand where uniformed bands play rousing tunes in the summer, and a rather intriguing collection of statues. Robert Burns needs no introduction to anyone, and he sits here on a tree-stump, busy being inspired by his muse. The effect of this statue is to turn a down-to-earth poet into a kind of super-Byron. Sir Wilfred Lawson and the Camel Corps are there. So is Robert Raikes, the founder of Sunday Schools, perhaps of less interest to most visitors than Sir Arthur Sullivan, of "Gilbert-and" fame.

But the two main things to remark in this stretch of the Embankment are the Old Watergate of York House and Cleopatra's Needle. The Watergate, which stands in the Gardens, not far from the tube station, was built in 1626 and was exactly what its name implies, the gate through which those arriving by river entered York House. It is interesting to see where the river used to reach until the 1860s and '70s, when the Embankment was built and the potentially destructive tides of the Thames controlled.

Cleopatra's Needle, first erected about 1450 B.C. in Heliopolis, has nothing whatever to do with Cleopatra. It is one of a trio given by Egypt to the Western democracies in 1875; the other two are in the Place de la Concorde in Paris and in New York's Central Park. The two sphinxes at the base of the Needle are pitted with holes resulting from a bomb in 1917. The needle almost never made it to London. During the journey, it was towed behind a tug in a torpedo-like case. In a storm in the Bay of Biscay, the tow line broke and for days the needle drifted. Astonishingly it was found, and amid great rejoicing completed its journey. Note the benches along here. Taking their cue from Cleopatra, they are exotically decorated with camels, sphinxes and palm trees.

From Waterloo Bridge to Blackfriars Bridge the walk is not quite so interesting. First comes the long, classical frontage of Somerset House, which looks wonderful from across the river, but is cliff-like to walk under. The Inner Temple Gardens cover a fair bit of the distance, not so characterful as the Embankment Gardens, but still delightful to ease the eye. Moored in this reach are several interesting ships. The mock-Gothic building, just before Blackfriars Bridge, is Sion College, an Anglican library and institution.

The South Bank

To Londoners "the South Bank" means inevitably the Festival Hall complex, built first as part of the post-Second World War wing-ding known as the Festival of Britain in 1951. For our purposes we are extending the expression to cover that part of the river from Lambeth Palace to the National Theatre. This is one of the walks in London that we consider an absolute essential for anyone who wants to see the gradually unfolding skyline of the very heart of the city.

Start from Lambeth Palace which stands at the other end of Lambeth Bridge from the Victoria Tower Gardens. You can get there quite easily by walking along from Parliament Square and then crossing Lambeth Bridge. The palace is a much neglected part of London's history, partly because it has been the residence of the Archbishop of Canterbury for seven-and-a-half centuries, and is still; which means that the palace can be visited only by appointment, and there are conducted parties (write to Palace Secretary, Mary Cryer, for details). The building was started at the very beginning of the 13th century, and has been growing ever since. Cranmer created the English Prayer book here; Wycliffe was tried here; it was the scene of power struggles for centuries between the secular and religious arms of government. Building continued until the 19th century, and the whole complex is a living museum of English architecture, with its own peaceful atmosphere.

Beside the palace is St. Mary's, naturally a church with a history. Captain Bligh, of the Bounty, lies buried in the churchyard. St. Mary's is now deconsecrated and has become a mecca for gardeners, for it is the home of the Museum of Garden History, run by the Tradescant Trust. The walk from here is gentle and interesting, not the least for the constantly changing views of Westminster across the river. This is called the Albert Embankment, and on the right are the new buildings of St. Thomas's Hospital. It is one of London's oldest established hospitals, having been originally founded in Southwark in 1213. It suffered terrible damage in the blitz, and the modern replacements are something of a triumph.

Across the foot of Westminster Bridge is County Hall. This mammoth building is the seat of the government of Greater London (by the Greater London Council—which is threatened with abolition at press-time). This means, basically, the whole of London *excluding* the City. The facade facing the river was built in 1932. The whole of this walk, now lying ahead, is fairly recent, and is part of the new consciousness of the beauties of the Thames and mercifully has at last percolated into the skulls of the planners. From the time of the Festival of Britain, this walk has been growing, a little at a time; trees have appeared and the whole promenade has become a matter for London pride.

Past the County Hall and standing a bit back, is Shell House. Under Hungerford Bridge, and the Festival Hall complex is now in view. Feelings are mixed about the architectural merits of the area, but no one can fault the artistic delights that it affords. Of the three concert halls, the Festival Hall has the biggest auditorium, used mainly for orchestral and ballet performances and other musical entertainment— including lunchtime chamber concerts and early-evening organ recitals during the week. It also has a restaurant with a marvelous view, and a good cafeteria where the visitor can stop for a snack. Next door is the Queen Elizabeth Hall, slightly smaller but also more relaxed. The tiny Purcell Room, which houses recitals, is in the same building.

Behind the Queen Elizabeth Hall is the Hayward Gallery, used for large-scale exhibitions of art, almost all of which break new ground in their choice of subject. The gallery is surmounted by a tall, skeletal sculpture made of neon tubing. At night rather hectic colors run up and down this erection, their speed and intensity being governed by the velocity of the wind playing on a small device at the top. The National Film Theatre is tucked away here too, partly under Waterloo Bridge. Its two auditoria present a quite staggering number of films, drawn from its huge archives. If you are interested in the art of the cinema, it is worth getting a temporary membership.

The National Theatre completes the South Bank riches. It lies on the other side of the foot of the Waterloo Bridge, but the steps and pathways tie it into the rest of the complex. You can complete your walk along the river by passing under the bridge on the promenade. The National Theatre had an excessive delayed birth, and there is a strong school in theatrical circles in Britain which feels that it should never have been born at all. Indeed, there is an undeniable anachronism in creating, in this day and age, a National Theatre which, for all its inventive modernity, is merely an updated version of the Comedie Française. However, there it is, and it is certainly exciting. The outside is a refined version of the rest of the South Bank; deftly used concrete, but less fortress-like than the Queen Elizabeth Hall. Inside, the foyers are elegant, intricately varied and full of both atmosphere and character; but their very intricacy can be extremely confusing to the first-time visitor. The three auditoria create expectation even before the performances start. This is essentially a building in which things can happen, where the brilliant disposition of space serves to foster a willingness on the part of the public to share in the making of an event. Go there, especially for a performance if you can, and wander around in the intermissions, absorbing the quality of one of the world's great theatrical buildings. There are also guided tours available during the day.

After an evening on the South Bank, walk back to the West End over either Waterloo Bridge or Hungerford Bridge. Look eastwards towards St. Paul's, which rides like a glowing vision over the city; it will convince you that London is still "the flower of cities all."

KEY TO MAP SECTIONS

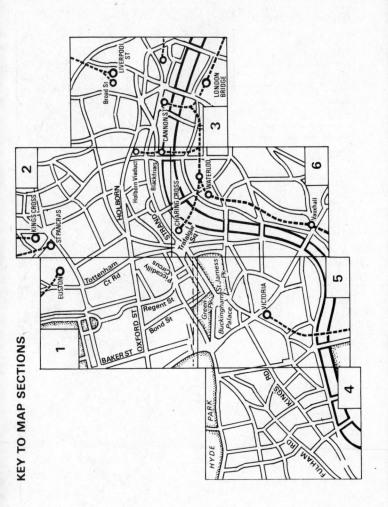

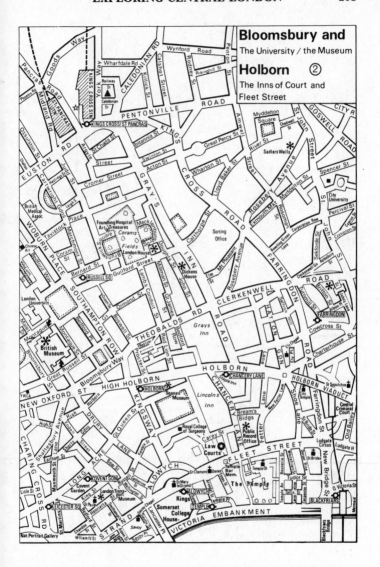

Bloomsbury and
The University / the Museum

Holborn ②
The Inns of Court and
Fleet Street

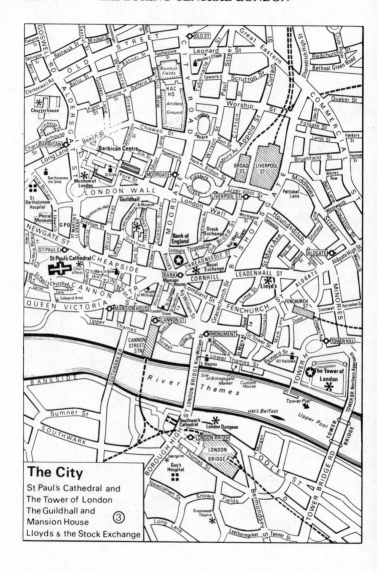

The City

St Paul's Cathedral and
The Tower of London
The Guildhall and
Mansion House ③
Lloyds & the Stock Exchange

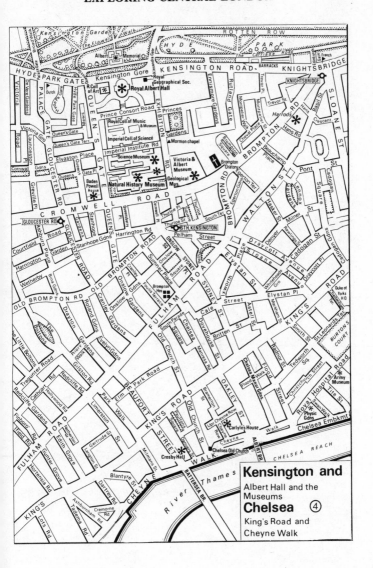

Kensington and
Albert Hall and the
Museums
Chelsea ④
King's Road and
Cheyne Walk

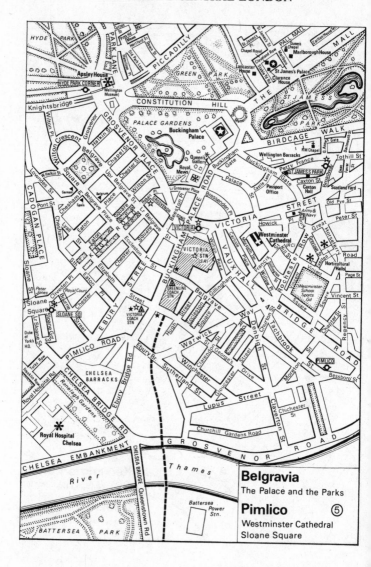

Belgravia

The Palace and the Parks

Pimlico ⑤

Westminster Cathedral
Sloane Square

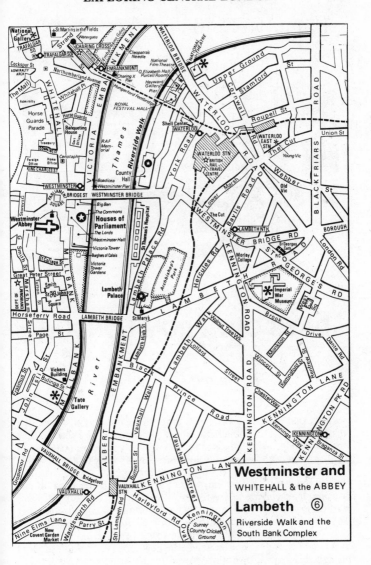

National Gallery
St Martins in the Fields
TRAFALGAR SQ
Strand
Watergate
CHARING CROSS
Cockspur St
ADMIRALTY
ADMIRALTY ARCH
Northumberland Avenue
The Mall
EMBANKMENT
Cleopatras Needle
Charing X Pier
National Film Theatre
WATERLOO BRIDGE
Hungerford Footbridge
Upper Ground
Cornwall
Stamford
Roupell St
Union St
Admiralty
Whitehall Pl
Horse Guards
Horse Guards Parade
Banqueting House
Treasury
Downing St
Foreign Office
Home Office
KING CHARLES ST
Cenotaph
RAF Memorial
Boadicea
Westminster Pier
Thames Riverside Walk
ROYAL FESTIVAL HALL
Shell Center
WATERLOO
York Road
County Hall
WATERLOO STN
BRITISH RAIL TRAVEL CENTRE
Marsh
Lower
The Cut
WATERLOO EAST STN
Young Vic
Webber St
Old Vic
BLACKFRIARS ROAD
BOROUGH
London Rd
WESTMINSTER
BRIDGE ST
WESTMINSTER BRIDGE
Big Ben
The Commons
HOUSES OF PARLIAMENT
The Lords
Westminster Hall
Victoria Tower
Burghers of Calais
Victoria Tower Gardens
Westminster Abbey
St College St
Great Peter Street
Smith Square
St John's
DEPT OF THE ENVIRONMENT
Horseferry Road
Page St
MILLBANK
Lambeth Palace
LAMBETH BRIDGE
St Marys
St Thomas's Hospital
Lambeth Palace Rd
Archbishop's Park
LAMBETH WALK
Hercules Rd
Baylis Rd
WESTMINSTER BRIDGE RD
LAMBETH NTH
St Georges Cath
Morley College
KENNINGTON ROAD
ST GEORGE'S RD
Imperial War Museum
Brook
Drive
Dante Rd
Vickers Building
Bullinga St
Tate Gallery
River
ALBERT EMBANKMENT
Lambeth High St
Black Prince Road
Vauxhall Walk
Lambeth Walk
Lollard Street
Walnut Tree Wk
Wincott St
Monkton St
Chester Way
Kennings Way
Renfrew Rd
KENNINGTON LANE
KENNINGTON
Way
KENNINGTON PK RD
Braganza St
John Islip St
VAUXHALL BRIDGE
Bridgefoot
VAUXHALL
VAUXHALL STN
Wandsworth Rd
Sth Lambeth Rd
Parry St
Harleyford Rd
KENNINGTON LANE
Burnett St
Kennington
Oval
Nine Elms Lane
New Covent Garden Market
Grosvenor Rd
Erasmus St
Surrey County Cricket Ground

Westminster and
WHITEHALL & the ABBEY

Lambeth ⑥
Riverside Walk and the
South Bank Complex

Hampton Court

DAYS OUT FROM LONDON

Varying the Capital Fare

It's not that there's a shortage of things to see in London, but getting outside the city gives you a better sense of perspective. "What do they know of London who only London know?" If you've been staying in a city or town for a few days as a visitor, coming back to it after a side trip is like coming home. It's a pleasant sensation.

Some routes out of London, by rail or bus, are better than others: for example, if you are interested in "1066 and All That," Hastings is two hours away by train, and worth the journey. Bath, on the other hand, can be reached by high-speed train in not much more than an hour. Along with the Edinburgh-Newcastle-York-London run, this West Country route is one on which the new super-fast trains are going through their paces, operating as part of the scheduled service.

Better still, though, is to spend a night away. Weekend bookings are usually no problem, even in midsummer, but if you have a particular hotel in mind for mid-week, like the University Arms in Cambridge, or the Randolph in Oxford, book a few days in advance, as the best rooms are sometimes snapped up by businessmen.

Travel costs in Britain have increased seriously in recent years, but day-trippers usually have it good. As long as you avoid getting to or from your destination during rush hours (7.30–9.30 A.M. and 4.30–6.30 P.M.) you'll find trains and buses uncrowded, and in any case, be very sure to check out all the possibilities for bargain tickets, every year there are more offers dreamed up. You can find that you save well over 50% on your trip.

Do not be misled by distances into thinking that a place is merely an extension of London. Richmond, for example, on a map looks like one of London's far-flung suburbs. In fact the town has quite an identity of its own. It is a bit like those English spas that grew up in the early 19th century and still enjoy a degree of elegance and prosperity.

You can even enjoy a sense of having arrived somewhere, after a shorter journey even than to Richmond, and that is if you take the Northern Line Underground to Hampstead. For collectors of useless information, Hampstead is the deepest station on the whole tube network—but you won't particularly notice it. Hampstead lies on the edge of the famous Heath, painted several times by John Constable, and is inhabited by the rich and the radical.

LONDON'S OUTSKIRTS

Hampstead

Hampstead, lying as it does high on a hill to the northwest of central London, has a clean, refreshing, countrified atmosphere (rather like a particularly charming English country town); it has literary associations, some beautiful houses, good shops, interesting pubs and several first-class restaurants.

If you go by underground, you will emerge at Hampstead tube station in the middle of Old Hampstead, halfway up the hill. This is the most picturesque part, not far from delightful streets like Flask Walk and Keats Grove, where the poet once lived. Also nearby is Church Row, with some grand Georgian houses; the streets behind the main roads also offer many architectural delights.

Hampstead is flanked by its Heath, a vast stretch of hilly parkland, mainly rough (that is, not divided into formal walks), from which there are spectacular views over all London; this is where kites are flown, swimming is done and where, on bank holidays, a fair is held. By the Heath, at the top of the hill, is Jack Straw's Castle, a big, plush pub with a Victorian ambience; further along is the 18th-century inn called The Spaniards, which contains, among other literary and historical associations, the pistols that Dick Turpin used—or so they say.

A little farther along to the east is Kenwood, a house with a library designed by Robert Adam and restored in 1970, set in a fine park bordering the Heath. The whole house constitutes the Iveagh Bequest, along with its excellent collection of paintings and furniture. In the summer, open-air concerts are held by the lake.

Near Hampstead, also topping a hill, is Highgate, again retaining a village atmosphere and some pretty houses. Highgate Cemetery is known as much for its elaboration of memorial and tombstone as for the famous buried here—the latter including Herbert Spencer, George Eliot, Karl Marx and Michael Faraday. The cemetery is closed to the public as a protection against vandalism, and a scheme to raise money to rehabilitate the cemetery is being organized by the Friends of Highgate Cemetery, who bought the place for £50 in 1981. It is a worthwhile project, for the area is full of superb Victorian monuments. Rod Stewart, the singer superstar, was once a gravedigger here and it was, fictionally, a haunt of Count Dracula.

Greenwich

If you have managed to catch a sunny day, and London summers can occasionally be blazingly hot, you should take the trip by boat from Westminster or Tower Pier downriver (eastward) to Greenwich. Not only will you see the remains of what used to be one of the busiest ports in the world as you chug along, but at the end of the voyage you will be in for a delightful surprise.

For Greenwich (pronounced *gren-ich*) is yet another spot where British history has coalesced. The heart of the historical area on the banks of the Thames is the Royal Naval College, housed in a former palace. This is some of the most splendid architecture and interior decoration anywhere in Britain. The Painted Hall is a triumph of breathtaking illusionism, painted by Thornhill. The Chapel is more restrained, but in its serious, 18th-century way, equally lovely. The whole complex was the work of several of Britain's greatest architects, Vanbrugh, Hawksmoor and, of course, the ubiquitous Wren among them. Here, too, is the National Maritime Museum, a treasurehouse of the days when Britain ruled the waves, with paintings, models, maps, intriguingly mysterious globes and sextants, relics of dead heroes, all that will fascinate anyone who has a taste for the sea.

The work of another great architect, Inigo Jones, can be seen in the Queen's House, which he built for Charles I's Queen, Henrietta Maria. This is one of the earliest, and best, flowerings of classicism in Britain, mathematically perfect, with a lovely central hall and staircase.

Actually on the edge of the river are two real ships, each of great historical interest. The *Cutty Sark* was the last the tea clippers, ships that raced from the East with their holds full of tea for the tables of England. Beside her is the *Gipsy Moth,* the small boat in which Sir Francis Chichester sailed alone round the world.

On the hill a little inland, with the sweeping grass of Greenwich Park leading up to it, is the Royal Observatory. It was here that Greenwich Mean Time was born. The work of the Observatory is now carried on at Herstmonceux Castle, away from the obscuring atmosphere of London, but the building remains as a musuem of the astronomer's science. The Prime Meridian runs through the center of the courtyard, so this building commemorates two basic universal measurements of the modern world. It was also designed by Wren . . . who else!

If you can stay for the evening, there is a lively theater where classics and modern plays are performed in a near-repertory way, with well-known actors doing their thing away from the West End. You can return to town either by the river (though not at night), by bus, or by train to London Bridge.

Kew Gardens

Just to get out of the built-up conglomeration of London for a few hours, and as a specific trip, try the Royal Botanic Gardens (known as Kew Gardens) which are especially popular during the spring and summer. The gardens cover 288 acres and contain more than 25,000 varieties of plants. There are strong Hanoverian associations here, as the gardens were actually begun (in 1759) by Princess Augusta, George III's mother. The Georges and their queens spent much time here and Kew Palace (the Dutch House), which has been restored to its former state, contains plenty of their relics.

The gardens have beautiful walks and the plants are housed in a series of sometimes spectacular buildings, such as the Orangery, the Palm House, built by Decimus Burton, and various hothouses. A literally outstanding feature is the Pagoda, built in 1761 by Sir William Chambers—a delicious folly that can be seen for miles around. Kew itself is on the river, with a village green fringed with 18th-century houses; the painters Gainsborough and Zoffany are buried in the churchyard. Gardens and museums open at 10, glasshouses at 11; closing times vary with the season, but average around 5. Tube: Kew Gardens (takes around 30 minutes from central London). By boat from

Westminster or Charing Cross in the summer. Bus: 27 from Kensington Church Street.

Chiswick

Quite close to Kew is Chiswick House, built by the 3rd Earl of Burlington in 1725 in the full flush of the Palladian craze. It is best reached by taking the tube to Hammersmith and then the 290 bus, which will drop you at the entrance to the House, on Burlington Lane, not far from the complex of the Hogarth's Corner spaghetti junction.

The interior of the house is quite lovely, designed by William Kent and magnificently restored. Pope, the poet who most closely echoes this period in his verse, was a frequent visitor here. The grounds are laced with delightful walks and avenues. There are temples, lakes, a bridge built by James Wyatt and a gateway designed by the greatest of 17th-century architects, Inigo Jones. If you can time your visit to coincide with the flowering of the camellias in the large conservatory, you will be rewarded by a really striking sight.

While in this area it is worth visiting Hogarth's House, at the back of Chiswick House, which, though there is not all that much to see, does give one an insight into the way the great painter lived. He and his family are buried in St. Nicholas church, back across the huge motorway complex (take the underpass), near the river. This is a pretty little enclave of houses, and one can spend a long time wandering along the side of the Thames here.

Richmond

The next stop on the way west through the outskirts of London is Richmond, which has been a favorite residential town since Henry VII (Duke of Richmond, in Yorkshire, before he became king) changed its name from "Sheen." It is picturesquely sited on the slope of a hill, at the top of which is Richmond Park. The hill commands a celebrated and fine view of the Thames and the park (2,350 acres), which is stocked with deer. The trees, especially the oaks, are ancient, the last vestiges of the once vast medieval forests that crowded in upon London. There are several private (and originally royal) residences in the park. White Lodge was once the home of the present Queen's parents and is now the Royal Ballet School.

Richmond is particularly rich in fine houses and literary associations. Leonard and Virginia Woolf, Dickens, George Eliot and Richard Burton, of *Arabian Nights* fame, all lived here. On the southwest side of Richmond Green is all that remains of Richmond Palace. The side streets of Richmond well merit exploring for their quaint alleyways.

An extension of Richmond Park is Ham Common, and just outside Richmond is Petersham, a delightful riverside village with more 17th- and 18th-century houses, including Ham House. This Jacobean house is most notable for its contents, which are almost totally original, giving a vivid impression of the life of the time. The house is managed by a combination of the National Trust and the Victoria and Albert Museum, with enviable results.

Hampton Court

Farther up river, on a loop of the Thames beyond Richmond, lies Hampton Court, a mellow redbrick palace, bristling with turrets and twisted chimneys in the very best Tudor tradition. It is one of the spots that should top every visitor's list of what to see near London and can easily be reached by train, bus or even by boat, perhaps the best way of all, though it takes quite a time.

The house was begun in 1514 by Cardinal Wolsey, who intended it to surpass in size and opulence all other private residences. Henry VIII coveted it and made the Cardinal an offer he couldn't refuse. The king added a great hall and chapel and lived much of his rumbustious life here. Further improvements were made by James I, but by the end of the 17th century the place was getting rather rundown. William III, the husband of Mary and equal monarch with her, was a Dutch Prince of Orange who decided that England should have its own Versailles. There was an epidemic of Versaillesmania at this time. In order to build a massive new palace, the existing Tudor one would have had to have been demolished, but money was short and the architect Wren had to produce a simpler, and in the event more effective, scheme. William and Mary, Mary especially, loved the palace. A lot of their life there is still in evidence, especially the collections of Delftware and other porcelain.

The site beside the slow-moving Thames is perfect, set in its great park full of dappled deer and tall ancestral trees, with magnificent ornamental gardens, elegant Orangery, the celebrated maze, and the old palace itself, steeped in history, hung with priceless paintings, full of echoing cobbled courtyards and cavernous Tudor kitchens, now restored to their original Tudor splendor at the cost of £50,000 and fascinating to visit—not to mention a couple of royal ghosts (the luckless shades of Jane Seymour and Catherine Howard, two of Henry's unfortunate queens).

In a very real way Hampton Court not only enshrines some of the best architecture that England can show, but also is a microcosm of much that was good in three centuries of English art and art collecting. To progress from the Tudor part of the palace, with its roundels of

Roman emperors, its symbolic tapestries, its ornate Jacobean wood-work, its tiny, almost claustrophobic, panelled chambers, into the end-less series of elegant rooms, opening one out of the other like a chain of airy boxes, with spacious views over the gardens and the park, is to walk through a central part of English history.

The rooms are furnished with many excellent pieces, especially the bedrooms, with their four-poster beds rearing like ornate catafalques surmounted by plumes. A great deal of fine art is hung here, too, including royal portraits and a fair number of Dutch still lifes.

Royalty ceased to live here with George III. He, poor man, preferred the seclusion of Kew, where he was finally confined during his madness. However, the private apartments which range down one side of the palace are occupied by pensioners of the crown. These "grace and favor" apartments must be among the most attractively placed resi-dences anywhere, having so much peaceful beauty and rich history on their very doorsteps.

Hampton Court

State Apartments
1. Entrance
2. King's Staircase
3. King's Guard Chamber
4. Wolsey Rooms
5. King's First Presence Chamber
6. King's Second Presence Chamber
7. Audience Chamber
8. King's Drawing Room
9. King's Bedroom (William III State Bedroom)
10. King's Dressing Room
11. King's Writing Closet
12. Queen Mary's Closet
13. Queen's Gallery
14. Queen's Bedroom
15. Queen's Drawing Room
16. Queen's Audience Chamber
17. Public Dining Room
18. Prince of Wales' Suite
19. Prince of Wales' Staircase
20. Queen's Presence Chamber
21. Queen's Guard Chamber

22. Queen's Private Chapel
23. Private Dining Room
24. Queen's Private Chamber
25. King's Private Dressing Room
26. George II's Private Chamber
27. Cartoon Gallery
28. Communication Gallery
29. Wolsey's Closet
30. Queen's Staircase
31. Haunted Gallery
32. Royal Pew
33. Chapel Royal
34. Henry VIII's Great Watching Chamber
35. Horn Room
36. Great Hall
37. Exit from State Apartments
38. King's Kitchen
39. Tudor Kitchen
40. Renaissance Picture Gallery

Hampton Court Palace
1. Main Entrance Trophy Gates

2. Outer Green Court
3. Moat
4. Great Gatehouse
5. Base Court
6. Anne Boleyn's Gateway
7. Clock Court
8. George II Gateway
9. Fountain Court
10. Great Fountain Garden
11. Flowerpot Garden
12. Privy Garden
13. Tijou Ironwork Screen
14. Banqueting House
15. Knot & Pond Gardens
16. Lower Orangery
17. Great Vine
18. Tennis Court
19. Wilderness
20. The Maze
21. Lion Gates
22. Tiltyard Gardens

P. Car Park
R. Refreshment
★ Lavatory, Male
☆ Lavatory, Female
† Lavatory, Disabled

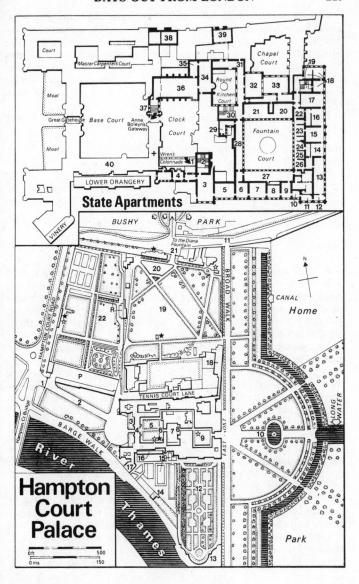

Court

Master Carpenters Court

38

39

Chapel Court

19

18

35

31

34

Round Kitchen Court

32

33

17

36

Moat

37

Clock Court

30

21

20

22

16

Great Gatehouse

Base Court

Anne Boleyn's Gateway

29

Fountain Court

23

15

28

24

14

Moat

Wren's Colonnade

1 2

Fountain Court

25

26

13

40

4

3

LOWER ORANGERY

5

6

7

8

9

27

State Apartments

10 11 12

VINERY

BUSHY   PARK

To the Diana Fountain

11

21

N

20

BROAD WALK

CANAL

Home

19

CANAL

R

22

18

EAST AVE

LONG WATER

P

TENNIS COURT LANE

1

3

5 6

7 8

10

2

4

9

16

15

17

14

12

Hampton Court Palace

13

Park

River

Thames

Hampton C. Bridge

BARGE WALK

Hampton Court Road

0 ft   500
0 ms   150

In the same area is the town of Twickenham, where the poet Alexander Pope lived—he is buried in the parish church. Turner and Tennyson both lived here for a while, and among the notable houses are Marble Hill House, a Palladian mansion built for George II, and Strawberry Hill, Horace Walpole's villa in the most delicately fanciful Gothick style of the mid-18th century. It is now a Roman Catholic teachers training college, but admission can be obtained on written application.

From Hampton Court, the River Thames bends and winds its way to Windsor.

FARTHER AFIELD

A great deal of southern England is reachable from London on a "Day Excursion" basis. You can either do this by taking one of the many coach trips available, most of which will include several places on their itinerary thus giving you a taste at least of what is available—or you can plan to see one major town and take an Intercity train there, or, if closer to London, a local train.

You would be surprised how far afield you can go on a day basis. Bath, in Avon, is quite possible, as are Winchester, Chichester (go there for a performance at the Festival Theater, even, and be back in London for a very late bedtime), Brighton, Hastings, Canterbury—all those to the west and south. To the north-west, north and east lie Oxford, St. Albans, Cambridge, Bury St. Edmund's, Norwich and Colchester—all destinations with much to see.

Those are only some of the main points that lie within easy reach; there are, of course, many smaller ones that are possible, but you should be warned that it is not always easy to get to a place and away again within a few hours. You should be sure to consult the latest schedules while planning your trips. For example, while Stratford-upon-Avon is theoretically reachable by train for a day's outing, in practice the turgid nature of the scheduling makes it a difficult trip—and indeed the station at Stratford is often closed on Sundays! Those interested in doing some shopping along with their sightseeing should check on the early closing day at their destination—it changes from place to place, though is mostly on Wednesdays or Thursdays.

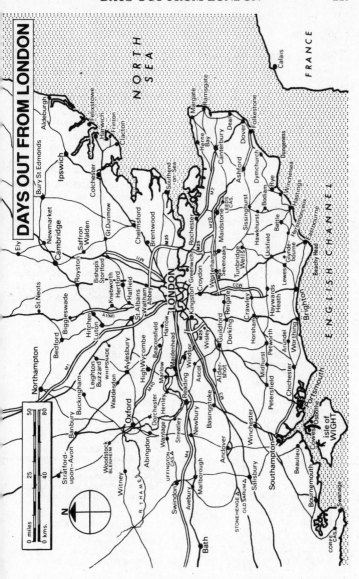

Windsor

Windsor has been the home of English kings at least since the times of Henry I, and possibly before. It is less than an hour from London by Green Line bus, train or on an organized coach tour. Tour operators make all-day trips, which take in Hampton Court, or, alternatively, very convenient half-day tours.

The gray stone castle dominates the town and looks out over the Thames. Naturally, the Royal Castle and the surrounding parks are the chief focus of interest, but the town round the castle has its own special charm and it is worth wandering in the narrow streets.

The first king recorded as living in the Windsor area was Edward the Confessor, who gave his palace at Old Windsor to Westminster Abbey before he died. William the Conqueror, realizing the military importance of the site, built himself a fortress. Timber fortifications were replaced by stone by Henry II and Henry III, who built the three drum towers.

Most medieval kings resided in Windsor, some for two or three weeks at a time. Edward I lived here and gave the town its royal charter, while Edward III—who was born in the castle and had a great affection for it—transformed the place adding much that is still standing and functional today. Edward IV began St George's Chapel, Henry

Windsor Castle

1. Henry VIII's Gateway
2. Salisbury Tower
3. Garter Tower
4. Curfew or Bell Tower
5. Winchester Tower
6. Norman Gateway
7. George IV's Tower
8. Cornwall Tower
9. Brunswick Tower
10. Prince of Wales' Tower
11. Chester Tower
12. Clarence Tower
13. Victoria Tower or Queen's Tower
14. Augusta Tower
15. York Tower
16. George IV's Gateway
17. Lancaster Tower
18. Edward III's Tower
19. St George's Gateway
20. Charles II Statue
21. Henry III's Tower
22. Horseshoe Cloisters
23. Canons' Cloisters
24. Dean's Cloisters
25. Albert Memorial Chapel
26. Superintendent's Office

State Apartments
1. Grand Staircase
2. State Anteroom
3. The King's State Bedchamber
4. The King's Closet
5. Queen's Closet
6. King's Drawing Room
7. Picture Gallery
8. The Queen's Ballroom
9. The Queen's Audience Chamber
10. The Queen's Presence Chamber
11. The Queen's Guard Chamber
12. St George's Hall
13. Private Chapel
14. The Grand Reception Room
15. Ante-Throne Room
16. The Garter Throne Room
17. The Waterloo Chamber
18. The Grand Vestibule

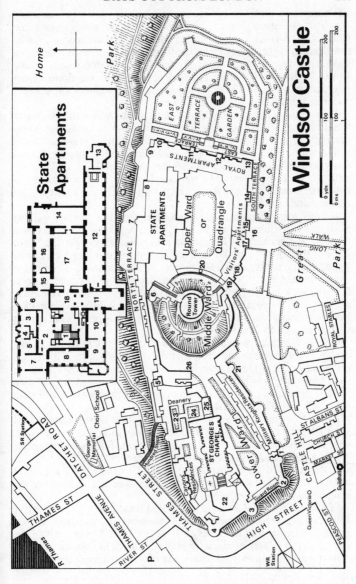

Windsor Castle

State Apartments

VII completed the nave and Henry VIII set the vault over the choir, and built the castle gateway. Elizabeth I built the north terrace and Charles II restored the state apartments. But it was George IV who transformed the essentially medieval castle into the royal palace you can visit today. Later William IV built the Waterloo Chamber and Queen Victoria (who continued to live here after the death of her husband, Albert, and was commonly called "the widder of Windsor") decorated the Albert Memorial Chapel.

Despite the multiplicity of hands that have gone into the making of Windsor, the palace has managed to retain a unity of style and a very marked character of its own. It is, in fact, the largest inhabited castle in the world. The Round Tower, which is actually not round, rises above the walls to the height of 280 feet above sea level, dividing the structure of the castle into two wards—the upper ward with the royal apartments and the lower ward, containing St. George's Chapel, the deanery and cloisters.

A great many famous Englishmen have spent their leisure walking along the castle terraces. Chaucer, for one, is said to have lived here while he was in charge of building improvements. It is from the North Terrace that entry is gained into the State Apartments, which can be visited by the public when the Queen is not in residence. The present Queen, in fact, uses the castle far more than any of her predecessors. It has become over the last decade a sort of country weekend residence, which allows the royal family a few days of relaxation and informality. On these occasions, Prince Charles often joins a polo team against visiting players in Windsor Great Park.

It is at Windsor, perhaps more than in any of the other royal residences that the public can visit, that one realizes just how incredible is the extent of the Queen's wealth of pictures, furniture, porcelain, in fact of anything worth collecting—all of it housed in buildings of deep historic significance. It makes the Pierpoint Morgans of the world seem like children with their first postage stamps.

Apart from the splendor of the various rooms of the State Apartments, a visit to Queen Mary's Dolls' House should not be missed. Given to Queen Mary in 1923, it is a perfect, fully-working palace within a palace. Electric lights work, the doors all have keys, the lifts are practical and there is running water. There is even a miniature library, with over two hundred tiny books specially written for the Lilliputian library.

St. George's Chapel is one of the noblest buildings in England. Over 230 feet long, with two tiers of great windows and hundreds of gargoyles, buttresses and pinnacles, it is quite grand. The exterior of the chapel is rivaled only by the interior. Light floods in from the stained-glass windows, and above the dark oak of the stalls hang the banners, swords and helmets of the Knights of the Order of the Garter. Here lie some of the most famous Kings of England, beginning with Henry VI, and including Charles I, Henry VIII (Jane Seymour, the mother of his only son, is also here) and many others, up to King George VI who has a chapel to himself. This arose from a personal decree by his daughter, the present Queen, and largely commemorates his prowess as a monarch during the Second World War. His brother, Edward VIII, who abdicated in 1936 to marry the woman he loved, and who was known to the world as the Duke of Windsor, is buried in nearby Frogmore Mausoleum, though there is a memorial to him here, before the choir. The Mausoleum is open to the public just three days a year; on a Wednesday and Thursday in May, and on the Wednesday nearest to Queen Victoria's birthday (May 23rd). Please check with the Windsor Tourist Information Center (tel. 95–52010) for precise dates.

The beauty of the church in the lower ward is matched by the exquisite reception rooms, a guard room, and a picture gallery. The Gobelin tapestries in the reception room are splendid and so is the collection of pictures, with a Rubens and a Van Dyck room. The royal library contains, among an almost unbelievable wealth of treasures, a fine collection of da Vinci's drawings and 87 portraits by Holbein. A new permanent exhibition has been mounted by Colonel Sir John Miller—Crown Equerry responsible for the running of the Royal Mews—in the Royal Mews at Windsor. As well as life-size models of horses, one of which wears the red and gold state harness normally used with the State Coach, there are many fascinating carriages and coaches, and a selection from the hundreds of gifts from all over the world presented to Queen Elizabeth II.

The walls of the castle itself enclose only 13 acres of land, but beyond the battlements are nearly 4,800 acres of Windsor Great Park. Charles II planted an avenue of elm trees, the Lond Walk, to join castle and park. On the southeast side of the castle is the smaller Home Park, filled with great oaks, some of which were planted in the time of the first Queen Elizabeth. It was here at Frogmore that Queen Victoria liked to spend her days. An added attraction at Windsor is the 140-acre Windsor Safari Park, situated two miles southwest of the castle on the B3022 road. The park is open daily all year, from 10 a.m. until an hour before dusk (from 9.30 on bank holidays), and contains within its grounds a drive-in lion reserve and a dolphinarium.

Windsor's links with the royal family are further exploited in Madame Tussaud's recreation of Queen Victoria's Diamond Jubilee Station, full of interest for rail buff and royalty freak alike. With audio-visual projections, resplendent settings from 1897, waxworks, robots and all the panoply of a historically accurate Disneyland treatment, this is an exhibit worth visiting. It is open from 9.30 to 5.30 daily, admission around £2.35 for adults, £1.60 for children.

Only a short walk over the Thames from the center of Windsor is Eton College—open to the public during spring and summer for daily guided tours in the afternoons (phone Eton College Tourist Office on Windsor 63593 for details)—and beautiful, 15th-century Eton College Chapel, which is impressively austere and intimate at one and the same time.

The best view of Eton and its famous playing fields is, in fact, from the battlements of Windsor Castle. Eton is an ancient institution (1440, founded by Henry VI) for which children must have their names put down for a place at birth. You will meet the current crop wearing their uniform of tailcoats and striped trousers, continuing to create the school's own private history surrounded by its ancient buildings. Eton town has an attractive High Street with some good restaurants and pubs for lunch.

Canterbury

It was through the gently rolling countryside of Kent that the early pilgrims went on their way to Canterbury and caught their first sight of the cathedral. The mother church of England, the seat of the Primate, it is a magnificent achievement of Gothic architecture (with remains of an earlier Norman structure), some rare early stained glass and a wonderfully serene crypt. Canterbury can be reached by train from Charing Cross, Victoria and Waterloo (about 80 minutes), or by car following the M3, which will take around 2 hours.

The history of Canterbury Cathedral goes back to the days of Ethelbert, King of Kent, who in 597 granted the site now occupied by the cathedral to St. Augustine, the Christian missionary from Rome. St. Augustine's church, despoiled by the Danes in 1011, was destroyed by fire in 1067. The oldest stones in the existing fabric of the cathedral belong to the church built by Lanfranc, who in 1070 became the first Norman archbishop of Canterbury. In 1175, William of Sens, a renowned French architect, was called in to design a splendid new choir and presbytery to house the tomb of Archbishop Thomas à Becket, who was murdered in the church in 1170. Stone was shipped from Caen, Normandy, and brought up the River Stour, at that time navigable as far as Fordwich. The shrine was destroyed by Henry VIII.

Behind the high altar in the Trinity Chapel is the tomb of the Black Prince, that redoubtable fighter who won his spurs at the Battle of Crecy in 1346. The high vaulted nave and beautiful choir, one of the longest in England, are among the most striking features. The whole of the cathedral is open free and the cathedral authorities rely on the visitors contributing voluntary offerings in the boxes placed at different points in the cathedral.

The city still retains much of its medieval character with the famous West Gateway, part of the ancient walls, old churches, houses and inns. It is also a modern town with plenty of diversion for the holiday-maker: excellent shops, cinemas and the Marlowe Theater (called after the Elizabethan poet and playwright Christopher Marlowe who was a native of the town). For the authentic atmosphere of medieval Canterbury, there are such inns as the 15th-century Falstaff, originally the parish clerk's house.

Canterbury contains many other ancient and lovely buildings: the Norman keep; the Church of St. Martin, one of the historic gems of British Christianity, which claims an unbroken pattern of worship lasting nearly 1,500 years; Christ Church Gateway, a lovely Tudor structure with 17th-century gates, and the Weaver's House, where the Huguenots plied their trade at the end of the 17th-century; these are but a small selection.

Canterbury is rich in literary associations, Chaucer's *Canterbury Tales* (c. 1380) being the most famous. Christopher Marlowe, Hugh Walpole and Somerset Maugham were at the King's School. Joseph Conrad is buried in the cemetery. The Canterbury Festival of the Arts is held at the end of September, with performances in the theater and in historic buildings including the cathedral.

Brighton, Lewes and Chichester

Easily reached from London, by train from Victoria (two trains an hour and the journey will take about an hour), Brighton is the self-proclaimed belle of the south coast. For anyone who does not mind a busy, lively resort, now developed into a big town with a broad coast road, Brighton and its continuation, Hove, can provide a delightful holiday for, quite apart from the obvious attractions of the huge new marina, good shops and restaurants, there is the maze of little alleys full of antique shops known as the Lanes. There is also the new entertainment and shopping center and some of the finest Regency architecture in the country. Brighton, in fact, developed from the impetus given it by the Prince Regent, later George IV, in the late 18th century, when he took up sea bathing there. Appropriately, it is his house—the Brighton Pavilion—which seems to be the epitome of the town. Built mainly by John Nash in a mock-oriental manner with domes and pinnacles abounding, it has never failed to shock and delight in equal measure, particularly against a background of the lovely little Regency houses that the Prince's more seemly friends built for themselves. The Chinese decor of the Pavilion's rooms is almost as astonishing as its exterior.

Today it is used for public functions and is well worth visiting, especially since the rooms have been refurnished with many pieces of Regency design from the Royal Collection. The nearby Dome, which was once the stables, is a concert hall. Besides its elegant centerpiece, Brighton has its brash area facing the sea, where there are funfairs and two piers—one sadly dilapidated—and cheap eating places, deckchairs on the beach (mainly shingle) and winking colored lights.

It is crude but vital, and if it is too much for you there are wonderfully quiet places to walk on the Downs just outside town. These are the low rolling hills beloved of Kipling, Chesterton and Belloc, who did not, however, have to walk so far as we do now to get outside the town, which has spread in all directions.

The ancient county town of Lewes, northeast of Brighton on A27, has very old churches and side streets almost too steep for a car to manage. Try to see the narrow but beautiful High Street here. Try also to wander around the green lanes behind the castle mount; they are the very essence of an old-fashioned English country town. For music lovers, Lewes is a good stepping-off place for Glyndebourne, which, in the summer season, offers some of the finest opera productions in the world, in a beautiful rustic setting.

Beyond Brighton, a number of resorts, Worthing, Littlehampton, Bognor Regis, enjoy equally good weather. Inland lies Chichester, with its Norman cathedral, fine old 18th-century houses and beautiful 16th-century market cross. It can be reached by train from Victoria Station (about 90 minutes), or by car following the A3 then the A283 or A286. The waters of Chichester harbor are always animated with small boats and yachts, all making a perfect setting for the excellent Festival Theatre, which has an open stage on which are performed outstanding productions of popular plays. Like Glyndebourne, it has an international reputation. Essential short side-trips from Chichester are to Bosham, a yachting village with a church depicted in the *Bayeux Tapestry,* and the excavated Roman Palace of Vespasian at Fishbourne.

Arundel Castle (about 1 hour, 20 minutes from Victoria), near Chichester, has been much restored and the great park with its attractive lake is always open to the public, though no cars are allowed in. Racing enthusiasts may like to visit Goodwood Park and racecourse, where fashionable meetings take place at the end of July (usually attended by the Royal Family).

Oxford

Oxford is an ideal target for a day out from London—as is its sister university, Cambridge. Oxford lies around an hour by train from Paddington Station, and there are trains every hour. The drive (by the A40/M40) is dead straight and takes less than two hours.

Whatever preconceived notions you may have about Oxford, your first sight of the city will doubtless confirm them all. Stop on one of the low hills that surround it, to look at the skyline. If you are fortunate, and the sun is shining, the towers, spires, turrets and pinnacles will look like a scene from a medieval fairy story. Here stretched out in front of you is Oxford, the home of erudition and scholarship, of Oxford English and—of Oxford marmalade. From here, time appears to have passed the city by and it must look much the same as it did 200 years or even longer ago.

First appearances are deceptive, however. The last 50 years have seen changes in Oxford that have revolutionized not only the town, but the very basis of university life itself. It is, in fact, one of the fastest-growing manufacturing towns in England. Although the average undergraduate can spend his three years at Oxford and only once a year, perhaps, pass the two vast industrial concerns that are responsible for the changes, he cannot remain unaffected by them. British Leyland motors (once "Morris-Cowley") and the equally enormous Pressed Steel factory that are situated in the outlying suburb of Cowley are behind the rapid growth of the city. This burgeoning of industry has brought changes which might not be apparent to the visitor, but which are felt most keenly by the shopkeepers and various trades people, who 50 years ago were totally reliant on the university for trade. Today, they have a vast pool of customers from the outlying housing estates, providing them with business throughout the year.

The exact date of the origins of the city of Oxford is not clear. It was most likely a late Saxon town that was part fortress and part market. No doubt the Saxon chieftains were attracted to its central position, and it became a favorite venue for royal conferences, a kind of Saxon convention center. During the early Middle Ages, the city thrived as a center of the flourishing wool trade—the earliest records date back to 1147, and can still be inspected in Oxford town hall.

At some time during the 12th century, Oxford became a meeting place for scholars. Some theories claim that it was founded by English students who had been expelled from the University of Paris in 1167, while others hold that it is an offshoot of the various monastic institutions in the immediate neighborhood. Whatever its origins, it is certain that by the end of the 12th century, the Royal Borough of Oxford was the home of the first established center of learning in England.

The earliest colleges founded in Oxford were University College (1249), Balliol (1263), and Merton College (1264). From the 13th century onwards a succession of royal charters strengthened the position of the university at the expense of the city; in many instances it was the university that ruled the town and not the other way round. Oxford became a power in the kingdom, as Canterbury once was, and its splendor was enhanced by new colleges built during the reign of the Tudors and by magnificent buildings of the later era (Sheldonian Theatre, Radcliffe Camera, etc.). There was a good deal of reconstructing and rebuilding of medieval and Renaissance Oxford in the 18th century, which destroyed some of the old streets that used to thread their way through the ancient "Latin Quarter" of the university. Many old almshouses, friaries, and houses inhabited in the Middle Ages by various religious bodies were sacrificed in the process, and the city that emerged from all those efforts was less compact, less uniform in its character than before. Nevertheless, even today a visitor will find no difficulty in discovering the real Oxford after wading from the railway station across nondescript approaches of a rather commercial city towards the stern beauty of the colleges.

The presence of the university ensures for the city standards of entertainment and cultural activity unusual in a provincial town. Few evenings pass without a choice of concert and theatrical performance. There is a famous bookshop, as well as schools of widespread renown, while the Clarendon Press is known the world over.

There is such a bewildering display of architetural styles in Oxford that the less good often takes the attention away from the best. You can, of course, just wander around and generally take in the atmosphere, but, assuming you wish to give one of the great cities of Europe its due, it is fairly easy to visit most of the more beautiful and historic buildings and to come away with a feeling for the university.

Start at the Carfax Tower, as this is the center of the city. Walk south down St. Aldate's Street towards Folly Bridge, with the Victorian Town Hall (you can examine the ancient records of the city if you wish to, including the Royal Charter of 1199) and the Public Library on the left. On the other side of the street is the City Information Center, one of the best equipped in the country and ready to advise on all aspects of the city's life and past; during the summer walking tours are organized. Book ahead if possible.

Continuing, you will soon come to the impressive Christ Church, known to its members as "the House." There was a time when the enormous college had only 101 students—Great Tom, its huge bell, can still be heard tolling 101 strokes at five past nine every evening to summon them home. General Oglethorpe, founder of the state of Georgia, studying at the much smaller Pembroke College, opposite, in the shadow of Wren's Tom Tower, must have heard these bells only too often. The chapel of Christ Church existed before the college and is also the cathedral of Oxford. The singing of its choir is justly famous (though keenly rivaled at Magdalen and New College). The college has

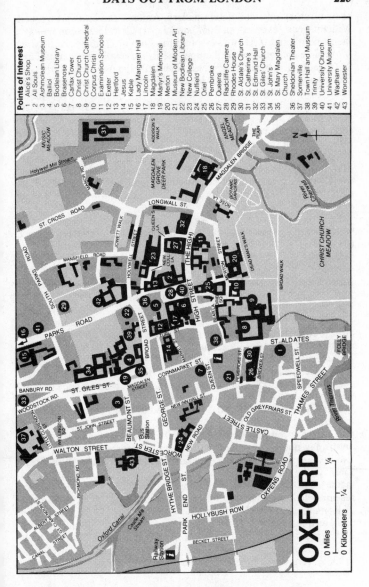

OXFORD

Points of Interest

1. Alice's Shop
2. All Souls
3. Ashmolean Museum
4. Balliol
5. Bodleian Library
6. Brasenose
7. Carfax Tower
8. Christ Church
9. Christ Church Cathedral
10. Corpus Christi
11. Examination Schools
12. Exeter
13. Hertford
14. Jesus
15. Keble
16. Lady Margaret Hall
17. Lincoln
18. Magdalen
19. Martyr's Memorial
20. Merton
21. Museum of Modern Art
22. New Bodleian Library
23. New College
24. Nuffield
25. Oriel
26. Pembroke
27. Queens
28. Radcliffe Camera
29. Rhodes House
30. St. Aldate's Church
31. St. Catherine's
32. St. Edmund Hall
33. St. Giles' Church
34. St. John's
35. St. Mary Magdalen Church
36. Sheldonian Theater
37. Somerville
38. Town Hall and Museum
39. Trinity
40. University Church
41. University Museum
42. Wadham
43. Worcester

its own rather splendid picture gallery. Among former members were William Penn (expelled, in 1661) and Lewis Carroll. A shop opposite the meadows in St. Aldate's inspired the shop in *Through the Looking Glass*. The college gardens flanking the Broad Walk are beautiful and the meadows extend to the river Cherwell. If you would rather see Oxford as a distant panorama across a foreground of greenery, continue to Folly Bridge and hire a boat.

On foot it is best to leave Christ Church beyond the cathedral, where you will soon find yourself in Corpus Christi, which introduced Latin and Greek to the university curriculum. Standing next door is Merton College, one of the richest and oldest. The Chapel and the 14th-century library are notable. T. S. Eliot was a member of this college. Henrietta Maria, the wife and queen of Charles I, was billeted at Merton during the Civil War, to be near her husband, who was staying at Christ Church. Oriel is Merton's neighbor, and is famous for its sons, among others, Sir Walter Raleigh.

Leaving Oriel, make your way up Bear Lane, past the Bear Inn, which boasts the lowest ceiling in Oxford, into the High Street, referred to as "the High." In fact, most streets in the town are known by their nicknames and abbreviations, so Turl Street is never referred to as anything but "the Turl," and then there are "the Corn" and "the Broad," etc. Crossing "the High" then, enter Brasenose College (or BNC for short), named from an ancient bronze nose-shaped knocker that used to hang on the front door.

Across the road from BNC is All Saints, which has no undergraduates. It consists almost entirely of appointed fellows, and is one of the most exclusive and erudite clubs in the world. Radcliffe Square (behind Brasenose), which is the heart of the university, boasts the third largest dome in England in its Radcliffe Camera. The building at the northern end of the square is the famous Bodleian Library, where a copy of every book published in England must be sent.

It takes its name from Sir Thomas Bodley, who presented his own fine collection to the university in 1602 and remodeled the earlier building to accommodate them. A splendid array of books is generally on display under the magnificent vault of the former Divinity School and in a second Exhibition Room, and a glimpse of Duke Humphrey's Library, the oldest part of the Bodleian, can be had above. Beyond, facing "the Broad" stands the Sheldonian Theatre, a fine classical assembly hall by Wren, recently restored with newly sculptured heads of Roman emperors. The corner between the new Bodleian extension and Hertford College is always a scene of flying bicycles and hurrying undergraduates. Hertford has a bridge modeled on the Bridge of Sighs in Venice which spans New College Lane. New College—new, that is, in 1379, from which time dates some of the stained glass in the chapel—

incorporates a long stretch of the medieval city wall in its gardens. It was the home of the famous Doctor Spooner and his spoonerisms; he is reputed to have told one dilettante student "You have hissed your mystery lectures and tasted a whole worm."

No tour of Oxford would be complete without a visit to Magdalen (pronounced *Maudlin*) College. To reach it from New College, walk down New College Lane into Queen's Lane, passing on your left St. Edmund Hall, and on your right, Queens. Turn left at "the High," pass the Examination Halls (known as schools), opposite, and find Magdalen College, a few minutes' walk further on. This is one of the richest colleges, with a magnificent main quadrangle and a supremely monastic air. A walk round the Deer Park and along Addison's Walk will lead you to envy the members of the college for the experience of living here. They have included such diverse people as Cardinal Wolsey, John Mason, founder of New Hampshire, Prince Rupert, Gibbon and Oscar Wilde. Magdalen Bridge is famous for the May Day celebrations after an evening of May Balls. Undergraduates gather in punts under the bridge at dawn to hear the choristers singing the May Day anthem from the tower.

The other principal colleges and the famous Ashmolean Museum all lie north of Carfax, so that after Magdalen, you should walk up "the High" back to the Carfax. When you reach Carfax, turn right up Cornmarket Street, through the main shopping center and soon the massive walls of St. John's and Balliol loom into sight. The latter's undistinguished 19th-century buildings do not reflect the fame it acquired at that time in the world of letters and politics. Opposite Balliol the Martyrs' Memorial marks the spot where Ridley, Latimer and Cranmer were burned by "Bloody Mary" in 1555 and 1556. St. John's has colonnades and a garden front that was designed by Inigo Jones.

Way beyond the north end of St. Giles, in virtual banishment, lie Lady Margaret Hall and Somerville, the earliest colleges founded for young ladies.

Beaumont Street, on the other side of St. Giles, leads to Worcester College. In this Regency street stands the Ashmolean Museum, with an outstanding collection of archeological finds from Greece, Crete, and the Near East, as well as famous paintings, prints, porcelain, and scientific curios. Among medieval items is the Alfred Jewel, found in a context that suggests a connection with King Alfred.

There remain other landmarks to be visited. The first is Keble College, unique for its remarkable Victorian architecture. Keble was the only men's college founded in the 19th century. More interesting and close by is Rhodes House with unique records of the colonial period in Africa. Much further out, beyond South Parks Road and St. Cross, lies St. Catherine's College, one of Oxford's newest.

Blenheim

If you have time to do so, there is one great house in the area of Oxford that you should try to visit, it is Blenheim Palace. This imposing palace was granted to the Duke of Marlborough after his victories in the Low Countries in 1704, which included the battle of the town of Blenheim—hence the name. The palace was designed by Vanbrugh, and the impressive gardens and lakes are mainly the fruits of 20 years of work by Capability Brown. This most famous of English landscape gardeners declared that his object at Blenheim was to "make the Thames look like a small stream compared with the winding Danube in Blenheim Park." At points, he almost succeeds—the scale of these grounds must be seen to be believed. The total cost of landscaping is reputed to have been in the region of £300,000. It was here that Winston Churchill was born, and in the nearby village of Bladon, in the simple churchyard, he lies buried.

Bath

Bath is easily reached from London by InterCity train in little over an hour; trains from Paddington Station. The city is undoubtedly one of the most beautiful and best-preserved of English 18th-century towns. But though its appearance is predominantly 18th century (inevitably a few modern buildings are scattered through the town), its history goes back to Roman times. The Romans were the first to discover the mineral springs that were ultimately to give the town both its name and fame. Their spectacular baths have survived to the present day. Nevertheless, it was in the 18th century that Bath reached its apogee. Its attraction was still the mineral springs—Dickens was later to describe them as tasting like "warm flat-irons"—and all polite society flocked there to gossip, be seen and, occasionally, to take the waters.

The architectural highlight of this delightful town is the Royal Crescent, a glorious and elegantly curving terrace built by John Wood. He was also largely responsible for much of the rest of the marvellous buildings still to be seen today including the Pump Room, the social hub of the 18th-century town, with its Chippendale furnishings, where Beau Nash entertained and made Bath the most fashionable resort of his day. Gainsborough, Queen Victoria, Lord Nelson and Jane Austen, among others, traveled here to sip the waters. See the beautiful abbey church and browse around the Abbey Green among the myriad of antique shops, and don't forget the remarkable Costume Museum, in the Assembly Rooms.

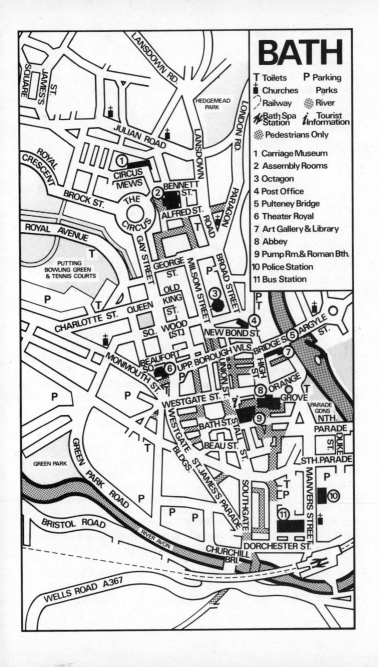

Bath is not merely a place for people groaning in the grip of rheumatism: it has a summer musical festival, where opera (Mozart in particular), symphonies and chamber music are presented together with other cultural attractions. Bath has latched on to the tourist boom in a very practical way and the city is well signposted to help you discover its attractions. In the summertime you may wish that it was not quite so popular.

Two miles away, in Claverton Manor, there is an American Museum, where each room is arranged by region and by period. The Georgian house is set in a splendid 55-acre estate.

Stratford-upon-Avon

Although it is not entirely easy to do an independent day trip to Stratford-upon-Avon, it is possible, and it features on most of the longer coach tours. By train you go from Paddington, but remember that the Stratford Station may be closed on a Sunday! How Britain's bureaucracy works out these little helpful details, we will never know.

This is "picture postcard" land, with its sleepy villages, tea gardens, thatched roofs and quiet vistas. But it is also the birthplace of that image of Britain which has been spread over the breadth of the world by the works of Shakespeare. The realm of the yeoman, the wooded land of Arden, the home of the prosperous small tradesman and the wealthier merchant. The region where landowners still pasture deer as they have done for the last nine hundred years.

Part of the region is indeed Shakespeare's England, and there is a fair number of cottages—now in the $150,000 bracket, if they have more than three bedrooms and all "mod cons"—that resemble the pretty cottage at Wilmcote, a few miles from Stratford, that used to belong to Shakespeare's mother.

Born in a half-timbered early-16th-century building in the town of Stratford-upon-Avon on April 23 1564, Shakespeare was buried in Holy Trinity Church after he had died (on his fifty-second birthday) in a more imposing house at New Place. Although he spent much of his life in London, where, of course, he became a leading figure of the Elizabethan theater, the world associates him with Stratford. Here, in the years between his birth and 1587, he played as a boy, attended the local grammar school and married Anne Hathaway; here he returned a man of prosperity, to the town with which his name is ineradicably linked.

Today, over three and a half centuries after he died, he remains the magnet that draws thousands of tourists each year to this south Warwickshire town. They come to visit the places with which he is iden-

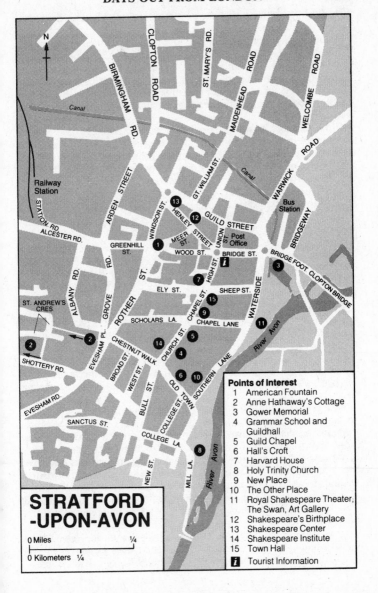

STRATFORD -UPON-AVON

0 Miles ¼

0 Kilometers ¼

Points of Interest

1 American Fountain
2 Anne Hathaway's Cottage
3 Gower Memorial
4 Grammar School and Guildhall
5 Guild Chapel
6 Hall's Croft
7 Harvard House
8 Holy Trinity Church
9 New Place
10 The Other Place
11 Royal Shakespeare Theater; The Swan, Art Gallery
12 Shakespeare's Birthplace
13 Shakespeare Center
14 Shakespeare Institute
15 Town Hall

ℹ Tourist Information

tified, and to attend a performance of one of his plays in the Royal Shakespeare Theatre.

Although the famous actor David Garrick instituted something in the way of a Shakespearean Festival in the town in 1769, and there were suitable commemorations on the occasion of the 300th anniversary of the poet's birth in 1864, it was not until 1874 that Charles Edward Flower formed the Shakespeare Memorial Association, with a view to establishing a permanent theater; the forerunner of the present building was opened in 1879.

From that time onwards, the Shakespeare season has grown in both size and prestige. In 1926 the original Victorian Memorial Theater was destroyed by fire. Bernard Shaw, when he heard the news of its destruction, sent a telegram that said simply "Congratulations." It had been a provincial version of the Albert Memorial, but with a sad tendency towards Tudor-Gothic. Part of it was saved and is now the Art Gallery. Productions in the town continued to be held in a converted cinema while a replacement was being built. For this a great amount of money was subscribed by the people of the United States, and in 1932 The Royal Shakespeare Theater designed by Elizabeth Scott was opened. With frequent internal changes, this is the theater that exists today. Further plans are in hand to rebuild the top story of the remains of the Victorian building as a new theater, in Elizabethan style, to present the plays in their original staging.

Although a good deal of restoration has been inevitable in the four centuries that have elapsed since 1564, the Henley Street birthplace itself, perhaps the most popular of Shakespearean shrines, still contains a good deal of the original timber framing, and that section of the building used as a residence is furnished in appropriate style. When Shakespeare was born, his father, John, used part of the premises for his work as glover and wood-dealer. The garden contains a unique collection of plants and trees mentioned in the poet's works.

New Place, on the other hand, was demolished in 1759, and only the site and foundations remain of what is said to have once been the most imposing residence in town. The gardens here are well cared for by the Trust and contain a mulberry tree alleged to have come from a cutting of the original one planted by Shakespeare; the original was destroyed by a later occupant said to have been annoyed by the number of visitors wishing to see it. The approach to these gardens is through Nash's House, the home of the poet's grand-daughter and her first husband, Thomas Nash, which again contains many interesting relics. Adjoining is a replica of an Elizabethan garden of great beauty.

Also administered by the Trust is Hall's Croft (in New Town), another fine old Tudor house, with an even lovelier garden, where the poet's daughter, Susanna, and her husband, Dr. John Hall, lived.

Quite apart from the places direclty associated with the poet, Stratford contains many other features well worth visiting. The Guild buildings at the corner of Church Street and Chapel Lane contain a chapel with a chancel dating from 1450 and incorporating part of the fabric of the original (built in 1269), the early 15th-century Guildhall, and the grammar school attended by the bard.

There is a fascinating link with the United States in the lovely half-timbered Harvard House, for not only was it owned by the parents of John Harvard, who gave his name to the famous American university, but it was actually bought and presented to the university by Edward Morris of Chicago in 1909. Holy Trinity church, beautifully situated by the Avon, contains the grave of Shakespeare, Anne Hathaway and other members of his family. The Town Hall, built of the lovely Cotswold stone from the hills to the south, was dedicated to the memory of the poet by David Garrick on the occasion of the forerunner of the famous festivals in 1769. A new, non-Shakespeare festival now takes place at Stratford each July, featuring a wide variety of the performing arts.

As is only to be expected, Stratford is well endowed with inns and hotels, including the Golden Lion, which was known as the Peacock until early in the 17th century; and the Shakespeare, which, under a different name, was actually there when the poet was born and is said to have been built as a residence by Sir Hugh Clopton, who later became Lord Mayor of London and who died in 1496.

Shakespeare was born in what was then a smallish town and his wanderings through the fields and woods so close to his boyhood home gave him a knowledge of nature and rural lore that so often reveals itself in his plays. One place he must have visited fairly often was Shottery, where his wife-to-be, Anne Hathaway, lived in the thatched farmhouse that, quite understandably, is one of the most photographed houses in the whole of Britain. Its garden is as close to the original as it is possible to make it. It is another of the possessions of the Birthplace Trust who have taken great pains to preserve the atmosphere of the key years of its story.

There is a regular bus service from the town to Shottery, but many will prefer the mile-long walk through the fields which, most probably, is the way Shakespeare used on those courtship journeys. North of Stratford, Warwickshire is at its best in the Forest of Arden, where the woodland glades and shady paths through the trees give little indication of the nearness of Birmingham.

Wilmcote, three miles from Stratford, contains another of the possessions of the Birthplace Trust, the Tudor farmhouse which was the home of Shakespeare's mother, Mary Arden, member of an old Warwickshire family whose earliest members lived at Aston (now a suburb of Birmingham). The family doubtless took its name from the wood-land environment, the very word "Arden" being used by the Celts for such a district. In the adjoining parish of Aston Cantlow, Mary and John Shakespeare, the poet's father, are said to have been married in the church of St. John the Baptist.

Tickets for the Royal Shakespeare Theater performances cost from £4.50 up to £15. You can use American Express credit cards by calling the box office on Stratford 295623 and quoting the card number. Book-ings are confirmed immediately. Standing room costs £2.50.

If you want to book seats before you arrive in Britain, you should pay by sterling check, obtainable from your bank, or by Eurocheck. Seats at the studio theater, The Other Place, are uniformly £5.50; box office number same as for Royal Shakespeare. The number for 24-hour booking information is 0789 69191.

The theater has a regular restaurant and a very handy cafeteria, which is ideal for those in a hurry after the performance.

St. Albans and Colchester

St. Albans lies just over 20 miles to the north of London and is accessible by train from St. Pancras Station and by Green Line bus. It is the successor to the capital of Roman Britain called Verulamium, built beside the little river called the Ver. The site of the Roman *municipium* (which lasted from A.D. 43 to about 410, surviving a sack-ing by the irrepressible Boadicea) is now occupied by a park and school playing fields, but much remains, including the major Roman finds of Britain.

Part of the city wall stands and archeological work is continuing at the site of the Amphitheater. Visit the Verulamium Museum, in which most of the finds are collected. Verulamium contains the Roman the-ater (the only one to be open to view in Britain) and the hypocaust, a Roman heating system of a private suite of baths, which has been excavated and preserved.

The major feature of the city is the 11th-century cathedral, which has one of the longest medieval naves in existence as well as a fine Norman tower; its west front is an unhappy 19th-century additon. St. Albans has considerable historical associations and was the site of two impor-tant battles during the Wars of the Roses. Its name derives from St. Alban, a Roman soldier who was the first Christian martyr in England; he was beheaded here in 303 and his shrine is in the cathedral.

Another fascinating town within easy reach of London (three trains an hour from Liverpool Street, trip taking just under an hour) is Colchester, the oldest recorded town in England, dating back to the Iron Age. It is famed for oysters, which the Romans enjoyed so much that they settled there and sent quantities home. One of the Roman founders was the Emperor Claudius, and the settlement was also attacked by Queen Boadicea, who is known today for the anti-pedestrian habit of fixing knives to the wheels of her chariots. Today the Roman walls still stand, together with a Norman castle, a Victorian town hall and Dutch-style houses, built by refugee weavers from the Low Countries in the late 16th century. It is an interesting, well-cared-for town, a delight to wander in.

Cambridge

This peaceful university city, whose Gothic spires are framed by broad meadows and great trees, is within easy range of a one-day excursion from London and is a convenient starting-point for exploring East Anglia. As the name suggests, from remotest antiquity Cambridge has been the site of a bridge on the river Cam (or Granta). Pre-Roman settlers placed their ford where the bridge is today, at the top of Bridge Street. The town became a market center for the surrounding farms. Over 700 years ago scholars began coming to Cambridge. At first they had no teachers, no organization, and no university. But the 13th century was a thriving period for education and research, and universities were springing up all over Europe—in Oxford, Paris, and Salamanca, among other places. The oldest colleges still in existence are Peterhouse (1284), Clare (1338), and Pembroke (1347). The newest is Robinson, a college for both men and women, ceremoniously opened by the Queen in 1977.

"Where is the University?" is a question hard to answer. The colleges are all over town. The oldest women's college, Girton, is three miles out in the fens, it was originally founded 15 miles away from the male perils of Cambridge, though most colleges are now co-educational, albeit often with just a small number of women.

In recent years the flood of visitors has proved a serious problem to the colleges, and reluctantly they have had to enforce regulations about entrance to their buildings, which are, after all, private property and places of study. It would be wise to contact the local Tourist Office (Wheeler Street, tel. Cambridge 358977) before beginning your visit.

We suggest you begin your tour where Cambridge itself began—at the top of Bridge Street, on the river. After a brief look at Magdalene College (pronounced *maudlin*), which contains the library of Samuel Pepys, walk down to the "Round Church" (dating from Norman times, perhaps founded by Crusaders). Then turn into St. John's College and stroll through its immense courts (quadrangles). Cross the river by the Bridge of Sighs, modeled on its counterpart in Venice.

You are now on the "Backs"—the beautiful green parkland that extends along the river behind several colleges. Here you will feel the essential quality of Cambridge. Resulting in part from the larger size of the colleges, and partly from the lack of industrialization, this atmosphere of broad sweeping openness is just what distinguishes Cambridge from Oxford.

Now make your way into Trinity College. If the weather is warm you can watch the people gliding along the river in punts, gondola-like boats, trademarks of Cambridge and Oxford. A few punts are available for hire from Trinity, if you would like to try it yourself; more can be had at Quayside (next to Magdalene) and at the Anchor Inn (near Queens' College).

Trinity is Sir Isaac Newton's college, and his statue is to be seen in the antechapel. The lovely Wren Library is open to the public and contains interesting displays. Outside the Great Gate stands an apple tree said to be a descendant of the one whose falling apple caused Newton to formulate the laws of gravity.

If you are a book lover, be sure not to miss Trinity Street, which contains one gigantic bookshop, almost unsurpassable in most subjects, plus two or three smaller shops.

Then be sure to visit Great St. Mary's, the official church of the University. Cambridge was the scene of considerable controversy during and after the Reformation, and this fact is reflected in the Great St Mary's pulpit, which moves on rails so that the Protestant-minded can preach from the center and the Catholic-minded can preach from the side.

Clare College, across the street behind the Senate House, is not without its delights, but you will probably prefer to go directly into King's College, whose majestic and huge chapel, dating from 1446, has been called the "finest flower of Gothic in Europe." Attend Evensong; the choir is world-famous.

If you have time, you can now cross the river again, behind King's College (a thing well worth doing for the view), and then look at some of the more controversial pieces of architecture in the University. Behind Clare College's Memorial Court is the University Library, a menacing-looking tower built in the 1930s.

To the south, on the Sidgwick Avenue site, is some quite good modern architecture, including a quadrangular building that stands on great pillars and has no ground floor. The History Faculty building, made of glass panes, is however often referred to as "the greenhouse." Newnham College, across the street, is a women's college with an atmosphere of cultivated elegance.

Return to the river at Queens' College and look at the quaint Mathematicians' Bridge. This is said to have been constructed on geometri-

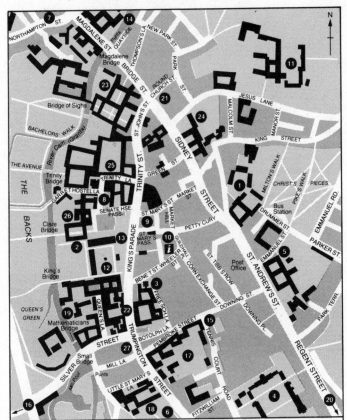

Points of Interest

1	Christ's	13	King's College Chapel
2	Clare	14	Magdalene
3	Corpus Christi	15	Museum of Archeology and Ethnology
4	Downing	16	Newnham
5	Emmanuel	17	Pembroke
6	Fitzwilliam Museum	18	Peterhouse
7	Folk Museum	19	Queen's
8	Gonville and Caius	20	Railway Station
9	Great St. Mary's University Church	21	Round Church
10	Guildhall	22	St. Catharine's
12	King's	23	St. John's

24	Sidney Sussex
25	Trinity
26	Trinity Hall
27	University Press
i	Tourist Information

CAMBRIDGE

0 Miles	⅛
0 Km	⅛

cal principles to hold together without nails, but a group of curious physicists took it apart one summer to see how it worked, and couldn't put it together again. It therefore now has nails. Queens' has superb Tudor architecture. In one corner of the attractive Pump Court is the Erasmus Tower, where the famous philosopher lived while teaching at the college (1510–13).

The Fitzwilliam Museum in Trumpington Street (open Tues.–Sun.: ground floor 10–2 only, Tues.–Sat.; upper floor 2–5 only, Tues.–Sat.; Sun., both floors, 2.15–5) is well worth a visit, having excellent collections of antiquities, paintings and *objets d'art.* The Museum of Archaeology and Anthropology, in Downing Street, is interesting, as is the Folk Museum in Castle Street, which contains objects illustrating everyday life over the past several centuries.

To see the way that a college has grown over the centuries you could not do better than visit Christ's. The Tudor main gateway, bearing a splendid coat of arms, leads into a fine courtyard, with the chapel framed by an ancient magnolia. The unfolding architecture leads you past a Fellows' Building credited to Inigo Jones, to the spacious garden (once the haunt of Milton), and finally to one of Cambridge's most modern buildings, a ziggurat-like confection that compels admiration.

If you enjoy walking, you can go to the villages of Coton (behind the University Library) and Grantchester (beyond Newnham) on pleasant country footpaths. The Tourist Information Office on Wheeler Street provides much useful advice, including maps and handy hints about bicycle rentals, for Cambridge is awash with bicycles.

There is an American Military Cemetery four miles out on Madingley Road, containing the graves of 3,811 American servicemen who were stationed in Britain during World War II. It is accessible by bus.

INDEX